URSULA FRANKLIN SPEAKS

Ursula Franklin Speaks

Thoughts and Afterthoughts,
1986–2012

Ursula Martius Franklin in collaboration with
Sarah Jane Freeman

Edited by Sarah Jane Freeman

McGill-Queen's University Press
Montreal & Kingston · London · Ithaca

ISBN 978-0-7735-4384-3 (cloth)
ISBN 978-0-7735-4387-4 (paper)
ISBN 978-0-7735-9200-1 (ePDF)
ISBN 978-0-7735-9201-8 (ePUB)

Legal deposit second quarter 2014
Bibliothèque nationale du Québec

Printed in Canada on acid-free paper that is 100% ancient forest free
(100% post-consumer recycled), processed chlorine free

McGill-Queen's University Press acknowledges the support of the
Canada Council for the Arts for our publishing program. We also
acknowledge the financial support of the Government of Canada
through the Canada Book Fund for our publishing activities.

Library and Archives Canada Cataloguing in Publication

Franklin, Ursula M., 1921–
[Works. Selections]

    Ursula Franklin speaks : thoughts and afterthoughts / Ursula Martius
Franklin in collaboration with Sarah Jane Freeman ; edited by Sarah
Jane Freeman.

A collection of twenty-two speeches and five interviews that have been
retrieved and restored from audio and visual recordings.

Includes bibliographical references and index.
Issued in print and electronic formats.
ISBN 978-0-7735-4384-3 (bound). – ISBN 978-0-7735-4387-4 (pbk.). –
ISBN 978-0-7735-9200-1 (ePDF). – ISBN 978-0-7735-9201-8 (ePUB)

    1. Technology – Social aspects. 2. Technology – Political aspects.
3. Social justice. 4. Feminism. 5. Civics, Canadian. 6. Education. 7.
Franklin, Ursula M., 1921– – Interviews. I. Freeman, Sarah Jane, 1957–,
writer of introduction, editor of compilation II. Title.

T14.5.F738 2014   303.48'3   C2014-900682-9
                                  C2014-900683-7

Typeset by Jay Tee Graphics Ltd. in 10.5/13 Sabon

Contents

Acknowledgments

This book is dedicated to the Massey College community in the broadest sense of the word: a community that has enriched us both with its stimulation and fellowship. It would not have been possible to bring this project to fruition without the wide variety of support and encouragement that we received from its members. While we cannot list all the people who assisted in transcribing the speeches and interviews assembled here, we remember with thankfulness each and every one of them. We want to record our special indebtedness to Kathy Chung, Eleanor Proctor, Michael Valpy, Alan Broadbent, and most of all to the ever-present Master of Massey College John Fraser.

URSULA FRANKLIN SPEAKS

Preface:
The How and Why of This Book

URSULA MARTIUS FRANKLIN

First and foremost this book is for me a testimony to the sustaining power of friendship and solidarity. Its pages grew from boxes of audio and video recordings – some of which were damaged, some of which were unlabelled, and many of which were difficult to retrieve – into an internally consistent text in a somewhat unexpected and unplanned manner. Initially nothing was further from my mind than authoring another book. As I went laboriously through my notes and papers years ago, I had to sort and prepare them for transfer to the University of Toronto Archives to join other documents transferred earlier. I found this sifting and assessing a lonely and demanding task.

At one point during this process, I asked Dr Jane Freeman, also a senior fellow at Massey College, for her help and advice. Jane's professional expertise in language, presentation, and communication as well as our personal friendship made it easy for me to turn to her. What had begun to trouble me was the accessibility of my public talks and lectures. They contained comments and reflections on issues of public concern, and I started to wonder whether they should be preserved and, if so, where and in what form.

Jane felt it was incumbent on us to at least go through the process of restoring the text of the speeches so I could leave to my students and their students an adequate record of the activities of an engaged Canadian academic. This meant recovery, transcription, and clarification of the tape-recorded talks, but most of all it meant finding a way to preserve the spoken voice in a written text, and this is where Jane's professional expertise and sensitivity were crucial. She was able to preserve my voice and the spirit of each occasion in a way I would not have been able to do. I would also like to record the sheer pleasure we had in slowly discovering the broad range of subjects and audiences that emerged from the harvesting of a rather ragtag collection of tapes. Against the background of my challenges of retirement, divestment, ill health, and old age, Jane dealt, in steadfast friendship, with the numerous challenges of retrieval and reconstruction, as well as with mobilizing transcribing help from the Massey community.

As the retrieval proceeded and we selected talks worth preserving, leitmotifs – i.e., basic connecting themes – began to emerge. Throughout the decades during which I taught and spoke, the political and social landscape of Canada changed drastically; yet the fundamental values that inform the conduct of engaged citizens remain part of our civic collectivity. The ongoing thinking about the relevance of these values within drastically changing social and political contexts is what connects much of my work.

It was in conversations with Jane about the content of the restored speeches and interviews that the idea emerged to publish a selection of them as a book. Such a collection could offer a way of preserving them as well as assuring easy public access to the material. This insight led me to the path I decided to take, having assured Jane's ongoing active collaboration as well as her continuing work as editor. Together we would retrieve, restore, and publish selected speeches of mine in one book.

This decision appeared to address the problems that I initially took to Jane. Little did we realize that new problems would surface as a consequence of this choice. I should have known better. Did I not learn enough from working all those years with Max Allen at CBC's *Ideas*? He taught me much about the differing needs of listeners and readers. Readers can go back over an opaque passage of a text; listeners cannot. Within a given talk, listeners need to have context and conclusions clearly stated, and the main building blocks of the argument have to be part of the talk. Readers can put a book aside and pick it up again. Listeners cannot return at will to a talk.

Because of my experience with radio, my talks were crafted to be self-contained units with a beginning, a clarification of context or purpose, my main thoughts, and the consequences of my approach ending with whatever conclusion or recommendation I could offer.

They were talks structured as talks that Jane and I tried to retrieve and restore, each a self-contained unit. One may call that the *archival task* of our endeavour. But we also worked hard to put the most interesting speeches together as a book, feeling that they have something to say to present-day Canadians. The book facet of the project, with readers as the intended audience, added a *communicative task* to the work.

At times, the communicative task of creating a text that is relevant to *readers in the here and now* created conflicts with the requirements of our archival mission of *restoring what listeners heard then*. The contradiction between archival needs and didactic savvy became most glaring in the case of "repetitions." When speaking to different audiences in the community, I had often taken care to use the same background example, the same stories or metaphors – not because I could not think of something different, but because I hoped to facilitate communication between groups by offering them a common vocabulary. I sought to achieve resonance among listeners. Yet, when reading speeches one after the other in a collection, common stories or identical examples don't induce resonance, they induce tedium.

It was again Jane, with her scholarship and experience, who analyzed, pruned, cross-referenced, and footnoted, resolving the conflicts between the archival and the communicative aspects of our joint task. These revisions took a great deal of work and skill. In many ways, the revised text became her book as much as mine. Her collaboration is manifest in every phase of this book's unorthodox growth and structuring. This is why I said at the beginning of this preface that this book is for me a testimony to the sustaining power of friendship and solidarity.

Introduction

SARAH JANE FREEMAN

Ursula Martius Franklin is well known and much admired in Toronto, Ontario, and Canada. Described by June Callwood as one of Canada's "national treasures," Ursula Franklin is a Holocaust survivor who came to Canada from Berlin in 1949. A highly respected physicist, feminist, pacifist, and public intellectual, she was the first woman at the University of Toronto to be named a University professor. By facilitating the collection of baby teeth in the early 1960s in order to determine their strontium-90 content, she helped provide the evidence needed to pass the treaty banning atmospheric nuclear tests. Through her investigation of ancient Chinese bronzes and pottery, she pioneered the field of study now known as archaeometry.

From 1952 to 1967, Dr Franklin worked as a senior scientist at the Ontario Research Foundation (ORF). From 1967 to 1989 she was a full-time member of the University of Toronto's Faculty of Engineering. During that time, she carried a full teaching load in Material Science, was a recipient of federal grants for her ongoing technical research, and became active in "the grant-giving business" in her roles as member of the Science Council, the National Research Council (NRC), and the Natural Sciences and Engineering Research Council of Canada (NSERC). As she notes, "It's from doing research oneself that one gets the knowledge and sense needed to examine the research proposals of others." A fellow of the Royal Society of Canada, she retired from the Faculty of Engineering in 1989 to become the director of Museum Studies, a post she held for two terms, until the mid-1990s.

In addition to scientific papers published in the fields of physics, engineering, archaeometry, and museum studies during the course of her career, Dr Franklin has also published two books for the general public: *The Real World of Technology*, based on her Massey Lectures, and *The Ursula Franklin Reader: Pacifism as a Map*, a collection of papers and previously published speeches on pacifism and feminism, published in 2006.

She has received more than twenty honorary doctorates from Canadian universities. She is a companion of the Order of Canada, a member of the Order of Ontario, and a recipient of both a Governor General's Award and the Pearson Peace Medal. She has appeared as a guest contributor many times on CBC Radio, most notably in delivering her Massey Lectures, *The Real World of Technology*. The Ursula Franklin Academy, a public high school in Toronto, was named in her honour by the city's Board of Education. In November 2012, she was inducted into the Canadian Hall of Fame for Science and Technology. In February 2013, she was awarded the Queen's Diamond Jubilee Medal. Married for over sixty years to Fred Franklin, she is the mother of two and the grandmother of four.

THE PRESENT COLLECTION

Throughout her career, Dr Franklin has been asked to give lectures many times a year to an unusually wide variety of audiences. *Ursula Franklin Speaks: Thoughts and Afterthoughts* contains twenty-two speeches and five interviews given by Ursula Martius Franklin between 1986 and 2012. While the material in *The Ursula Franklin Reader* focuses on pacifism and feminism, the speeches and interviews collected here address a wide range of topics, and the audiences vary considerably. Some of these speeches were originally delivered as keynote conference addresses, others were given as convocation addresses, at public gatherings, or on CBC Radio.

Dr Franklin usually speaks from only minimal point-form notes, does not write out her lectures, and does not use PowerPoint. As a result, most of her speeches have existed only in audio or video recordings. The shifting technological context she so often discusses is reflected in the range of methods used to record and preserve the speeches and interviews assembled here: while the earliest were recorded on 8-mm video cassettes, VHS tapes, and cassette tapes, the later ones were recorded on CDs, DVDs, websites, and YouTube. Many of the earlier recordings have been damaged, or are of poor audio quality, and the ideas she shared in spoken form were in danger of being lost.

With the help of Dr Franklin's point-form speaking notes and her prodigious memory, she and I have worked to restore the lost material from these speeches in order to share the ideas she presented to her original audiences. With the exception of one lecture that was printed in a revised form in an academic journal, none of the material collected here has previously been available to the public except through the ears and memories of those who were in the original audiences. The collection does not include all the unpublished speeches she gave during the twenty-six-year period between 1986 and 2012 – only a selection of the ones that, by our good luck, someone had the foresight to record.

Somewhere in the process of assembling this collection, Ursula and I realized that the speeches, when assembled, totalled more than the sum of the parts. Each speech was prepared on a specific topic, at a specific time, for a specific audience. When juxtaposed with one another, however, the collected speeches reveal both the breadth of Ursula's expertise and the evolution of her perspective in a way that none of the speeches reveals alone. Each speech is thought-provoking on its own but when read in sequence, or in thematic clusters, the collected speeches allow readers to see the development of Franklin's point of view across twenty-six years of her work for human betterment. She often discusses the importance of cultivating *discernment* – the ongoing weighing and assessing of what is around us – and the speeches and interviews assembled here reveal the ways in which Franklin's own ongoing cultivation of discernment has influenced her approach to certain topics when speaking in different contexts and different decades to a wide range of audiences. The two overriding themes of the collection might be described as "Working for Human Betterment" and "Cultivating Discernment."

We have divided the speeches according to the audiences for whom they were first intended: those who work for human betterment through their roles as *citizens*; *youth* who have yet to decide how best to make their contributions; and those who work for human betterment through their roles as *professionals*. Within each of these groupings, the speeches are listed chronologically. In addition to the table of contents, we have grouped the speeches by theme in an appendix in order to allow readers to read the collection either chronologically or thematically. The introduction and conclusion of the book are based on excerpts from a series of conversations Dr Franklin and I had while preparing this book. We believe it is worthwhile to share this work with the public because it deals with four decades of reflection and action on pressing public issues. The introductory conversational excerpts are intentionally broad while those in the conclusion focus on specific issues raised in the speeches.

IN CONVERSATION WITH URSULA FRANKLIN

JANE: Ursula, the speeches and interviews in this collection took place over the space of almost three decades. What are your thoughts on publishing now speeches that you gave several years ago?

URSULA: It is right and proper to ask why somebody like me – as she cleans out her papers past her ninetieth birthday – would think of publishing things that were said decades ago and publishing them for the here and now. Do I have anything to say that hasn't been said, and what are the thoughts I bring now to what I said then?

The reason for me to do it, and to do it under the overall title of *Thoughts and Afterthoughts*, is that I, like others of my generation, have for decades walked around problems of the same nature in a rapidly changing environment. The world in which I started as a young academic, feminist, and pacifist is drastically different from the world I am leaving. Yet, the issues remain. There is still war. There is still discrimination. The academic life, while different, is still constantly under scrutiny about the relevance of what is taught and studied.

The privilege of having been able to work, think, write, talk, and, most of all, listen and observe brings with it the obligation of thoughtfully comparing the here and now with the then and before. That's why I like the notion of "thoughts and afterthoughts." The wish that any citizen, any conscious scholar, any feminist has is to be useful: to be relevant. That means that what we say as matters of principle must be applicable to current situations.

What we try to do both in terms of the papers and their interrelationships is to say that, however much the world changes, there are basic thoughts and principles one brings to the task of being a responsible citizen. Those can be discerned over the clutter of the daily conversation, the daily arguments, the changing venues, the

changing rhetoric. What remains is our deep commitment to each
other as human beings, to the Earth that nurtures us, to the principles that have guided us, and to the need to continue handing these
principles on to those who come afterward in a manner that makes
them useful rather than quaint.

JANE: Certain themes arise regularly in the book because of your
deep commitment to topics such as pacifism, feminism, and the
social impact of technology. In our ordering of the speeches we
have taken care not simply to group the speeches into thematic
clusters, or even to separate them into two books – one for citizens
one for academics – because of the essential interconnectedness of
the topics you discuss and of the relevance to all readers of topics
such as technology, peace, and justice. Could you talk a bit about
the danger of reductionism we tried to avoid by not simply sub-
dividing the speeches into groups according to their dominant
themes?

URSULA: At the beginning of my career, it became very apparent
there is a limit to the usefulness of experts. Let me rephrase that:
it became clear that the life of the community cannot be left to the
sum of the knowledge of experts in various regions. As both the
peace and the environment movements had to be of concern to
citizens, it became apparent that more than expertise was needed;
therefore I have always tried not to equate expertise with discernment but to keep on linking knowledge in terms of fact and
understanding in terms of issues. The link between knowledge and
understanding that I think cannot be broken is often twisted with
overspecialization, with the overemphasis on detail that reductionism brings. Reductionism makes it possible to deal with specifics in
sophisticated detail but leaves other things out.

In terms of thought and afterthought, it is very clear that the
things that have been left out through an overly reductionist, specialized, expert-based approach are the very things that give us
trouble later. The afterthought is the awareness that what was first
considered trivial later became the dominant source of problems.
Forgetting the whole for the sake of looking in greater clarity at
detail has its profound limits. If anything comes out of thought and
afterthought it is "Don't consider the whole to be only the sum of
the parts." If necessary give on detail but don't give on the totality.

JANE: Perhaps it is because you have so consciously linked your
knowledge as a specialist and your understanding as a citizen that

you are so often asked to speak both to expert and to citizen audiences. The original audiences of your speeches are remarkably diverse. They include groups such as deans of fine arts, members of the public, university faculty members, physicists, and students of the Ursula Franklin Academy. Could you talk a bit about the ways you approach speaking to different audiences?

URSULA: Being a scientist, I started by talking to my colleagues at a time when the results of our work became of public interest and public significance. We talked about nuclear issues and the social responsibility of scientists. At that point, I very frequently used the image of the scientist as "a citizen with a toolbox." Depending on the issues, in many cases scholars develop their toolbox at the expense of developing their citizenship. On the other hand, the lay public may be good citizens with a limited toolbox.

Whether or not I articulate it in those terms, I would say that as I speak to audiences I always think of them as "citizens with a toolbox." I try to address the balance between the two because a good and effective citizen, in a good and effective system, should be literate both in their expertise and in their obligation and limitations as citizens. So the audiences to me are young or old, all citizens, all having a toolbox, with the parameters of their being active citizens, and I am trying to strengthen the part of their existence that needs the extra attention.

JANE: I wonder if we could talk a bit about what you call your "fussiness about language." In the speeches in this collection you often pause to define certain terms. Why are definitions so important to you?

URSULA: The older I get the more fussy I get about language. It isn't a question of being right or correct; in a sense it's a conflict-resolution issue. It is at the beginning to say, are we talking about the same thing? This is why I became so interested in things that are defined by what they are not, but it's also something I learned from my Chinese life.

The Chinese had a strong philosophical school somewhere around the time of Confucius concerned with "the Rectification of Names." As a form of justice, as a form of peacemaking, it is incumbent on whoever has to adjudicate or make peace first of all to see if it is a question of names. There's a long, deep philosophical tradition on the Rectification of Names in which the socially more responsible, the socially more powerful, are the ones who can rectify names but also have to be correct in what they say and name. We can only talk when we understand what others mean, so both as a means to assuring a peaceful structure and a dialogue, definitions are helpful.

JANE: Would you say definitions are even more important when we reach across divides to talk to people out of our disciplines and to those whose backgrounds we don't share?

URSULA: Absolutely. We only have to define. We don't have to agree. To define, to understand that's what they mean when they use a word, and then to give feedback. I'm getting increasingly fussy, and I'm also increasingly looking for words that aren't mortgaged by previous meaning. This is why I like the term "scrupling," which I talk about in the interview with Anna Maria Tremonti.

JANE: You often mention the importance of discernment, and we have talked about the fact that throughout this book you model for readers the importance of cultivating discernment as a daily activity. The speeches in this collection were given in different decades, to different audiences, on different subjects. What stays the same is your commitment to gaining and applying clarity – in whatever context you find yourself – in order to understand the impacts of technology, to increase pacifist activity ...

URSULA: ... And to understand the meaning of justice. That's correct. Discernment is a daily activity. The process of discernment is an ongoing one, because the context in which we work changes. Whether we like it or not, we are part of a changing environment. There is a Quaker phrase often used among the members of the Society of Friends that says: "Be present where you are." For much of my life I thought this meant, "Act your principles wherever you find yourself." I tried to be clear about my basic principles, and it seemed the challenge was to be present: to express one's views through action and argument when you're in a minority, as I was when I refused to do classified work. But as life went on I found it much harder to know *where* I was. This little phrase of "Be present where you are" at first to the young sounds like you have to know *who* you are. Increasingly for me, it has become a question of *where* am I? What is the reality in which I am present? Am I acting a script that society projects over the true reality, which I call the "vernacular reality" in the *Real World of Technology*? You will see more and more of my interests going into understanding exactly where we are. That is, what can a teacher do? What can a politician do? What does a grant-funding structure do? What can you do if your government is suddenly deaf? Discernment for me now is the double part of that little phrase of "Be present where you are." First of all, one has to be present and ask *who* am I, but also *where* am I? What is going on in the world? Discernment requires both individual responsibility and an analysis of context.

JANE: How do you hope this book will be used?

URSULA: I hope this book will be used as a friend. I hope it will be used as if you had a good friend with whom, and through whom, you could explore a question. If you are a teacher, you may ask your friend for examples or rely on her experience and eloquence. On the other hand, if you are by yourself, you may want to say, "Aach, isn't it nice, I am not alone. There is somebody else worrying about the same thing." If you are a student, you say, "Hmmm. There is somebody else who may elaborate that part of the course where I didn't really get the point." I hope the book will be a friend to those who teach, to those who are being taught, and most of all to those who are worried: those who want to be good and informed citizens who look for community and don't want to be alone if they think about something that is not the current flavour of the month.

I

Interview with June Callwood*

(*National Treasures*, Vision TV, season 4, episode 11, 29
November 1994)

JC: Every Canadian can make a list of national treasures, and what
I think those lists would have in common is that the people we
admire most are people who live a life of responsibility for others.
The human race wouldn't have survived very long if most of us
weren't opposed to what Gandhi described as "untruth, injustice
and humbug." In this series you'll meet some of the people that
I think exemplify a useful life, a well-lived life– the givers, the
treasures.

   Dr Ursula Franklin is an amazing woman. She is an intellectual
of international standards, a physicist at the University of Toronto
who also helped pioneer the new science of archaeometry: the
examination and analysis of ancient materials. A prominent and
lifelong feminist and pacifist, she is also an inspiration to women
across this county.

   Ursula, most people know you for your ideas about how social
systems work, about the peace movement, and about militarism.
Most of us don't even ask about your scientific work because we
assume we can't figure it out. I want to start by asking, how did
you get from being a physicist working in metallurgy to looking at
ancient ruins?
UF: I began as a crystallographer, and one of the things that always
fascinated me in physics is the notion of structure. Whatever discipline you are in, once you get a knowledge and a feeling for how

---

* We gratefully acknowledge the producer of Vision TV's *National Treasures* series for permitting us to include this interview.

the whole and the parts relate – how a whole can be more or less than the sum of the parts depending on what and where the parts are – once you understand the nature of structure, then the behaviour of materials starts to make sense. You know why when you hit a piece of copper it makes a thin sheet, and when you hit a piece of rock salt it makes all sorts of little crystals of rock salt. You can grind the rock salt, but you can't possibly grind a piece of copper. You begin to understand that underneath those properties are *structures*.

That awareness of structure is equally relevant when you observe social systems. As you look at how people arrange their lives with respect to each other, you consider not only *whether* it matters who links to whom but also *how* it matters. When you then think about what makes the difference between peace and war, between prejudice and respect, you begin to see that it's not all just personal stance but that there's a structure. As you and I know, there are elaborate social structures that change constantly. On the other hand, materials structures only change by external interventions otherwise they are preserved and subject to our study. This is why I became so interested in ancient technology. Artifacts reveal what people have done just as texts tell us what people thought others were doing.

JC: What can you learn in archaeometry?

UF: You can learn an awful lot. For instance, you can determine relations of trade. You can analyze pottery to the point at which you can say, "This clay comes from that particular area." There have always been questions such as, "Did the pot travel? Did the potter travel?" The knowledge of the raw materials reveals part of a trade pattern.

JC: You're following migrations of people too, right?

UF: You follow migrations, but you also have to be very critical of hearsay, because very often history is written by the winners rather than the losers, and they tend to denigrate the losers and suggest the winners have done it all. Very often you find no record of the ingenuity of the people on the ground. If you examine materials, however, you find, for instance, that a certain type of pottery may originally come from Cyprus. It may be traded into the Levant but very soon the local people make stuff that looks the same. It is only the tools of the scientists that can tell you this isn't really a Cypriote pot, this is something that looks like a Cypriote pot, and –

pure Jane Jacobs – eventually the people in the Levant get very
good at making it, and they export it back to Cyprus.

JC: Isn't that fascinating. Can you discover women's history
through these pieces of pottery?

UF: You can often discover women's history through weaving, textiles, things that – like women's history – may disappear except
that they leave imprints. The pots as they are being made are put
on mats, and sometimes you see the mats' patterns on the bottom
of the pots.

JC: The cloth is gone so there's only the pattern on the clay?

UF: Yes. It's just a footprint. There are some beautiful things in
China; in fact there are pieces here in the Royal Ontario Museum –
metal mirrors that have corroded, and they were wrapped in silk.
The silk is long gone, but its imprint in the patina is good enough
to reconstruct, and John Vollmer and myself and others have recon-
structed the weave of some of the early Chinese textile patterns.

JC: Was it your science that was examining the Shroud of Turin?

UF: We stayed out of the Shroud of Turin. We felt that this wasn't
the place for science. Facts were not so much the issue, and not
only myself, who would only have been involved marginally, but
also other colleagues in Toronto declined that opportunity. Knowledge is not necessarily helpful to solve all problems. Some problems
don't arise from lack of knowledge, and we felt that this wasn't a
problem in which knowledge would help; it would only make the
divisions sharper.

JC: You have a multidisciplinary approach to everything you
do. You were you able to head up a team at the University of
Toronto that pulled together very unusual disciplines to work in
collaboration.

UF: Yes.

JC: Is this still happening?

UF: No, unfortunately it isn't. When I retired, my position was not
filled by the university. Although there were good people, people I
had been able to bring along who could have made competent and
dedicated successors, that position wasn't filled.

JC: So that fell apart? Let's talk about it anyway. I've learned at
your feet on this, that people working together, especially the col-
laborations of people with different skills, different backgrounds, is
very rich. What did your team do?

UF: It's very rich and it's very rewarding. I can probably illustrate it best with the example of team teaching. It wasn't that colleague A did the first three lectures and colleague B did the next three lectures. I taught a graduate course on ancient materials with my friend and colleague Maxine Kleindienst, who was then the chair of anthropology and archaeology. The course was essentially a conversation between the two of us. We were both there in every class. There were times when my knowledge was the first to be put on the table. For instance, I would talk about how things break. Maxine would pick up that topic immediately and talk about early stone tools and what the development of flint and stone tools tells us historically about people, their settlements, and their work. Then I would discuss the microscopic examination of existing stone tools. Using a microscope and modern techniques, you can see how an ancient tool worked and what it was used for – whether it was grass cutting or wood cutting or whatever. The discussion was like a good, pleasurable, interesting conversation between friends, and hopefully what came out of that for the students, as it did for us, was a real understanding, and that's what collaboration is all about.

I was asked recently to open a conference on interdisciplinarity at the University of British Columbia, and I opened it with a talk I called "Going Fishing Together." I think collaborative, interdisciplinary work is like going fishing together. One may have the boat, and one may have the knowledge of where the fish are, and no one can do it alone. There's also the fact that they are likely friends, and they enjoy each other's company. They freely share in what they have, and that seems to me the crux, rather than to define a new area in which one builds a new little enterprise and a new little empire.

JC: We should all go fishing together.

UF: I think we do in many ways. That is the pleasure of friendship, of doing things together. It means a level of equality, a level at which one knows that all have something to contribute and all have something to gain.

JC: Now you have many extraordinary honours. You are a companion of the Order of Canada and of the Order of Ontario. You have a lot of honorary doctorates and many other things, but it began with you being the first woman professor in the Engineering Faculty at the University of Toronto, didn't it?

UF: I wasn't the first woman professor, but I was the first woman to be appointed a University Professor. This is a rank that is a bit like the Senate. The university appoints a small group out of its own number as a way of saying you really belong to the university as a whole, not solely to your own discipline. That group includes people like Northrop Frye, C.B. Macpherson, and others.

JC: What I was going back to was when you first came to teach at the University of Toronto. I didn't think there were any other women teaching in that faculty.

UF: There were other women. They weren't in the Department of Metallurgy, but you mustn't forget that during the war there was a very large number of women in the technical fields at the university, including physics, and they were perfectly capable of filling in for the men, except that after the war they were slowly elbowed out, and some left. You may recall Elizabeth Allen, who was a very fine and devoted member of the Physics Department. She died last year. There was also Elsie McGill and others. Some of them came in at that time, a few immediately after, and then there was that great gap when the university chose not to hire women in the sciences and in engineering.

JC: Did you have a difficult time? We're so conscious now of women being harassed.

UF: I don't think my difficulties were that great, largely because I took a reasonably dim view of engineers as a collectivity. You know just because you are excluded from something that doesn't by itself make it particularly desirable.

JC: You didn't get your nose out of joint too easily!

UF: Not only that, but in all phases of life I have a style of living, as does my husband, where we choose a few good friends for who they are as human beings. Belonging to a clan – I'm just not a good type for that. They have as much good reason to think I just don't fit in. It's not all prejudice; they have to put up with somebody who doesn't do military research in a faculty where *everybody* runs after military research. They have to put up with somebody who takes a very dim view of girly pictures in graduate and undergraduate offices. The fact that I was different was for me a given and not a horrible revelation.

JC: And you knew who you were.

UF: Quite, and that was nonnegotiable.

JC: Another one of the amazing things for me in learning about you was finding out you were in Berlin through the war and only came here after.

UF: Yes.

JC: Your mother was Jewish?

UF: Yes.

JC: How did you survive that war, Ursula?

UF: Painfully. There's only one word for it. My mother was Jewish, and my father came from an old German family. In the sort of mixture of bureaucracy and cruelty that the Germans practised, they went after the people of complete Jewish background first, and once those people were eliminated they began to round up the mixed couples. Both my parents were in concentration camps, in separate ones, and I was in one of those forced labour camps during the war. It is more miracle than anything else that we all survived.

JC: You were a teenager at this time, Ursula?

UF: Yes. I was a teenager when the war began. I was born in 1921. My parents were very anxious to get me out of Germany even if they couldn't get out. In fact I had a place in a college in England, but the Brits did not allow a student visa for somebody who wasn't eighteen. I turned eighteen two weeks after the war broke out, and nothing could push the bureaucracy to allow me to get out. I wasn't as unhappy about it as my parents were, particularly my mother. We were separated toward the end of the war, and it was only after Berlin had fallen that we met again in our old house that had been taken from us. We had said that whoever survived would try to get back to the house.

JC : That must have been something when you found you had all survived. What a moment for you all.

UF: It was. I had had news from my mother, but no news from my father. You know the way the grapevine works. There is no rationale in life in terms of who perished and who was saved, but of course it leaves an imprint on all one's life. You say, "What am I going to do with a life that really is a gift beyond anybody's deserving and merit?" There were so many people who perished. I didn't.

JC: Many survivors suffer from irrational guilt, but nevertheless guilt that they survived.

UF: I never felt guilt so much as I felt obligation. That is, there were things I was obliged to do because the others weren't there. I think

some of the things I feel very strongly about – in terms of the public domain, of being useful, of being concerned about things that
aren't just in my own interest – I think these concerns come out of
that basic question, how does one conduct a responsible life that
really has been given by an accident of history? It could just as well
have been given to somebody else, but you have it, and you better
do something.

JC: Why were you in science? Your family was not.

UF: I think that was precisely a political reaction. I might have
gone into history, but I went to school at a time when history was
already censored, and the only things that couldn't be censored, of
course, were mathematics and physics. I was very clear on that. I
remember a sort of real subversive pleasure that there was no word
of authority that could change either the laws of physics or the
conduct of mathematics. It was because of that, I think, that I had
so much pleasure in learning, and because the teachers could be
much less corrupt than the teachers of history.

JC: Where did you get so much self-reliance? Did your family raise
you that way?

UF: I would think so. I was the only child and my parents were
incredibly good parents. As a child if I had any criticism of my
parents, it was that they were *too* good parents. I often wished my
mother wouldn't take me so seriously, that she wouldn't remember so much, that I could be much more casual, but ours wasn't a
casual family. I think it was my parents who, without necessarily
saying so, raised me in an atmosphere of respect that gave me the
feeling I had the potential, the obligation, and the tools to do things
decently.

JC: You already had a Ph.D. when you came to Canada. How did
you come here?

UF: I came on a postdoctoral fellowship that emerged, in fact, from
an article I wrote in 1947 or 1948, when it began to be clear how
the German universities developed. I was in Berlin, which was one
of the most stimulating places – though one of the most miserable
in terms of physical setting – where people really thought about
what a university should be like and drew conclusions from the
past. There was a group of people who, just because things were
physically so difficult in a destroyed city, had to break from the
normal German segregation of professors and students, and they
all sat around the table and all talked and all worried.

JC: You used that experience directly when you did multidisciplinary teaching.
UF: Yes, and I probably learned more in those two years than I ever
learned per unit time in all my life. But after 1947, when I went
to my first meeting of the German Physical Society in Goettingen
while still a doctoral student and began to have contact with people in other universities, I realized that there was really very little
hope for a genuinely new beginning, for really drawing conclusions
from evidence. I wrote that up in a little article, and I began to
look for opportunities to leave Germany. I thought it was impossible to stay, both for me and for my parents, who had very serious
health scars from the time in the concentration camps. I would not
have thought at the end of the war that there would be any excuse
for me not to stay; it took me two-and-a-half years to realize that
I couldn't, and also that there was no place for me. There was
no place for people who wanted a radical, profound change that
would make a repetition of the past impossible.
JC: Your passionate opposition not only to what the military does
but also to military structures comes from that experience, that
wartime experience, and the devastation.
UF: And from the experience of an authoritarian government, of
oppression. As we said before, there are people but there are also
structures; you cannot have oppressive structures and not destroy
good people. Out of that little article, which I sent to a good friend
of my mother's who was a professor of physics in Oxford, more
for his information than anything else, came a response that drew
my attention to The Lady Davis Fellowship Trust here in Canada,
which sent people to a number of universities. The University of
Toronto had put in for somebody in my area. I had just finished
doctoral research that was good science and that, together with
the work of my supervisor, got some very high acclaim. I was able
to apply, and I came here on that scholarship, which, to the ever-
lasting blessing of Lady Davis and her husband, had a provision
for immigration; that is, I had the chance to immigrate. I had other
opportunities, but I was looking for a place to park my loyalty.
JC: To park your loyalty. Were they astonished that a person could
qualify for that scholarship and be a woman?
UF: I don't know. If they were they didn't show it. I was the only
woman, but they were compassionate and very polite people, and
if they were surprised they didn't show it. I was also pretty dumb

in the sense that I didn't expect prejudice. My mother and her three
sisters were all academics. I didn't come out of an atmosphere
where it was a surprise if women used their minds, so the subtle
hints may have completely escaped me.

JC: You were in the perfect position to help Voice of Women (VOW)
when it started. Very few of them had any scientific training, and
yet they were trying to prevent the testing of nuclear weapons in
the atmosphere. They had to find someone who knew what they
were trying to do, and that was *you*.

UF: That's true, but you could also just take the whole thing and
turn it around. The VOW [now Canadian Voice of Women for
Peace] came into my life at the absolutely perfect moment to keep
me from just being one of the boys and doing what everyone else
did. It gave me an opportunity to put my knowledge into a broader
context, and I have always had an enormous feeling of gratitude
and debt for VOW and for the fellowship of the women's movement. Science is a competitive thing, and to be in an atmosphere
where people trust you as a human being – they can't really check
what you're doing – an atmosphere where the prime requirement is
to establish and maintain and exchange trust, was a great gift. One
brings respective talents to the task. Mine was only one of many,
and it so happened that mine was rare in terms of other people's.

JC: It was dead on.

UF: But there was Helen Cunningham. There were others.

JC: Kay Macpherson.

UF: Kay Macpherson.

JC: Your contribution as the scientist, and that was a singular contribution, came when they were trying to establish that there was
harm, and most particularly to children, from testing in the atmosphere. You had that insight regarding how they could prove it. Isn't
this the baby-tooth story?

UF: That's the baby-tooth story, and of course one of the sad things
is that what seemed to us self-evident was so very difficult to translate into policies and government action.

JC: I remember that the cows were eating grass that was saturated
with strontium-90, and it was getting in the milk, and into the food
chain, and into the babies – but how to prove it? It all sounded so
subjective, and *you* said, "It'll be in the teeth."

UF: Yes, and it was, and we did the tooth survey as well as saying
to the mothers, "Just use powdered milk. The radioactivity decays."

That brief, "Fallout Monitoring in Canada," was the first brief I
wrote, and we brought to the government. In that case it was first
the provincial and then the federal government, and that was when
I first learned about the lack of follow-up and monitoring. Voice
of Women and the Quakers, including myself, did all this stuff:
we took the brief to the government, we appeared before the Joint
Committee Reviewing Canadian Foreign Policy, and in between
are *thirty years*. You would think in the course of thirty years,
an organization like Voice of Women, which had been correct,
which had been right, would have some standing. We were there
to appear before the Joint Committee. It was the last session of
the last day of a longish meeting of the committee, and there were
the *pacifists*. It was the only organization speaking for women and
thirty years later we were still...

JC: ... Still at it.

UF: Not only were we still *at it* but we were *again* shunted into
the 4:00–5:30 session of the very last day when minds are made
up. Reports are essentially clear in the minds of those who have
to write them, and then they have to deal with *those pacifists*.
That's the sort of thing I would not have foreseen when we began.
I believed then that the government was basically ill-informed but
well-intentioned, and now I believe that governments are well-
informed and ill-intentioned.

JC: Let's leave that, that's beautiful. What a sad commentary. You
mentioned that you are a Quaker and went on to something else.
When did you become a Quaker?

UF: Somewhere the early 1950s. I married in 1952, and my husband had had exposure to Quakerism in England. When our children were born, we didn't really have any family here, and we
looked for something that would be a spiritual home as well as
an extended family. While we wished to stay within the Christian
spectrum, we both felt we could not live in a church that blesses
flags and weapons. We were pacifists before we were Quakers, but
it was a very easy transition to Quakerism for us, and it has been a
very good home and an extended family for us and our children.

JC: Where did the core of Quakerism fit with who you are?

UF: There are two things that I found so very easy about Quakerism. One is the respect for every person regardless of his or her
beliefs. Friends say that there is "that of God in every person," and
that – whoever they are, wherever they are – it is possible to appeal

to that: as Quakers say, "to answer to that of God in every person."
The other is the openness to inquiry. Since Friends believe God
reveals herself to everybody in each person's particular way, there's
no limit to inquiry, to science, to knowledge. There is an encouragement to use both heart and mind, not one alone. I found this
very easy and very much part of who I was, reinforcing my belief
that one is essentially, and has to look at oneself as, a responsible
instrument.

JC: Is this a faith without a deity?

UF: No, not at all. It is a part of the Christian spectrum. Think
what the Reformation had done in moving responsibility back to
the believers. This has always been important to me because my
father's family came from a long line of Protestants who really
thought they had singlehandedly produced the Reformation, so I
was brought up in that tradition.

JC: They were all at the church door!

UF: Essentially what the Reformation had done was to establish
a sense that every human being is able to discern the divine and
the difference between right and wrong without an edict, without
somebody being specially put in a position to tell them what to do,
that their conscience was perfectly capable of doing this.

JC: How do you get a conscience that's so exquisitely developed?

UF: You tune it like an instrument. You know, when people start
singing they develop their ear. They develop their voice. They begin
to hear dissonances that they didn't hear before. You become
attuned to having to make responsible and moral decisions. One of
the interesting things about Quakers is their concept of what they
call "a sacramental life." You don't have a creed, you don't sign
something; the only proof of your faith or lack of faith is how you
conduct your life. Consequently it's like singing. At every point you
say, "Am I in tune?" You develop your conscience as you develop
your hearing, and then you begin to hear smaller dissonances that
you didn't used to hear. It's like tuning one's mind, and it becomes
quite natural in the conduct of one's daily life.

JC: I was struck by something you said in a speech. I think it comes
from the Quaker tradition. You were speaking about the military,
about the military mindset that has dominated our economy and
part of our society for a long time. You said the military hierarchy
had been replaced by a similar kind of economic hierarchy, and

that what we needed – this is the phrase I'm grabbing for – is
"horizontal solidarity."

UF: Yes.

JC: Horizontal solidarity – that's great, Ursula!

UF: It is that people have to look around on the plane where they
are and see who else is there, see with whom one shares a life,
rather than that vertical loyalty that salutes. I think normal life has
a great deal of scope for that and one just has to cultivate it. Where
women come in is in the difference in their view of rank. I've been
among those who have encouraged women to take positions of
responsibility, to move up and become mayors or professors, yet it
isn't that they will become better people because they are professors or mayors. Rank is like a postal code; it defines their responsibility, their work. It's not, as it is in the hierarchical structure, an
extra button on the shoulder that means their judgment is superior.
You ask the bank president what he thinks of whatever – whether
kids can spell – and he probably hasn't spelled anything for the last
thirty years.

JC: But he has an opinion.

UF: He has an opinion, which he is entitled to, but because he's a
bank president it's seen as much more important than it would be
if he were the person who operates the elevator.

JC: In the beginning the Women's Movement certainly aspired to
that collaborative model. It seemed to be such a wonderful time
because we did care for one another, and now something has happened, something has poisoned the garden, and I don't know where
to begin to sweeten it again.

UF: It's very difficult. I see, as you do, the erosion of the public
sphere with enormous apprehension. I have grown up with a conviction that people have an obligation to struggle with others for
the welfare of those who are not in a position to struggle for themselves. I don't have to remind you that slavery was abolished by
middle-class women and men who probably hadn't the slightest
idea what it was like to be a slave, but who had that conviction –
this is not right, and it just isn't done.

JC: But there came a time when there was a collective will to do
that.

UF: Yes, but the collective will grew out of the fact that people
who were not slaves could not in good conscience lead a full and

honourable life when there were others who were still slaves. You know, Karl Marx didn't write during the night shift at the salt mine. He wrote in the Library of the British Museum, yet his work created a collective consciousness that in turn liberated workers around the world.

What I see, with considerable apprehension, is what I consider to be the privatization of the public sphere: that people feel that they have only the right to speak for themselves, and that it's intrusive to worry about other people's wellbeing. I find that eroding because there are so many problems that are common to all of us and are indivisible.

JC: The human tribe survived by caring, supporting one another.

UF: Also the human tribe collectively made the mess that one has to clean up, and there is no ownership of the environment. There is no ownership of water. There's no ownership of justice or peace. These are things I consider indivisible benefits; there's either justice for all, peace for all, or there's no justice. There's clean air for all or there is none. With this trend for appropriation and for ownership, what suffers are these things that are essentially the common good. You and I grew up with a conviction that when one has any spare energy, or any spare talent, or any spare money, it is an *obligation*, it is the essence of citizenship, to use it for the common good.

JC: You don't have a choice; you just have to do it.

UF: You do it and that's life. That's citizenship, and that is the notion of collaboration, and you know others do it, too. It isn't an issue of "white man's burden"; it is collaboration. In the foreword to *The Real World of Technology* I said something that I've said umpteen times, and that I still believe: that the image of the peaceful world is a potluck supper.

JC: I love that.

UF: People bring what they do best. It would be a disaster if everybody brought the same. Those who don't cook still have essential things to do, and people who come, however modest it may be, have the rightful expectation to have nourishment and fellowship. A real world has to be a world in which people can bring what they do well, that is respected *because of* not *in spite of* its being different. There's room for all, and everybody can feel that they contribute.

JC: You have lovely metaphors: the fishing trip, the potluck supper. Another one is earthworms. What is it we learn from earthworms?

UF: Well, I think from earthworms we learn that before anything grows there has to be a prepared soil. When we were talking about that endless process of bringing briefs and information to governments, and so on, the only thing that can keep us going is the notion that it prepares the soil. It may not change minds, but it will provide the arguments for a time when minds are changed. I think until and unless there is that prepared soil, no new thoughts and no new ways of dealing with problems will ever arise.

JC: Ursula, we're both in our seventies. I don't know whether it's the way we were raised or our great ages, but I find myself growing discouraged more than I used to. I thought that there would be a kinder world by now. How do you handle that?

UF: Well, I, too, get discouraged. Sometimes my friends quote me back to myself reminding me I once said, "We cannot afford the luxury of despair." As I get older I realize how little one really knows and how little one really understands.

The timeframe we see is short; historical developments are long. You think how desperate many people must have been in various times of history that must have seemed to them eternal, though in fact they lasted only five years. When you think about the whole period of my childhood. Hitler came to power in 1933, and it was all over in 1945. That was a period of just *twelve years*. The French Revolution took twenty-five years, and you can see what it did to history. What I say to myself is we are in an incredible social transition, and we have expectations that it will go at the pace and with the predictability of Victorian England, and it just doesn't go like that. It's very hard to see one's own time. It's very hard to see what are just fireworks, and what are real glimmers of hope, so I think one just has to believe that people have always muddled through. They will muddle through with or without our advice.

JC: Generally without!

UF: That is the only way I get around that: to recall the depths of disillusionment and despair that must have happened in other, often very recent, times of history.

JC: And if we hang on it will be all right?

UF: It'll muddle itself out, hopefully, and if it doesn't it won't be because you or I didn't try.

JC: I guess that's the point. Someone said, T.S. Eliot I think, "For us there is only the trying, the rest is not our business."

UF: Quite. I sometimes say it in a much less elegant way: "I'm not God, I just work here." You know that's all one can do, and in many ways it's a great relief, because just imagine if you were responsible for the universe.

JC: You're only responsible for what you do yourself.

UF: Yes, and that's all. You work here. You try to do a decent honourable job. That's all.

JC: Ursula Franklin, a scholar and a philosopher, thank you. It's been wonderful talking to you, Ursula.

2

When the Seven Deadly Sins Became the Seven Cardinal Virtues

(Acceptance speech on receiving the YWCA Women of Distinction Award, Toronto, 1986)

I would like to begin with a few historical reflections because it behoves us to see where the roots of our activities and concerns come from. It is really of interest to see how closely the movements for women's rights, for peace, and for social change have historically been linked.

I would like to take you back to the earlier part of the nineteenth century. Through the almost 150 to 200 years of the developing Industrial Revolution, women had come into a very different social setting and had become a very strong force in their respective communities. That was a time when women looked at the world around them not so much with a practical concern but with a kind of mental and religious concern. Profoundly striking was the increasing unacceptability of slavery. If you look into the abolition movement, which started out of profound religious considerations, you see the enormous role women played in raising consciousness about the social institution of slavery. Human beings ought not to be owned by other human beings; whatever the economics, it was morally, religiously, and socially unacceptable.

Eventually world consciousness rose to a point that in 1840 the first World Anti-Slavery Convention was held in London. At that point something really striking happened. The women who had done all the work were not allowed to speak, and they did not wish to attend the convention if they could not speak. Their exclusion brought home what many of them had seen before: there are not just slaves somewhere in far-off countries. Women saw their own role with increasing criticism. They too were subjected to forces beyond their control. Much of the impetus of these same women who worked so hard to bring about a worldwide movement for the abolition of slavery was then channelled into the suffrage movement and the movement for women's rights for equal participation.

At the same time, and out of that same root of common humanity, there was a strong worldwide peace movement beginning, including women who had seen the effects of the Crimean War and of the Civil War in the United States. In 1848, only eight years after the Anti-Slavery Convention, the International Peace Congress was held in Brussels, and it was opened with the words "Mesdames et Messieurs." It was in the work for peace that women – for the first time – had equality in a world forum.

From there on you will understand why the concerns for equality, development, and peace for many women were one. At the root of all of them was the concept of justice, and justice is essentially a moral and a religious concept. It's not a legal concept. It's a firm belief in common humanity whether it is expressed, as it is in my own Quaker tradition, where people speak of "that of God in every person," or whether it is expressed in any other tradition. There is a belief in common humanity – that all of us are God's children, equally precious in His or Her sight. That provides a code of conduct for every human being, because if we are equally precious and equally important to God, then who are we to classify people into those who matter and those who don't? I think that's the root, the real religious, moral root of justice.

Equality really means that all people matter equally. As we consider daily, local, or world issues, the very central thing justice demands is that all people matter, and that all people matter equally. Long before that can be translated into legal equality at every point, it has to translate itself into caring. That's one of the things the YWCA has done so extraordinarily well is to put that feeling of common justice into terms of caring.

The caring function of justice that goes into development must also redress the injustices of the past. The social and political barriers that stand in the way of realizing that all people matter must be removed. Again the anti-slavery work is probably the best example, and there are many economic examples in the Third World now and in our own country. We can also stress the belief that people matter by giving people opportunities, providing education, providing a space for them to show what they are capable of, or providing that bit of shield and shelter needed for them to come into their own. That work, I think, is a caring function of justice.

If we look at removing barriers to execute that common caring and feeling that people matter equally, we see that most of the barriers are manmade – and I say that advisedly – and they are barriers we have the absolute obligation to remove. That isn't done in far-away countries; it has to be done here in our own territory, on our own turf. Many of those barriers were erected for private, corporate, national reasons, and so it is those who are part of the private, corporate, and national entities who have to work toward dismantling them. It cannot be the victims who are charged with dismantling the barriers that keep them from equal participation. The YWCA has been exemplary, and has to continue to be exemplary, in pointing out the many practical barriers to justice. Our mission then, in the development for justice, is at home, in the broadest sense of the word, to make it possible for those who could perfectly well exert their own worth to have the space to do so and the barriers to that exertion removed.

One of the greatest barriers to justice is the arms race. I don't know whether any one of us will live long enough to see on television well-fed children and starving and shoeless soldiers, but at the moment, regardless of country, nation, or denomination, it is the women, the old, and the children who are starving, and the young men in uniform who have clothes, have food, have shoes, and are fine. One of the profound barriers to justice is the misuse of the world's resources and the misuse of the world's talents for purposes of destruction and not purposes of caring. That's something that can only be changed by a combination of practical and moral action. It is my firm belief that no amount of practical action will make a difference if it is not combined with the admittance that there are moral standards – religious, ethical beliefs that matter as much as people matter. We have to stand not only in favour of practical measures but also in favour of a moral standard that is not negotiable: people's lives are not negotiable; the fact that we are brothers and sisters is not negotiable; and the inequality of suffering is not acceptable. We have to say that both in our words and in our lives.

Elise Boulding in her history of women called *The Underside of History: A View of Women through Time*, spoke of that movement in the mid-eighteenth century that founded the YWCA and other similar women's organizations saying that the common twin concept of spiritual and economic welfare has always been, and continues to be, a theme and a guide to these groups. I think we have to think in terms of that twin concept of spiritual and economic welfare, and it's not only other people's spiritual welfare. We may have the economic welfare, but we have to be very concerned about our spiritual welfare and be willing to see where our economic welfare comes from.

Lewis Mumford, the great historian of technology, once pointed out that a very quick way to describe the transition into the modern industrial society – and he spoke about the Industrial Revolution – is to say that the Seven Deadly Sins of the Middle Ages have become the Seven Cardinal Virtues of the Industrial Age. That is very well put, but it is more than a facile sentence. Suddenly greed and envy, avarice and luxury, gluttony and all those things that the Middle Ages considered deadly sins are the very things that drive the machinery of a consumer society that puts private gain before communal welfare, and that isn't that recent. I remind you that a member of the Canadian Cabinet said to a group of Aboriginal people that they had to learn to become greedy, while they still believed that greed was, in fact, one of those cardinal sins rather than one of those great virtues.

Personally, I think we have come to the end of a time in history where this inversion of values has any social utility. We now begin to come into a time at which the very survival of this planet requires that we go back and say: "No. Greed and envy, avarice and gluttony, the love of self and luxury – these are not good things, and we will not survive, all of us, if we believe that these are virtues." We have to get back to the spirit of concern that brought the YWCA into being, that brought women's organizations into the public scene: that caring for a concept of justice. While we do so, we have to work in this world to alleviate the effects of injustice.

You can say, "That's all fine, but how do you do it?" In response to that question, there are three thoughts I would like to leave with you. One is the consideration of structures. One of the great barriers to justice is very often not people but structures. By structures I mean the way people divide up authority and responsibility. There are such things as evil structures. As we work, we have to be very clear about the structural problems that make it difficult to achieve justice.

Being in such an interdependent world, we also have to look not only at what we do but also at how we do it. Again, the YWCA has been exemplary in seeing very early that one cannot do things *for* people, one has to do things *with* people. The great command of anyone who wants to be effective in the field of development, is to listen – not to accept one's own definition of a problem, but to listen to victims and accept the definition of the problem of those who are on the receiving end of development. So one barrier is structure, and another is information: get information from those who feel the impact of what is done, not from those who dole it out.

A third point I feel very strongly about is that we need a very much more profound understanding of technology. That doesn't mean devices and switches and plugs but what these things do to a society: their place in the social fabric. I want to remind you that not only certain sectors but also our whole society has basically an anti-people trend. When you look at policies, when you look at pronouncements, you find that people are considered sources of problems: they get married, they have children, they need schools, they need them in certain places, they want jobs, and then they get old and we have to worry about hospital beds. Essentially, people are looked upon as a perpetual source of problems. On the other hand, where does one turn? One turns to devices: we need more computers in the school; we need a databank for your doctors. Once you are attuned to it, you see our whole society is permeated with the concept that people are a source of problems and devices are where you turn for solutions.

Now something is obviously blatantly wrong. We can very well make a case that frequently devices are sources of problems, and even more so that people are sources of solutions. If we think in terms of development with justice then the first rule is "People are the sources of the solutions." People are resources. People aren't a nuisance to have around. Some of my colleagues design plants with the desire to have nobody in them. What is the point whether it's cheaper or not? It is a question of *cheaper for whom.*

With that same sense of justice as we defined it – that people matter – we also have to approach other aspects of technology. We cannot be part of a discussion on *what* risks a certain technology has without asking *whose* risks. It makes an awful lot of difference. Assume you are talking about video display terminals, for example; the great discussion is "Are they or are they not putting the operator's health or eyes at risk?" You don't discuss *whether* there are risks; you discuss *whose* risks. Who is it that is at risk? It's quite pointless to talk about risk-benefit without saying "Are those who are at risk also getting the benefits, or are those who are getting the benefits very far removed from the risk?" This is particularly the case if you look at development in the Third World, for example, where women are often in the end more disadvantaged than they were before. The questions to ask are "Whose benefits? Whose risks?" rather than "What benefits? What risks?"

If we wish to think and act for development with justice, then for our own sake as much as for the sake of anyone else, we have to realize we do this because it is a moral imperative for us – not because it is a benefit for someone else, but because it is a dictate of our own moral and religious background. This imperative comes out of a tradition in which women have identified themselves with those who are the subjects of slavery, and with those women, children, and men who were victims of war. In its modern tradition this stance is no more than a century and a half old, but during that time, particularly through the development of science and technology, the means of oppression, the means of war, the means to do injustice have increased immensely. So has the resistance, but we have to realize – and it really is so – that all we hope to do can only be done when the greatest threat to development, and that is war, is removed from the scene. There is no development without the assurance of peace.

For me peace is defined in two ways. One is that it is a commitment to the future. Anyone who has on any level a commitment to the future has, by necessity, the commitment to actively work for peace, because there is no future without peace. Then there comes a second definition, and that is the definition of peace not as the absence of war but as the absence of fear. That definition links us to all those of our sisters and brothers who have reasons to fear the knock on the door at night: to those who have reasons to fear there will not be enough food tomorrow morning for their families; those who have to fear missiles; those who have to fear pollution; and all of us who have to fear nuclear war.

Working to eliminate fear links us very profoundly, because as we work to eliminate one level of fear we work for justice and peace *provided* we do not do this by making others more fearful. There's no way to be secure when others are more insecure; there's no way to reduce fear through means that make the burden on others greater. In that sense of equality that all people matter equally, when we work to eliminate a source of fear somewhere, using means that are just and equal, we remove one barrier to the realization of peace. We can only do that when we watch the means by which do it, and the best way to watch the means by which we do it is not practical, it is not technical, but it is a moral means. It is to remember the roots from which we came. It is, in my opinion, to remember that the time for the Seven Deadly Sins to be the Seven Cardinal Virtues is over. We have to remember again that it may be a sin to be greedy, that it may not be right to love luxury, that it may not be right to be envious, but to be caring, humble and modest. Thank you.

3

The Legacies of War

(Keynote address, Voice of Women Conference, Ottawa,
1990)

Thirty years ago, when the Voice of Women (VOW) entered into
the arena of public discussion, peace was on everybody's mind. We
had the effects of nuclear testing, and world peace was a subject
of discussion much more than it is today. For many of us in Voice
of Women, our preoccupation throughout the decades has been the
issue of peace, and one can rightfully ask what it is that occupies us
today.

I want to maintain that it still is, in fact, the issue of peace that
brings us together. I want to reinforce that peace is not the absence
of war. Peace is the absence of fear. Peace is the presence of justice.
Throughout the work we have all done, we are very clear that peace
is, in fact, a consequence. As somebody put it, "Peace is a by-product
of the persistent application of social truth and justice and the strong
and intelligent application of love." The price of peace is the price of
justice. It is very clear not only that do we not have peace but also
that all the issues before us are very much issues of justice – justice
for people, justice with respect to the environment – that allow a
condition in which there is freedom from fear: be it the fear of war
and the military, fear of oppression, economic or political, cultural,
or sexual, fear of not knowing whether there will be meaningful
work for oneself or for one's children, or whether there will be a
public sphere in which issues of justice will have priority over issues
of profit. Peace is the overriding issue.

Now, we can ask why is it so difficult in this day and age to work
effectively for peace? What, for instance, has the collapse of the
Soviet empire done? Has it brought us closer to peace? I want to
consider with you what is in a sense the legacy – the mortgage –

of forty years of non-peace, of Cold War. It is often forgotten that the problems we address today, the problems that bring women together – be they in Beijing, in Toronto, or in the former Yugoslavia – are problems related to the legacy of a Cold War, as well as to the legacy of many hot wars. I want to innumerate five areas of that legacy because that is the political, economic, and emotional landscape in which we have to work.

The first part of that legacy is that the world is full of weapons: weapons to which more are being added. Strong and ripe weapons development and weapons trade are going on internationally. The world is full of easily available weapons, but because of the legacy of the Cold War, because of the preoccupation with weapons, the world is also full of unresolved problems.

It is easy to forget that for decades the priorities of a Cold War, and of a militarized world, have allowed governments to postpone the rightful demands of their citizens and not to do a great number of things that are, in fact, the obligations of government. We remember that governments are there for people and not people for governments. We aren't their source of income; they are our servants. For decades we were told the service a national government would provide would be to arm the country physically, and in terms of mindset and propaganda, to keep those evil empires from reaching over the pole into our minds and corrupting our soil and our thoughts. That isn't quite the job description of what Canadians expect from governments, but together with the incredible production and supply of arms around the world it has led, over the decades, to an equally large supply of unresolved problems.

The second part of the legacy of forty years of non-peace is the legacy of things undone, not done for decades, and that is a pretty awful mortgage for the world to carry. These are mortgages of social policies and opportunities that women in particular feel very strongly: missed openings and access to education, to training, to jobs, to taking part in public life on terms that are appropriate for women rather than appropriate for governments. Of course, there are also the unresolved problems of sustainable development, a healthy environment, dealing with the toxic legacies of arms production. There is also the research not done: the questions not asked and explored. Having spent much of my life at universities, that is something I find particularly troublesome: the questions not asked, the research not done, the money not available to pursue essential explorations of alternate medicine, of alternate technologies, and of different ways of arranging our lives together.

My third point is that the legacy of the Cold War has left us with a tremendous lack of bridges. Dividing the world, often against people's will, into ideological islands and blocs has essentially made it impossible for two generations to speak freely to each other: to build friendships, exchange thoughts, and build the bridges that are essential for development of a peaceful society. We must never forget that there have been forty years of physical, intellectual, and emotional isolation.

In many parts of the world that isolation came on top of old colonial barriers. The people never were together because the independence of countries in the Third World came almost simultaneously and overlapped the postwar activities that gave both the arms race and the Cold War. There are people who historically were first artificially separated by colonial powers and then equally artificially separated by the ideology of the Cold War. Whether in Bosnia or in various places in Africa, we need not be surprised when we find animosities and hostilities that began to be fostered by colonial powers in a divide-and-rule situation perpetuated during the Cold War that now, with the help of arms and the pressure of economic needs, break out into active fighting and the lack of peace. What is there, again as that legacy, is the lack of bridges, and some of the very few existing bridges are those among women that the peace movement over decades has fostered. Those are trusted bridges. They are the very few bridges we have, and we should not begrudge the time needed to continue to build and expand them.

Such bridges are particularly important because of another legacy, and that is my fourth point: the lack of non-military perspectives. For decades everything has been focused, and continues to be focused, on winning. Now, in many ways, winning is one of the more pointless things in life. Do you have kids who play hockey? Mine had other competitive sports and very early had the good sense to be on the losing teams, which gave them the opportunity to do something else with their Saturday mornings. An artificial emphasis on winning is quite unconstructive, to put it mildly. If you allow an oxymoron, to focus life on winning is a losing proposition. That perspective on winning is a military perspective that has taken over public life and public discourse to what I consider to be an absolutely destructive and detrimental extent. There are always far more losers than winners.

To me there is a significant difference between success and achievement because achievement is always built on the cooperation of a group of people. One achieves with and through the assistance of others. People learn from each other. They begin to excel because there is support, learning, and understanding. Achievement is always obtained with people, by people, and through people. Success, on the other hand, is very frequently dependent on the absence of more competent or more aggressive people. If I succeed with my meringues it is only because there is nobody else who makes better ones, and so I hope and pray that there is nobody who makes better meringues, and then those little lumps of not quite happy egg white will be my success.

Unfortunately, that concept of success as a solo venture applies to many other situations as well. I see that with profound sadness among my students who begin to think very negatively about their classmates who are as able, or more able, than they are. Their success very much depends on the fact that there may be nobody around who is better than they are. Many young people are urged to be successful, to be lean and mean, and that translates into a situation in which people see each other not as sources of support but as hindrances in their own paths. If there is anything I find frightening in the social development I try to outline, it is the view of people looking at other people as being in the way. That is the military view. The military loves to walk into empty, uncontested spaces. What they do when they get there is another question.

The lack of non-military perspective that has come as a legacy of decades of Cold War has a much stronger impact than we may recognize. In the military emphasis on winning, the world has forgotten in many of its quarters that, in fact, we need each other quite desperately. It is unhelpful to look at everything on the local and global scene in a conflict model. Forty years of looking at the world with nothing but the glasses of the conflict model results in every problem being cast as if it were a conflict; somebody has to win, and by that same token somebody has to lose. It is always somebody's fault; if somebody were to leave, then the world would be a happier place.

There has been a severe lack of work on non-conflict models, on coping models that say, "There are problems in the world. That is how life is rigged." How does one cope? Where is knowledge? Where is support? Where is the assessment of what it is that one really has to cope with? We are now faced with forty years' worth of non-learning in a cooperative model, and that is why negotiations are so difficult. It's like people who haven't run around the block for decades and now have to do it, and everything aches, they limp, and they can't get up to speed at all.

Our work for peace is doubly difficult because there is a lack of articulated experience in the cooperative model. Everything in the public sphere is cast in the conflict model. A friend once pointed out that even the weather forecast is frequently cast in a conflict model. There is the *threat* of thunderstorms rather the *probability* of thunderstorms. As we articulate the problems we need to address, let's avoid this kind of model that leads to the seemingly inevitable conclusion that might is right. Over the last few years, the world has moved with incredible and unbelievable ease from the belief that *military* might is right to the belief that *economic* might is right. To my way of thinking, none of that is valid, but we are in a phase in which the conflict model is well and living in every newspaper and in every government. The substitution of the military might by economic might seems to me somewhat cosmetic and not a change of substance.

That brings me to my last point in the legacy. Over these decades we have seen the public purse funding an enormous amount of high technology that was primarily of use to the military but with spin-offs and the need to apply them to the civilian sector in order to make the appropriate profits. I would suggest the touted information superhighway is, in fact, the civilian continuation of Star Wars. It's an equally harebrained scheme put together in order to meet *created* needs, just as the strategic defence initiatives *created the need* for an umbrella of missiles that nobody asked for. We are now being provided with a stream of irrelevant information that nobody has asked for, and it might be quite wise to look at that as an extension of Star Wars designed primarily to support the same type of industry. One should be clear on one's position as a citizen, and say, "Is that what we want?"

Having laid out those five legacies of the Cold War that we have to cope with, I would like to switch focus now to what we might do and how we might do it, because we need peace. We need peace for the task of healing both people and the Earth. One of the steps in this task is the need for us to name: to be very clear and articulate about how we got where we are. The current mess didn't come in a plain brown envelope by public post. It was created primarily by men who didn't listen.

From the perspective of the peace movement, we see that what is morally and humanly wrong is in fact also dysfunctional, and we need to carry that perspective into the next phase of our work. The leanness, the meanness, the focus on the bottom line obviously didn't work for all those guys who were after power. One can't conceivably think that someone designed the state of the world as it is now. What they thought they were doing, whatever it was, didn't work out, and it didn't work out, I would suggest to you, because the means were wrong. It is wrong to bully people. It is wrong to get security by making others insecure.

Those who do not share with us the feeling that this is a family of humanity in which no one can live forever at the expense of everybody else have to be reminded that the alternatives of exploitation, brutality, and oppression in fact *do not work*. They have never worked. The Romans didn't get away with it. The slaveholders didn't get away with it. However much it looks tempting in the short run to yield to what is pragmatic, in the long run the immoral *does not work*. It's impractical. It's dysfunctional, and from the current vantage point one must articulate that. We must say (a) how we got to where we are, and (b) the means by which we got there are no longer acceptable means, not only because we think they are wrong but also because they don't work. They are dysfunctional, and we do not wish to continue that mess.

Of course we know there are other ways of doing things, and many women have done things differently. Hierarchy, patriarchy – determining things from the top down – has outlived its usefulness. What we bring now is a horizontal solidarity. It's what you have here today and what all of you carry into your own work. There is such a thing as horizontal solidarity. It is something that goes across boundaries and in which the solidarity is based essentially on *an agreement on means*: regardless of what the situation might be, there are certain things, such as violence, that are not acceptable.

If I had the time I would have spoken about the roles of the NGOs, because I find it increasingly unacceptable to think of international organizations and name them by what they are not. It's very nice to say that these are not governmental organizations; fine, we aren't like governments, which is a great compliment, but there are positive ways to characterize NGOs, too. Most international voluntary organizations are cooperative, and they are preoccupied with facilitating social change.

We need to work with the people in those organizations in order to change the world from the imperial model in which it still operates. The UN still takes the position that Queen Victoria once thought she had to take – to send expeditionary forces to where the natives are unruly and tell everybody what to do. From that imperial model we have to get to a cooperative, tolerant, confederated model, and women must take a leading role in facilitating that shift. You will be working on that and I will be working on that, and I hope our work will not only build bridges of friendship but also give us the confidence our past work so very richly justifies: confidence that we can facilitate change, and we will facilitate change. Thank you.

4

Coexistence and Technology: Society between Bitsphere and Biosphere

(Polanyi Lectures, Concordia University, Montreal, 1994 and 1995)

This paper is an amalgamation of two Polanyi Lectures by Dr Franklin, given in March 1994 and 1995 respectively, at Concordia University. Both addresses were given to an audience well acquainted with the work of Karl Polanyi and fully cognizant of the politics and issues of the Cold War era. In considering these talks for publication Dr Franklin realized that present-day readers may not be similarly prepared. She decided to step back from the more detailed arguments intended for the participants of the Polanyi Conferences and to combine, in one paper, the fundamental considerations advanced in the original presentations, as these, she feels, still deserve attention.

May I, first and foremost, thank the Polanyi Institute[1] for the opportunity to address this gathering. Over and above the academic ties that bind me to the Polanyi Institute I have an enormous personal debt of gratitude to Karl and Ilona Polanyi, a debt I will never be able to discharge adequately. It is in their memory and informed by their thinking and concerns that I invite you to consider the issues that created the unique international journal *Co-existence*[2] in light of today's problems and in the context of the work of the Polanyis. It is an invitation to illuminate these problems again rather than a prescription for their solution. I will try to make the case that it is incumbent upon us to consider seriously the patterns of thought and inquiries embedded in *Co-existence* and in the community that created it, not so much in spite of but because of what happened in the intervening years.

Let me first speak about coexistence, the journal and the concept. It was about thirty years ago that the first of the three existing issues of *Co-existence* was delivered to its subscribers, just a week after Karl Polanyi died [23 April 1964]. The publication of the journal was the outcome of a unique enterprise that brought together an international group of scholars all deeply concerned about problems of a workable global peace: problems that have not gone away. The preparation for the journal as well as its actual printing centred around the Polanyis. All was achieved without external grants or funding. There were no sponsors, no grant applications, but rather contributions from individuals through both work and gifts.

The journal was born out of two overriding trains of thought that developed among an international group of senior scholars in the late 1950s. First was the fact that nuclear war had totally changed the environment that had been the basis of previous discussions and conventions about war. Nuclear weapons made it finally clear that there was no longer the option of neutrality, no more bystanders or noncombatants: no "them" and "us." No longer was it feasible to think in terms of preventive war, "a just war," "our war," or "their war." All this had become obsolete. On the other hand, in the real world polarities were finding their expression in nation-states governed by different political systems but with corresponding powerful means to inflict harm.

If there was to be any quality of life for ordinary people wherever they lived, then one of the essential prerequisites for an internationally sustainable peace was coexistence. It meant contesting groups had first and foremost to say if we wish to exist then life has to continue, and we have to accept the premise of coexistence, which is the legitimate existence of others. Coexistence, then, is the beginning: a prerequisite of a new modernity.

The Polanyis were very deeply concerned with issues of peace. It was, in fact, the peace issue that first brought me into contact with them. They felt very strongly that it was no longer possible to consider war. If life were to go on and war was no longer an instrument to settle disputes, one had to look at the roots of problems much earlier and more seriously. Karl and Ilona saw very clearly that if the then existing blocs of socialist and capitalist powers were to live together in peace based on that idea of peaceful coexistence in which systems built on different value systems would be respectful partners then a great number of boundary issues had to be settled.

Issues that dealt, for instance, with banking and law, with passports and economic situations, as much as they dealt with planning and politics – not to speak of ways to curtail weapons, armaments, and nuclear forces.

It was the Polanyis' opinion, which I shared, that the best minds would need to focus on problems of coexistence, and that one way of facilitating this focus was to create a forum outside and beyond political rhetoric. An unaffiliated, international scholarly journal seemed to be an appropriate venue. It was for this purpose that the journal *Co-existence* was created. I was present when the question of the journal's title was discussed, and I remember Karl Polanyi's impatient rejection of "Problems of Coexistence" saying, "Of course there will be problems, but what matters is that the submissions deal with coexistence and nothing else."

In the first issue of the journal we find a paper by Jan Timbergen[3] in which he outlines the concrete prerequisites of coexistence. He advances four conditions to achieve a workable state of peaceful coexistence. (1) Social systems of different values have to grant each other the right to exist. Parties may not like each other but they have to grant to each other the legitimate right to exist more or less in perpetuity. (2) Out of this consent comes the respect for, and the acceptance of, the basic needs of the other. The other has needs. One may like them or not. One may agree or disagree with what the other considers needs, but each party has to accept that others have needs. (3) Accepting these two requisites results in accepting the third very important condition of coexistence: self-limitation, a reciprocal constraint on the use of expansion and power, which is an essential part of the fabric of coexistence. (4) The fourth prerequisite Timberger advances for a practical coexistence is genuine communication. This does not mean talking about the weather with people one doesn't like but a focused attempt to understand the language, culture, and history of the partners in coexistence.[4]

One of the issues of *Co-existence* contains a wonderful paper[5] by Paul Bohannan on colonialism in which the colonizing powers see themselves in a form of coexistence with the local population. Based on his experience in Africa, Bohannan describes debates and disputes between the colonial administrators and local representatives. He coins the lovely phrase "working misunderstanding" to illustrate how the parties work with each other, though on the basis of profoundly misunderstanding why each party does what it does.

In terms of the fourth prerequisite of coexistence – genuine communication – that paper points to the need to avoid working misunderstandings and to be clear and open about assumptions and intentions.

I would suggest that even today these four criteria are valid: coexisting partners need to grant each other the right to exist, to accept the basic needs of the other, to accept the need for self-limiting constraints, and to strive for genuine communication. These criteria are valid on the macro as well as on the micro level. On the micro level, in the community for instance, consent to exist has to be granted to people of different attributes and backgrounds. They have the right to exist as whole persons. Others have to respect and acknowledge their presence and their needs. The obligatory self-limitation of expansion applies to personal elbowroom as much as it applies to national armies, and genuine communication will be necessary in dealing with interpersonal relationships as well as in achieving a functional multinational organization.

For the purpose of this discussion, let us define coexistence as a set of conditions that make it possible for fundamentally different groups or societies to live respectfully in the presence of each other and to agree that the acceptance of the conditions of coexistence is a prerequisite for genuine peace. In the late 1950s and throughout the 1960s, considerations of peaceful coexistence referred mainly to the coexistence of nation-states built on different ideologies and priorities. As I said before, the Polanyis and their friends saw the great need to focus the best minds within all such nation-states to look critically at institutional and intellectual roadblocks as well as opportunities to make coexistence work. We are most fortunate that the archives of the Karl Polanyi Institute provide us with archival material that documents their thinking and outreach.

Reconstructing the process of soliciting contributors and contributions for the journal from their correspondence provides some extraordinarily interesting insights. It is not only of interest who within an extensive international network on both sides of the ideological boundaries was approached by the Polanyis but who was not. We find in the archives the carbon copies of Ilona's letters as well as many of the replies. The cross-references are particularly illuminating. Some names of suggested contributors appear to come up again and again from different constituencies since the initial network of the Polanyis was very interdisciplinary, including theologians, scientists, political economists, historians, linguists, and artists. But even more extraordinary is the absence of some names as well as some disciplines.

I would now like to turn your attention to an issue close to my heart and that is technology and coexistence. What emerges from the overall picture is what I would call a really cavalier attitude toward technology. To me, this is quite extraordinary because by the 1960s there were many very serious critiques of modern technology appearing within the intellectual community that the journal tried to involve. For instance, the work of Lewis Mumford[6] had influenced many of those now interested in issues of coexistence. One has also to remember that Jacques Ellul's *The Technological Society* was published in 1954; then there was the work of Nigel Calder, not to speak of his father, Ritchie Calder.[7] One could give many other examples. Yet, on going through the files, I did not find their names or references to their work.

This absence of attention to the social and political impact of technology is especially surprising to me, knowing Karl Polanyi's deep interest in the consequences of industrialization and his own activities in the Worker's Educational Association in Britain. Karl himself pointed out that socialism and capitalism were two responses of society to industrialization. He hoped in the end socialism would humanize an industrial civilization; however, looking at the three issues of *Co-existence*, we find no direct discussion of technology. Yet even in 1960 it must have been clear that technology is social instruction. If societies that are based on profoundly different ideologies are to coexist, can they do so while using the same technologies, which inevitably structure work and social life?

Let me restate here my working definition of technology: technology is practice – "the way we do things around here." The use of machines, computers, and electronic controls is commonplace, but technology is more than the sum of all gadgets. Technology is *how* we work with each other on common tasks. Technology structures social and political life as it is the practice that changes even when the task remains the same. Dwellings, for instance, have been built for a very long time but how these homes were built, by who, and for whom has changed profoundly as societies have changed.

In the existing three issues of *Co-existence*, it is within the discussions on planning that we find the closest approach to a discourse on the social impact of technology. Apparently, the presence or absence of state planning was regarded as one of the crucial features that distinguished the political and economic systems attempting to coexist. A paper on planning in the first issue of *Co-existence* begins with the sentence "The impact of the Soviet Union on the rest of the world can be summarized in one word: *planning*."[8] Industrial planning was not specifically considered nor does one find a general awareness that, for instance, the division of labour imposed by or facilitated through particular technical advances is a form of implicit planning. Nevertheless, any technology in and of itself is binding social instruction. With this perspective in mind, the discussions related to statistics in *Co-existence* are particularly interesting.

In a paper on the prospective planning in India,[9] the great statistician Mahalanobis provides his insights into the whole apparatus needed to deal with large sets of numbers: the raw material for planning. For the contributors and the readers of *Co-existence*, the gathering of numerical information was an important task. Was it done by the state and kept secret? Was it done casually and openly, by private or commercial institutions? Why was it gathered at all? These issues define one of the crucial interfaces to be negotiated between coexisting systems. Thus, the scholars *planning* the journal and hoping for discussions arising from its content, were consciously trying to struggle with the issue of how to deal with the inevitable structuring by the planning process itself. The agency of planning as well as the premises guiding it would be fundamentally different depending on the ideologies and premises involved.

I find it almost mind-boggling how much the very umbrella of planning hypnotized the contributors. While there are substantial discussions on the historical principles of planning, there is no discussion of the role of those Kenneth Boulding calls "the planees," i.e., those impacted by plans and schemes; yet whether or not plans work will depend almost totally on the response of the planees. To carry out any plan successfully, consent and conformity by the planees are essential. Consideration of technology – of *how* things are done and *how* people relate to each other because of their way of doing things – would have greatly helped in the task of illuminating the problems of peaceful coexistence.

Allow me to take a moment to explore the question of whether groups based on fundamentally different principles can in fact exist (and therefore coexist) as being distinctly different when the groups utilize essentially the same technologies. As examples, I will briefly consider the fate of two intentional communities legally embedded in the larger society, recalling that Karl Polanyi himself was strongly influenced by Robert Owen and the impact of his thinking on his contemporaries.

Let's consider the Kibbutzims in Israel and the Hutterite colonies in Alberta. Though they are profoundly different, both are intentional communities that exist legally. There are laws in Israel and Canada, respectively that guarantee and safeguard the existence of these communities. They are assured the larger society will not overtly take them over or obliterate them provided the detailed rules of coexistence are accepted and adhered to, yet in Israel the Kibbutzims are increasingly disappearing as genuine social or political alternatives. In Canada, Hutterite colonies continue to exist, but they do so by enforcing a separation and isolation of their members, denying them the liberty to coexist with others. In the face of this reality, my question is this: have the technological decisions made by these intentional communities threatened or prevented their genuine survival, in spite of the favourable conditions for coexistence that had been established?

There is a wonderful book entitled, *The Forgotten People: A Year among the Hutterites*,[10] from which I learned a great deal. It was written by a young German conscientious objector who lived for a year in a Hutterite community close to Lethbridge, Alberta, and wrote a book about his experience. Having the same Hutterite background, he is very respectful in his approach, but he also understands how impossible it would be for him to live permanently in that world of the sixteenth/seventeenth century as the members of the present-day colonies do.

Hutterites see their surroundings as evil: "the world" is intrinsically evil. There are irreconcilable differences between them and their surroundings. For instance, Hutterrites have no private property. Their view of education is that it, too, is of "the world." They wish to educate their own young and comply only with the absolute minimum legal obligations that Canada requires. According to the author of *The Forgotten People*, a two-levelled approach prevailed in the Hutterite Colonies regarding the use of modern technologies: decisions on the use of modern equipment were arrived at by a very authoritarian and hierarchal process, and modern, high-tech farm machinery and equipment was purchased if and when it helped increase revenues for the colony. Decisions were usually made by very few members, all of them male, and most of them old. What mattered was the financial strength of the community, which was seen by its leaders as the protective barrier that shielded their settlement and the settlements of other Hutterites from the encroachment of "the world." That is what mattered and that alone.

Internally, that is within the colony, there are no modern technologies and no technological decisions have to be made. Work is carried out using traditional low-tech and gendered labour practices, patterned after the European agricultural communities of the sixteenth century. Labour is collective and there are no private enterprises. Ordinary members have very limited contact with the outside world, and environmental concerns are not part of decisions on agricultural activities. The author of *The Forgotten People* found among those Hutterites remaining in their colonies no concerns about the soil, their animals, or the impact of their activities on those outside the colony.

In Israel, on the other hand, Kibbutzims were formed before there was a State of Israel. Kibbutzim members had a positive view of "the world." They welcomed the State of Israel, seeing themselves as being of the same cloth as those on the outside. They hoped to be leading the way. The state surrounding them was respectful and supportive. In the early days, Kibbutzim members believed the state was teachable and would move gradually to more collective and less patriarchal structures.

Like Hutterites, original Kibbutzim members had little private property or private space. One of the fundamental and important differences that set them apart from the state was their collective decision-making processes, which included technological decisions. The choice and use of machinery and devices was based on collective decisions that were guided, as a first priority, by the needs and abilities of the members to serve their community throughout the various phases of their personal lives. It was the attempts at integration of the productivity of the Kibbutzims into the general economy of Israel that began to erode the distinctive difference between the collectives and the technological society in which the intentional communities were embedded.

Kibbutzims welcomed the arrival of labour-saving devices, as many socialists did, as providing ways to take the drudgery out of their labour. This development was welcome provided two conditions were met. One was the assurance of the community's authority to distribute gains and equity of return among its members, and the other was that the community retained control of the labour process, and particularly of the division of labour. Provided these conditions were met, the decisions on technology were collective and welcoming in the same way as the Kibbutzims welcomed schools – as something that enlarged the horizons of the collectivity. Nevertheless, the new technologies were not holistic technologies but prescriptive technologies that fit into an increasingly globalized economy. They required certifiable expertise, specifications, and differentiation of labour processes. They needed managers and normative planning.

The fundamentally egalitarian structure of the Kibbutzims began to crack under the load of these demands. Again and again, individual Kibbutzims tried to make an industrial contribution to the country while maintaining their structure. It did not work. In the end, the prescriptive structuring of technology essentially forced the technocratic class system on the intentional communities and destroyed the egalitarian base that was their distinguishing attribute.

I cite these examples to show why I feel that genuine coexistence, in terms of the four criteria outlined earlier, appears only possible if the coexisting entities use genuinely different technologies. The structuring impacts of modern production technologies are so strong that they override the ideological and moral differences that led to the formation and cohesion of the very entities attempting to coexist.

I see only two options for groups that attempt to coexist as they choose the technological processes by which their collective activities are conducted. As they prepare for coexistence, the group has to make a very conscious attempt to adopt "different ways of doing things," i.e., different technologies. The groups will need a clear awareness of the structuring properties of technological changes. Each group can, of course, modify its own technological apparatus in response to changes in the coexisting environment; however, they have to know that regardless of how the eventual fruits of their labour are distributed, every society bears the imprint of how those gains were achieved. Hutterites, for instance, could have chosen the path their Mennonite brethren followed. Mennonites, to varying degrees, have interpreted their own beliefs against the framework of modernity and have arrived at a spectrum of compromises that permitted their communities to survive in a modern world. For Kibbutzims in Israel, the price of meaningful existence as well as coexistence would involve opting out of participation in the globalized economy in spite of the drive of the State of Israel to seek a prominent place in the global technological order.

The second option, one that the orthodox Hutterites have taken, requires the isolation of the community as the prerequisite for its survival. This option basically imprisons the members of the group by making them unfit for the very interaction that true coexistence requires.

In the mid-1990s, we see ideologies retreating in the face of technological dominance. Increasingly, ideological struggles have turned into issues of economic competition while the nuclear arms race and wars continues. The prescriptive technologies of industrial systems have become *the* dominant social forces. Globalization with all its planning, management structures, and subcontractors has turned much of this world into an industrial production site.

This giant global mechanism, that looks like a vastly magnified and elaborated set of clockworks linked by sinews of instant communication, is what I call the *bitsphere*: a world that operates in terms of sophisticated productions and transactions. The world has become, in fact, more and more transactional. Motorcars, for example, are assembled from parts supplied by very different sources and subcontractors, but not just cars. I want to recall for you what happened to a friend of mine in Toronto who was buying a pair of winter boots a couple of years ago. She is the sort of person who likes to know who has made the shoes she wears, so she looked at the boots and found the left one was made in South Korea and the right one was made in India. Being the conscientious type, she went back to the sales person and said, "Have your orders been mixed up?" to which the sales person replied, "Oh no, this is how they come. That's their production. Aren't they clever? Nobody can steal or divert their products." I have the nightmare of a developing country celebrating the acquisition of a model shoe factory and all they make are left boots. You can visualize all those left boots looking for their mates from South India.

Such a scheme of economic development is not a step toward coexistence, not even a step toward the betterment of one nation-state or the other. In fact, nation-states seem to have gone. One may make the case that there are, in fact, no longer contesting nation-states shaping the world politics as the Polanyis had assumed. The overall structuring effect of modern technologies has drastically changed the division and the nature of power and of political/commercial decision-making.

However, don't entertain the thought that coexistence, that is the survival of all through their adherence to the prerequisites I outlined earlier, is no longer of importance: au contraire. The importance of coexistence on the micro level, such as within a community, school, or organization made up of distinctly different groups and individuals, is fairly obvious. More hidden but also more urgent, is the realization of the need for coexistence on the macro level.

I want to highlight here the need to think again about the dynamics of a possible coexistence of super-powers in terms of the work of the Polanyis but with a very different understanding of who the contesting super-powers are. Karl and Ilona Polanyi and their friends saw that nuclear weapons had put the fate of the world at risk. Understanding the magnitude of this risk as well as the fact that coexistence, however difficult, offered the only way to mitigate and eventually eliminate the risk, motivated them to ask likeminded scholars to dedicate their best resources to a collaborative effort of clarification and problem-solving. The issue to them was human survival.

Today we are faced with the issue of global survival anew. The global use of similar or identical technologies has resulted in a *bitsphere* beyond national boundaries and jurisdictions that acts like a global super-power. This super-power is in conflict with, and contesting the supremacy of, the second existing super-power, *nature*: that is, the *biosphere*.

In my darker moments I think that if I had one request of the government of Canada it would be that Canadian policymakers would treat nature the way they treat the Americans – with caution, as a large and irrational power. At every step there is a need for Canadian policymakers to look over their shoulders and say "Will they be miffed? Will they be offended? Will they retaliate?"

In the real world today, ordinary people feel and see the consequences of the increasing hostility between the biosphere (nature) and the bitsphere. As the bitsphere expands, attacks, and affronts nature, the biosphere retaliates. We see the ice caps melting, we experience global warming, we witness the disappearance of populations of plants and animals.

We are, I suggest, in the presence of an escalating arms race between an aggressive bitsphere and a resentful and retaliating biosphere.

Maybe we need to think again of those four criteria I outlined earlier. Maybe we need to accept and support the presence of the biosphere, its right to exist. Maybe we have to respect and acknowledge
its needs. Maybe we have to practise self-limitation. Most of all, we
have to relearn nature's language. Learning the language of the biosphere is not just to finance environmental studies. What is required
of us, I suggest, is the understanding of nature in terms of power
relationships. The bitsphere has to come to terms with the retalia-
tory power of the biosphere as well as with its ancient culture and
ways of achieving its goals. For these reasons, it is not hard for me
to make the case for revisiting and reapplying the search for coexistence, and in doing so to honour the memory of Karl and Ilona
Polanyi and their friends.

NOTES

1　The full name of the Polanyi Institute at Concordia University is the Karl
　Polanyi Institute of Political Economy.

2　The full name of the journal referred to throughout this paper as
　Co-existence is Co-existence: A Journal for the Comparative Study of
　Economics, Sociology and Politics in a Changing World. The publisher is
　Co-existence, Pickering Ontario, 1964.

3　Jan Timbergen, "Concrete Concepts of Coexistence," Co-existence, vol-
　ume 1, May 1964.

4　The subject of the prerequisites for coexistence was taken up again and
　expanded in a brilliant paper by B. Landheer, "Power Structure and
　Coexistence," Co-existence, volume 2, November 1964.

5　Paul Bohannan, "Lessons from Cross-Cultural Communication,"
　Co-existence, volume 3, May 1965.

6　Some of the works of Lewis Mumford relevant here include The Condi-
　tion of Man (1944), The Conduct of Life (1951), The Transformations of
　Man (1956), and Myth and the Machine: Technics and Human Develop-
　ment (1967).

7　Works of Nigel Calder relevant to this discussion include, for example,
　Robots (1957) and his editorials in The New Scientist; relevant works of
　his father, Ritchie Calder, include Living with the Atom (1962) and The
　Invasion of the Machine (1968).

8　V.B. Singh, "Need for Planning," Co-existence, volume 1, May 1964.

9   P.C. Mahalanobis, "Perspective Planning in India: Statistical Tools,"
    Co-existence, volume 1, May 1964.

10 Michael Holzach, *The Forgotten People: A Year among the Hutterites*,
    translated by Stephan Lhotzky (Sioux Falls, SD: Ex Machina Publish-
    ing Company 1993; original German version: Hamburg: Hoffman und
    Campe Verlag 1980.)

5

Canada and Social Justice

(An address given to Companions of the Holy Cross at a
Retreat of Anglican Women in 1997)

I have been asked to talk about "Canada and Social Justice," and I'd like to make this as informal as possible. Please feel free to interrupt at any time. There's no point if I lose you in the first five minutes and then keep on going for another fifty, so please interrupt. When I noted this down I was thinking of the emphasis in your case statement on intersessional prayers. I can only say if you feel free to interrupt God, for heaven's sake feel free to interrupt me.

In terms of the emphasis on social justice in Canada, I'd like to emphasize the urban and multicultural environment as that's what I know. Because I believe social justice is a religious issue, I come to this from a Christian perspective – from the perspective of Quakers. While Quaker theology has often rightly been considered reasonably wobbly, Quaker social practice has always been pretty solid and firm. It's from the belief that one's faith is witnessed to by one's practice that I look at social justice.

I bring to that a Canadian perspective. Ours is a country of immigrants, a country that considers the separate gifts immigrants bring to be some of the most important assets and treasures of the country. It's a country that has very much defined itself as *not* being a "melting pot" country, having tried to treasure and encourage the cultures from which immigrants come, to bring them into the schools to ensure the next generation would know the language of their grandparents and the history of the societies and the cultures from which they came.

That dream of multicultural society has perhaps been made easier through the presence of two founding European nations. This country always had the presence of French and English, both as people and as languages. If you look into Hansard, which is our equivalent of a congressional record, you will see it comes in French and English, two columns side by side. When I was on the National Research Council and on the Science Council we had simultaneous translation so that people could speak in the language in which they were comfortable and choose their language for the repartee. It is assumed that those who aspire to be entrusted with governance in Canada will be adequate in both official languages.

A fact we too often forget is that the immigrants did not come into an empty country. The Aboriginal people who inhabited this part of North America got a very inadequate treatment in this multicultural society, and it is one of the things that cries out for both a practical and political rectification. This society cannot continue to be a vibrant society without being very much more just to the ongoing contribution of this country's First Nations.

While I hold very much that social justice is a religious concept, it is also very much embedded in the laws of a country. One must not forget the law has two aspects: a punitive and a normative aspect. We say with our laws, "This is what we expect from citizens, and if you don't do it there is a law that may have penalizing aspects." But we forget the law also has a normative aspect. When we say we don't hit people over the head, it isn't because you may be convicted of assault but because we live in a society in which this isn't done. In most cases one hesitates to invoke law, but in some cases one may have to invoke the law to assure justice.

While social justice is a religiously based concept – it is based very much in the concept of all the religions – it does not require a particular faith. It is my opinion that at this time in the world the difference between religions in the sense of the consequences people draw from their faith is much less big that the difference between the religious and the secular view of the world. The really great gap in the outlook and attitude of people is essentially between those who have a religious worldview and those who do not.

I would suggest there are two touchstones: these two groups of people differ in their view of power and of time. If you have a religious view of the world, then you know there is power beyond human power. Whatever way you label it, whatever tradition you come from, the human person is not the ultimate power. If yours is a secular view, however, power is the aggregation of human power. The same goes for the view of time. Anyone with a religious view of the world has a long view of time. It's God's time; it's nature's time. Anyone who is secular views time in terms of the time between elections, between annual reports or quarterly statements, or between fluctuations on the stock exchange. Regardless of what people profess, the ways in which they view time and power gives you an idea of whether religion is for them a facade or a fact of life.

For Quakers – for Friends – social justice rests on the core of their Christian belief that "there is that of God in every person." We believe that, however hidden, however difficult to discern or to come out, there is that of God in every person. If you truly believe that then everything else is brutally simple because you can't kill God. You can't oppress God. You can't starve God. You can't inflict suffering. You can't deny the expression of God in other people, and that's that. That is very simple, but of course it's also very difficult because it specifies means. It doesn't say as much *what* you should do but *how* you should do it. If you believe in that of God in every person, then whatever you do, for whatever noble purposes, it cannot involve means that kill God.

This is why Quakers have always been steadfastly against war and every form of violence and oppression. Because you just can't do it. You can't do it to God. For that reason, you can't allow your government to employ means that involve oppression. The commandment "Thou shall not kill" does not speak of weapons. People can be killed by starvation. Their spirit can be killed by hopelessness, by demeaning, by depraving. One cannot allow oneself to be involved in those means. The outcome of that belief, of course, is a view of social justice. A society has to be arranged in a way in which means are found that are consistent with one's beliefs; you cannot do the things that give you anguish in your heart because they involve transgression of your most profound beliefs. So social justice is driven by the religious conviction of citizens and, of course, unfortunately, by the lack of religious convictions.

Let me come back to Canada. Canada's social philosophy has essentially two roots from which it comes. One root is Britain. Canada is, and has always been, part of the Commonwealth. It has the stamp of its British heritage, the heritage of people who left Britain very frequently in opposition to a structure of class but with respect for social institutions such as schools, judicial system, and parliament. The second formative force in Canadian political philosophy, which comes out of the Western Canada of the 1920s and '30s, is the

Social Gospel: the belief that the testimony of faith is action, action in public, and action that is transparent as being driven by the belief that all are God's children, all are equal, and all work together – one for all and all for one. Out of that philosophy have come Canadian institutions such as the cooperatives, often inspired by corresponding British institutions, an early unemployment insurance scheme, and Medicare, which came out of Western Canada and were then transformed and transferred to the rest of the country.

The Social Gospel has given the country's emphasis on public schools, public hospitals, and public universities. To this point, and it may change, this country has only public universities. We have always believed that the great seedbed of citizenship and mutual responsibility is bringing up young people together in the knowledge of each other and each others' family, because they learn from each other as much, or more, than they learn from their teachers. Gifted youngsters in any part of this country and of any origin – and this works more in theory than in practice, but it does work – should not be denied the higher education from which their gifts would allow them to benefit.

The country has immensely benefitted from this approach because it has given us citizens, and now teachers, doctors, lawyers, who have learned with each other and have for that reason been sensitized to the problems of others. We feel strongly about the value of public education from kindergarten to university. It allows a mixing that is not only of practical use but also in keeping with our religious beliefs; if we believe all are God's children then there is no other choice. You don't segregate God.

While historically Canada's foundations were shaped by both Christian and British structures, in the last three decades a large number of immigrants have come who were imbued with ideas that were neither Christian nor British. The country, and especially the City of Toronto, absorbed a very large number of immigrants of very different languages and backgrounds. Now how is that done? I want to spend a bit of time on this because while Canada has in its rhetoric an image of a rural agricultural society with wide open spaces, the reality is that most Canadians live in large cities. The back and forth of social tensions, the need to adapt, to test ideas, to see areas of potential and actual conflict – those things are most experienced in the cities. It's in the urban environment in which the new and the old meet, both in terms of people and in terms of ideas and institutions, so I will talk about Toronto.

First I want to talk about the people who have come out of faith communities that are not Judeo-Christian. Many faith traditions, of course, place a great deal of emphasis on respect and kindness for strangers, on the duties of hospitality and of caring. Kindness is important, but for an immigrant country it is not enough. It is not enough to divide the world into "us" and "strangers" and be nice to strangers. The real test of a country and city that absorbs immigrants is that the strangers have to become us. You can't just be nice to them and say, "Oh yes, they are green, or black, or chequered, and they are from far away and they stutter, and they don't know what we mean when we say PMO. Poor dears, let's be nice to them." The strangers *are us* and have to become us. Beyond the openness, it is necessary to think of us together with the strangers – to give up that appeal to "be nice to others" and to see the others are us. The Chinese little girl who sits next to your son in class is not "other." She's just one more grade 3 child. It's that change of perspective that is the task, and of course it's a task of social justice.

Again, I want to emphasize the importance of public schools. Everyone cares about their children, and for many immigrants it is because of the better life for their children that they go through a great deal of suffering, uprooting, finding work that is often well below their qualifications. What keeps them going is the hope for their children. It is on that basis that citizens meet in each other's houses. It is the birthday party of the little Chang girl that brings her friends from school into her house or into the picnic in the park. It is Mrs Fitzgibbons who goes and asks who will go with the class when they go to the zoo. Does Mrs Singh or one of the Singh boys have time? It's there that people meet as people, and it is there that they see that of God in each other.

If you were to go into the school where my son teaches you would see that every notice that goes to the parents of students in Grades 1–3 goes out in six languages: Chinese, Korean, Farsi, English, French, and Spanish. If your child were to go to that school and speak at home a language that wasn't one of those it would be quite all right and understandable and legal to ask, "Could he get the notices in Polish?" And he would get the notices in Polish, because it may be his Polish grandmother who looks after the kids. I think this willingness to communicate in the languages spoken in children's homes is really important. Of course it may mean that people in Toronto pay more taxes than they might, although it's a relatively small expense, but that is willingly done because that's the source not only of social justice but also of social peace.

This country and this city have absorbed an enormous number of immigrants. Almost two thirds of the people who live in Toronto were not born or raised here. Half the children in my son's class do not speak English at home. To bring adults together without any violence, without any fights, without any social tension comes, in my judgment, from that fact that the children are together. You have something truly in common, and that is the welfare of your children. That is the swim team. That is the choir. That is something you do together for what is most important to you, and it is there that you begin to see that of God and practise it. So we treasure the schools and their respect for the language and the culture of the parents.

We treasure our libraries. If you go into a library in Toronto you will find quite sizeable holdings in languages that are not French and English. These aren't just Dante but short stories in Italian, so people who work hard can go to the library for a good read in their language. This is particularly important for women, many of whom work very hard and are often confined to their homes either with children or elders. That there is a library – a free public library that has books and reading material in their language – is extremely important particularly for the sense of self-worth of women. The fact that these libraries will also guide people when they have to do their income tax or translate forms is an additional help. A well-rooted community is a prerequisite for social justice, and public institutions such as schools and libraries safeguard the communal roots.

In contrast to countries where there may be dominant groups that are white or black or Hispanic, Canada's immigrant population is very multiracial, very multicoloured. There are no overriding groups that become centres of gravity as the black citizens of the United States had to become, so it is not a dichotomy or even a triangle. It is a spectrum of people of all colours, origins, and religions, and their cultures have found a place in the public sphere. Of course, they sometimes take their own expressions. For Aboriginal people in particular, for example, there are Aboriginal Health Centres in the city where Native Peoples can find nurses, counsellors, doctors in their own tradition without having to explain themselves to people from a culture they consider alien.

Social justice then begins at the bottom. Of course, it doesn't end there. It becomes very much part of economic justice. The social justice we care about is not purely answered through respectful multicultural conditions. There are overriding injustices that are economic. Economic justice requires not only the part that religious and social justice required – respect for that of God in every person – but also the right for meaningful work, for lives that can contribute.

One of my friends in the school system always said it is the dream of parents that their children be "personally happy and publicly useful." While those two things may not appear simultaneously – one cannot hope one's children are *always* personally happy or *always* publicly useful – they have something to do with each other. In the end you cannot be personally happy and have no community, no contribution to make. Even if you have all the money in the world you need to be publicly useful. You need to know that somebody waits for you. Somebody needs your work, your contribution. At the same time, you cannot be publicly useful when you are hateful and grudging.

One of the things the broader aspect of social and economic justice demands of us is to worry about meaningful work: to realize that God has created the human mind and the human hands and the human soul for contributions. There's is nothing worse in the terms of "Thou shall not kill" than to give young people in particular the feeling they don't matter. There's no work for them; there are machines around that do what their fathers did. There is no meaning to their work life. This issue transcends cultural barriers. It is not just immigrants who need to worry about work. It is not just Native Canadians. It is all our young people about whose future we have to worry. All of us have to worry about the way in which people work and the way in which industry and automation go: what that does to nature, what that does to our environment.

What we see ahead as a central question of social justice has a religious component of justice: that all are able to access God's grace, and all parts of God's creation are deserving of equal care. In addition to the issues of justice and fairness I outlined, in Canada we increasingly worry about access to decision-making. That is a Canadian preoccupation. Decisions vital for Canadians are increasingly taken outside the country through many links including NAFTA and the Free Trade Agreement. With the best of all wishes, it becomes increasingly impossible for a country like Canada to make moral decisions. The constraints on moral decision making are not only internal but external: constraints on what we offer to our young people in terms of work in a technological world.

Those are the things we are worrying about. Those are the things about which we are praying for wisdom and guidance to set our sights straight and to know what is big and what is small, and this is where you and all our prayers are constantly needed. Thank you.

6

A Drive to Know: The Glory and Hell of Science – Reflections in Memory of Jacob Bronowski

(The Jacob Bronowski Memorial Lecture, New College,
University of Toronto, 29 March 2000)

Jacob Bronowski died in 1974. In the intervening years much has happened, and both personal and institutional memories have faded. I would like to use the time I have with you not only to reflect on science and human values as Bronowski would have done but also to see them through the biography and life of Jacob Bronowski. Although I'm quite aware I probably bit off a bit more than I can chew in my title, I would like to consider the three strands in the title: the drive to know, the glory and hell of science, and Jacob Bronowski.

I would like us to reflect on the drive to know. Why on Earth, we should ask ourselves, does anybody want to know anything? It's a question that is sometimes quite good to ask at a university, and my answer is people basically need and want to know something because they have to cope. Whether it is the "Why?" of a young child who has to cope with a very peculiar world around her, or the collection of bits of gossip when you want to make a good impression at the dean's sherry party, it is usually the need to cope that stands behind the drive to know. That doesn't mean you cope with the great mysteries of life and death, but there is a personal relationship between the drive for knowledge and the need to cope. I think we also have to talk about science: what we mean by science – its practice, its practitioners, its methods, and the critique of those methods. Most of all I want to talk about Jacob Bronowski, and I will try to weave these three strands together.

There's no biography of Bronowski, which surprised me. He died young. He was born in 1908 and died in 1974. Before going further, I want to acknowledge my sources. I've read much of Bronowski's writing, certainly not all. I've benefited greatly from the fact that the library, as a gift from his widow, possesses four half-hour interviews with him taken within a year of his death by a TV station in California. I have seen not only Bronowski's written work and his dramatiz-ation on the BBC of *The Ascent of Man* but also his own comments on his life at a very mature stage. I also want to acknowledge my great indebtedness to Professor Natalie Zemon Davis. She elicited comments from Bronowski's daughter, Lisa Jardine, who is scholar in her own right, an academic as well as a communicator in Britain. It is on these sources that my comments are based. My critiques, if there are any, come really from the reflection of those .things that happened in the twenty-five years after Bronowski's death.

As we reflect on the quest for knowledge, the drive to know, I also want to register the importance of the questions not asked. There is a category Mary Daly very rightly calls "non-questions" – those things that seem so self-evident, so secure, so unchallenged as not to need to be coped with. When such issues are raised, those encapsu-lated in the establishment of a particular culture and thought pro-cess find it difficult even to acknowledge a question has been asked. That happens to women, that happens in racism. That happens, indeed, to many questions related to the basis of science in which scientists, including frequently Bronowski, say, "I can't see the prob-lem. What's the matter with you?" Knowledge is very often extended by those who have the audacity of raising non-questions, and those non-questions often come from a new need to cope.

Bronowski was of a generation like no other generation. Born in 1908, in what was probably then Poland or Russia, he was a child in the First World War under the profound impact of the Depression. His parents took him to Germany, and in the 1920s they moved to England, where his grandfather had a modest textile business in East End London. Bronowski grew up in England. A brilliant student, he won a scholarship to Cambridge, where he studied mathematics and physics, but at the same time he was constantly involved in litera-ture and was – as was his generation – formed first by the Spanish Civil War and then by the advent of fascism, which was particu-larly important for him as a Jew, as a European. Those experiences formed the young Bronowski. When the Second World War broke out, he enthusiastically did war work in operations research with Blackett and the very famous British team. Then came a turning event in his life.

He was on the first mission of scientists that the British government sent to assess the damage in Hiroshima and Nagasaki. Now he was an operations research man. In the four previous years, he had expanded scientific understanding to make bombing more precise, and suddenly he was faced with Hiroshima and Nagasaki. I don't know what he expected, but what he saw changed his life. He saw a degree of devastation of civilization that made him decide not to continue research in atomic physics. He also saw what happened in Auschwitz: not only the extermination through the Holocaust but also that experiments were done, that people were trying to do medical science on those who were incarcerated and condemned to death.

That double impact of the Holocaust and the bomb changed many in his generation, and most eloquently and clearly changed Jacob Bronowski. Bronowski then decided a great part of his ongoing work would be devoted not to *doing* science but to *explaining* science, to probing publicly, in lay and philosophical language, the enterprise of science. In the subsequent twenty-five years of his life until his untimely death in 1974, that is what he did.

When I looked again at his work I was thinking, what was he doing? What does one say of a creative life that encompassed his book on Blake, his play *The Face of Violence: An Essay with a Play* (1954), his innumerable talks and lectures on human values and science, on civilization, on the process of science? How does all this hang together? Is there a subtext? What on Earth was he doing?

I think there is a subtext. I think what Jacob Bronowski was trying to do – not only as a person but also as a scholar and a scientist of his generation and background – was *to redeem science* as a social and cultural activity. In other words, he was trying to recover, rediscover, and explain the glory of science – the light science had brought in terms of advances in knowledge, in human betterment and progress. At the same time he was drawing attention away from the dark side of science, the hell that science had brought. He was striving to redeem and restore the light, and with that the self-respect of the practitioners as well as the collective reverence for them. He was trying to put the darkness in its place, to put the hell, or some of the hell at least, onto somebody else's plate, and say something like, "Circumstances beyond our control led to those outcomes."

Implicitly and explicitly, this quest to redeem science is evident in much of Bronowski's work. Here's a question I find interesting: what do you do with a collective social enterprise when you believe in its pure core, a core of reason and light, when at the periphery the practice becomes rotten? That's a genuine problem, and it's not just a problem of science. Most Churches at one time or another find it difficult to protect the clarity and value of the core from the worldly practices of the periphery that frequently become inconsistent with the values of the core. The noble aims, ideas, and practices of democracy are not, in my mind, all too sure to survive the practices of so-called democratic governments. How does a core that may have been impeccable and clear, though limited, protect itself from the worldly practices of the periphery? It's a genuine problem that occurs in history again and again.

Bronowski would probably not see the challenge in those terms, but in the last twenty-five years of his work one sees a very genuine shift of emphasis. In his early work there is an emphasis on the truth-seeking pure science that is in many ways a self-correcting enterprise, in which scientists in their own integrity, morality, and truthfulness revise their own and their colleagues' findings. In later work he looks much more at the larger context – at the historical contributions of both reason and organized knowledge as seen in *The Ascent of Man*.

He ends with a very interesting, little-discussed paper in *Encounter* (July 1971) that speaks of what he calls "The Disestablishment of Science" where that self-same Jacob Bronowski suddenly says maybe it's a good idea for scientists not to work for the military. Maybe it's a good idea not to accept this money and then sneak in some basic research. Why shouldn't we have money for basic research that we ourselves give out? One sees echoes of things like the Canadian granting councils when he advocates that the government might trust scientists enough to give them a hunk of money and let them distribute it among themselves. Now fortunately or unfortunately for both of us we never had a chance to talk about it, but Bronowski felt, and felt only very tentatively in 1971, that it might not be such a bad idea if scientists would decouple themselves a little bit from the most overt sources of power.

However, not only had Bronowski changed; the world around him had profoundly changed. Questions were raised that were in many ways those non-questions that Bronowski and his friends did not feel were valid questions to ask. The questions were raised outside the scientific establishment by Rachel Carson and many others who felt the need to know, the need to cope – whether it was to cope with radiation and deterioration of nature, or whether it was to cope with women's questions on their place and knowledge in the scheme of things. The questions came from those who had to cope with the consequences of the accelerated growth of organized knowledge under the rubric of science.

Those who raised questions raised them in terms of whether science brings us good knowledge that might have fallen into bad hands, or whether is there possibly something fishy about that establishment of science in and of itself. Although there is a great deal of work that could be discussed, I will focus only on the critique of science and the scientific method: the critique that attempts to link and not to decouple the glory and the hell of science.

I owe you some definitions. What is it that I and others mean when we speak about science? For Bronowski science is an activity. It's a collective activity but collective only within the scientific community. It's an activity with the aim, as he says in his late interviews with students, "to read nature," to find out how the natural world is put together. He put this type of creativity next to the task of art that he defines as "addressing the riddle of man." For Bronowski then, science is that self-correcting system in which scientists are the truth seekers, the truth keepers, and in many ways the truth amenders. In that same period he defined science as "the attempt to find conceptual order in the endless chaos of facts."

If you turn to the contemporary critique of science on the other hand, and I could quote Evelyn Fox Keller or Ruth Hubbard, but here I follow what I still think is the most succinct and readable critique of the scientific method from a feminist point of view, and that we owe to Margaret Benston. She came out of theoretical chemistry, taught both women's studies and science at Simon Fraser University, and in the later part of her life focused mainly on computer science. In a brilliant paper she laid out some of the assumptions of modern science. She characterized science as a method of creating and verifying facts about the natural world and pointed out that under the rubric "science" we can find people who see it as a systematically connected body of knowledge. "Science" also includes a body of practitioners, which in turn has its own sociology, its own selection and training. Science in that modern Baconian sense is an enterprise for a purpose. The discussion of that purpose from the point of view of those in the 1960s also has to include both the funding of scientific work as a source of livelihood and the end use of scientific knowledge.

However, inherent in the scientific method (evolved during what is called the Scientific Revolution, starting in the mid-eighteenth century and earlier), there is a component Bronowski doesn't mention, and that is reductionism. In the early eighteenth century the dominant issue was probably that people had the audacity to take nature under their own roof not totally but in part: that part of the natural world could be studied, separately and in detail, with equipment and devices specially built for that purpose. The new knowledge, abstracted and removed from its context, could then be certified and put back into the larger whole. The putting back is a particularly difficult issue, but taking part of nature and studying it is an incredibly important and fruitful enterprise because modern science works. That practice has produced enormous advances in both the understanding and utilization of the natural world, but most important I think one has to realize that science provides a method of separating knowledge from experience.

On the basis of modern science, you can indeed separate knowledge from experience. You can go to a university and learn to build bridges from somebody who has never built a bridge. That's the nature of the enterprise, and it works provided you know you only learn how to build a bridge – nothing less but also nothing more. That is reductionism: taking part of nature into the lab and studying it separately in its minutiae. Already before the 1960s, this process had been a target of critique, particularly for philosophers who pointed out, as Jenkins did in 1942, that this method of investigation gives people a reduced, restricted, and, as he put it, "impoverished reality."

It is that impoverished reality that becomes the life and work of science. The critique of science came mostly from those at the receiving end of the study of that impoverished reality, in contrast to Bronowski's view of scientists as dedicated truth tellers and truth seekers, which was the dominant view at the time he wrote *The Ascent of Man*.

I want to stop for a moment on that terminology, because I know I'm not the only one who says *The Ascent of "Man"*? Hmm. Professor Natalie Zemon Davis's friendship with Jacob Bronowski's oldest daughter allowed her to inquire about this choice of terms. Professor Jardine warmly remembers and acknowledges that her father's personal support was unfailing in all her intellectual and scholarly endeavours. She explained that he was genuinely puzzled by the feminists' objection to naming the series *The Ascent of Man*. When they argued, "Well, what about women?" he felt women were included and that this debate was quite pointless. It was one of those obvious non-questions to which Mary Daly had drawn our attention. Bronowski was so encapsulated in his environment – and I'm sure we are equally encapsulated in our thoughts, in our concerns, in our soil – that he didn't see the point.

Others, however, most certainly did, and the point was not the issue of equality, though that was difficult enough in the scientific establishment. The essence of this non-question is something else. In that drive to know is there no place for anyone to contribute creatively except when coming from the brotherhood of well trained, usually white, usually male scholars who learn from the same books, use the same instruments, and lo and behold agree on the "truth"? Where, one asks, is the understanding that there is a contribution to be made to knowledge by farmers because they are farmers, by metal workers because of the knowledge of the hand, by women, not in spite of their being women, but because of their being women? Where, in that world of learning, is the recognition of learning from experience? The knowledge of the hand and the knowledge of the heart are part and parcel of the knowledge one needs to cope and not something peripheral.

If one were to put in vernacular language the state of things as they were when *The Ascent of Man* was put together, one would probably say, "Brother, you're kidding yourself. A good part of that wonderful truth seeking, truth telling, self-correcting system may be a figment of your imagination. Your band of heroic practitioners is not really very representative." But also you may ask, "Why do you want to know these things? What do you do with the facts once you've found them? When you find those things you consider truth, what do you do in the lab? Do you break out into the 'Hallelujah Chorus' because you found the truth or part of the truth? Do your elders begin to orchestrate a drive for the Nobel Prize? Is that group seeking 'the truth' not much more like a well-financed spying operation into nature on behalf of those who wish to use the research results? Are you not part of a spy network? Are you mercenaries rather than truth keepers? And will you remember your elder, Francis Bacon, who was very clear about wrestling with nature, appropriating her secrets for the benefits of mankind?"

It is necessary to re-examine the impoverished reality that the scientific method produced, and I'm quite sure that had Jacob Bronowski lived longer he would have looked much more at the mercenary spy aspect of the scientific enterprise. He didn't, and we can only honour and respect his drive for knowledge, his wish to redeem, as it must be redeemed, the enterprise of science, not as *the* way to know but as *a* way to know.

Twenty-five years later, however, we are entitled to some further reflection. Bronowski would have seen the profound grief that the acceptance of the impoverished reality of science and the application of science have brought both to nature and to a large part of the human family. Where we are now, the drive to know and the drive to cope bring a different and additional landscape to us.

In concluding, I would like to say again how much I admire and respect Jacob Bronowski's work, both in and of itself and in the context of his time. I admire how he placed science and the arts side by side, his stress on cultivating the imagination, his profound and very deep preoccupation with violence, his play *The Face of Violence*. In his last interview Bronowski stated to the young that violence is not as much an issue as a manifestation. To him the root cause of violence was repression (he did not say "oppression"), and he urged tolerance as a response, yet he did not seem to see the repression of the drive to know by the reductionism of modern science. It must have been hard for him to acknowledge that the diminished reality science depicted facilitated the drive to material gain, the clearly mercenary side of the enterprise Bronowski so much longed to redeem.

Where we stand today, if you accept my interpretation of it, we know very clearly that side by side there's a knowledge of the brain, there's a knowledge of the hand, there's a knowledge of the heart. What seems to me profoundly important in our situation is not to see these as a cafeteria menu, to dip into this or to dip into that in our drive to know, but rather to realize that the fabric of life can only be assessed from an interaction of these knowledges. It is not good enough that the artist deals with this, and the scientist deals with that, and the person whose greatest strength is the knowledge of the heart deals with that. What is required is an integration: the working together on a problem with these different insights.

In the last volume of his essays, *A Sense of the Future: Essays in Natural Philosophy* (1978), published after Jacob Bronowski's death, one of the essays is entitled "A Sense of the Future." He saw the future as being shaped by science and science being shaped by broadly educated scientists who like Professor Potts in Bronowski's play, *The Abacus and the Rose: A New Dialogue on Two World Systems*,[1] would say, "I, having built a house, reject / The feud of eye and intellect." From today's experience we have to conclude, sadly, that the future did not turn out like that.

NOTE

1   Bronowski's radio drama, first aired on the BBC in 1962, was later retitled *The Abacus and the Rose* and put into the second edition of the book *Science and Human Values* (1965).

7

Thinking about Technology

(A public "University Lecture," University of Toronto, 2004)

This lecture is an honour for me, and I'm intending to use it to honour someone else. Please regard this lecture as my tribute to James Ham, formerly dean of the Faculty of Applied Science and Engineering, royal commissioner, president of the University of Toronto, and someone who spent his life thinking and teaching about technology in a most exemplary way. If I can pay a small tribute to him in this lecture, it would be most gratifying for me.

I'll spend some of our time on definitions. Partly for the sake of clarity and partly because I would very much like to encourage people to an ongoing process of thinking about technology. I would like you to take what I'm saying in no way too literally. I'm not engaged in a praising/blaming exercise but rather in a looking/puzzling type of endeavour, because while we are in a most interesting, fascinating, and certainly perilous time, I don't think we are sitting helplessly on either an up or down escalator. When I compare observations and insights, I do so not so much in an either-or mode but rather as a point-counterpoint of a complex orchestration.

Now let me come to definitions. What do I mean when I say we are thinking about technology? I think of "thinking" not only as a very enjoyable activity but also as something akin to taking your mind for a walk around a question the way you might take a dog around the block for a walk. Thinking in that sense is the intellectual equivalent of scratching and sniffing, of digging and barking, of picking up and following scents, and the enjoyment of finding real and imaginary treasures. One can walk alone. One can walk with others. One gets pretty addicted to that sort of thing. I'm sure the dean will know the sound of collective barking and yelping on the finding of imaginary and real treasures that is the sound of research and graduate school. It's a good thing, it's a joyful thing, and it's something much to be recommended.

The block, the question, around which we walk is technology. Here I find myself consciously in the company of Jim Ham, who was dean of engineering when I began at the University of Toronto and who changed the curriculum in a manner to encourage and even compel engineering students to think about technology. He gave myself and colleagues like Morris Wayman and Bill Vanderburg opportunities to develop the scholarship, the information, and the course on thinking about technology, so I find myself in his company on this walk.

How do I define "technology"? I define technology as practice: *the way we do things around here.* There are a lot of advantages of this definition, which is, in fact, borrowed from Kenneth Boulding. There's a historical dimension. There have always been people doing things together, and we can learn a lot about groups of people when we look at what they did and how they did it. Defining technology as practice allows us not only to think about what was done but also, and much more importantly, *how it was done* and gives historical dimension to the political, social, and human structuring that sits in technology. I would like to talk to you about ancient technologies, but here I'll concentrate on modern technologies, and take you, quite arbitrarily, to the Britain of the Industrial Revolution. It is not where technological considerations should start – there are Roman and Chinese practices of great interest – but I will start with the Industrial Revolution because we don't have much time.

I take you to 1682 to the City of London because at that time there was an inquiry headed by Sir William Petty on the growth of the City of London,[1] its wellbeing and its economics. In Petty's report he suggested that much could be improved if work – labour – would be organized differently. Petty's suggestion of a different division of labour is important to all considerations, and that is why I begin with Petty. He considered production and used the making of a clock, the watchmaker's task, as an example, saying, "Wouldn't it be much more sensible not to have watch makers laboriously making a watch but to have different people make the dial, the springs, the works, the casings, and have somebody else assemble it?" This new practice was adopted, and it is much of the fabric of the Industrial Revolution.

Petty saw very quickly that dividing labour according to the requirements and utility of production was really very advantageous.

No worker had to know it all. One could employ more workers to do just one thing, but – and this was a big but at that time – if you do that, *things have to fit*. It's no more somebody's individual idiosyncrasies that make the watch like this or like that. Once you go into that division of labour there come new requirements well worth having if one wants the returns of more production, lower skill, greater output, and efficiency. But there were specifications: things had to fit. There had to be tolerance and fit. Notice the language.

With the specifications came other important social inventions. There came management. Somebody had to be in charge of all this. There came the need for resources. The workers needed to have stuff to do their work. There came the need for capital. There came the need for control, and thus with an obvious increase in production and many other very good things came the social inventions of management, control, and planning. These features distinguished the industrial technologies of the time that I call "prescriptive technologies" because these are prescriptions: the *how to – or else*. These new prescriptive technologies lent themselves exceedingly well to the incorporation of machines, of devices. As we look back over the last 200 years, we find the increasing incorporation of nonhuman devices into existing prescriptive technologies.

These prescriptive technologies were different from "holistic technologies," the craft specializations of earlier times. As we sniff around the block of technological development, the substitution of holistic with prescriptive technologies is a place where we have to stop for a minute because *the way things were done* changed drastically. That division of labour, which turned out to be very advantageous, spread quite quickly from the direct manufacturing of clocks and other things to other activities – to political and social activities – and led eventually to a recognition of the utility of prescription to interlocking systems that really characterized the technological world: systems so persuasive and pervasive that Jacques Ellul very rightly called them a "milieu." We now live in a world in which there are prescriptions for almost anything and everything.

With the spread of prescriptive technologies, planning, management, and control became legitimate, rightful things. You couldn't do things differently. Everything had to fit, and that is the last and possibly most important part of the acculturation caused by these technologies, these prescriptions. The workplace taught *the need to comply*: not only did the part need to fit to low tolerance, so did the worker, and the need to comply was self-evident. There wasn't a tyrant standing there with a sword saying, "You do as I say, or else," there was just a silly little screw that had to be right, to fit, so the worker could earn his living. This culture of compliance – the notion that conformity was safety – permeated Western society from there because compliance is safety, even if you comply to something that doesn't seem appropriate: the Brits still drive on the wrong side of the road but you better do it. So conformity becomes safety, self-evident, and that conformity is the price of an incredibly increased production.

One has to think how real the technological enthusiasm of the nineteenth century was: enthusiasm for *the new way of doing it*, the new science that would undergird more and more sophisticated ways of doing things. Increased production appeared to be the road to plenty; prescriptive technologies with their science were so obviously going to help eliminate hardship and need. Even when it became apparent that things might go horribly wrong, when these same types of prescriptions produced war, when that compliance produced fascism, the search was for better and more enlightened prescriptions: different planning. Gunnar Myrdal's cumulative causation type of global planning was thoroughly committed to social justice, and it was global planning that would get us there: better prescriptions, more enlightened ways of doing it.

The thought that there was something much more profoundly wrong is very much the thought of our time, of our sniffing around and saying, "No, that isn't really the plenty, the delivery from slavery that the nineteenth century had thought." Yet, I want to show you that the conceptual framework and ideas that let us now see what it is that was so profoundly missed were there at the time of Petty.

They were there, and I'll quote to you the people whose business it was to think, the philosophers. I'll quote Immanuel Kant, the German philosopher born just barely a generation after Petty, in 1724. Kant makes it very clear that basically one needs to distinguish very precisely between what is a mechanism and what is an organism. A mechanism states Kant, is *a functional unit in which the parts exist for each other in the performance of a particular function*. Kant showed that the mechanism, for which the clock was the prototype in that era, is a functional unit; it's something designed to do a specific task, composed of parts that all work together in the performance of that task. Each part is designed for a particular function within the whole, but it is made externally and assembled, and the presence of all functional parts produces the mechanism. That's a mechanism: parts working together, designed to work together, externally fabricated, and then assembled.

A mechanism is fundamentally different from an organism. An organism is *a functional and structural unit, in which the parts exist for and by means of each other in the expression of the particular nature of the organism*. It also does something. It also has parts, but its parts – such as the roots, the leaves, the flowers of a plant, or the limbs, the eyes, the brain of an animal – are not made separately and then assembled as in a machine: they arise out of an interaction with each other in the developing organism.

That is a fundamental difference. While parts designed for a specific purpose within a mechanism are assembled, the parts of an organism grow in concert with each other through internal interaction and only so they can function, and the whole organism withstands time, notwithstanding the odd false tooth or hip replacement. We know, and Kant's time knew, the difference between a mechanism and an organism. These are prototypes, pure prototypes, and nothing is pure prototype in real life. Yet we know to this day, carts are assembled, horses are raised, and there are a lot more carts than horses.

Here I again feel very much the presence of Jim Ham. When he finished his tenure as dean of engineering, he spent some time at MIT with a friend of both his and mine, the late Cyril S. Smith, to study transitions from holistic to prescriptive technologies. They looked at books of non-prescriptive technologies that described artisans and non-prescriptive technologies used in different parts of the world. Jim knew very keenly that there was a transition from holistic to prescriptive technologies in all parts of the world, and that it was a fundamental transition.

I take you from the definition of these archetypes of mechanism and organism to the here and now because we see the historical trajectory. We can see how those prescriptive technologies worked: they worked in terms of output, stuff, and wealth; they worked in terms of acculturation to compliance and conformity; and they worked in terms of scope of management and control. As a result of their effectiveness, they were very quickly and then very extensively transferred to non-production activities, to human and social activities

such as administration and communication that need *not* be looked
at as production, and that in fact are diminished if we look at them
as merely production activities. For human and social activities the
mechanism is not the appropriate model, but prescriptive technologies depend on mechanisms, so we go from "agriculture" to "food
production," we go from "education" to "skill production." Three
hundred years of that brings us to look at our world and say, "Wow!
Isn't this whole globe a giant production site with very fancy mechanisms, and what does it do? It makes *money*." It makes money for
some.

Well, that's the historical trajectory; nevertheless, the organisms
are still there. Trees are trees, fish are fish, and people are people,
and they do what trees, fish, and people and all organisms have
always done. They function and respond to increasingly complex
prescriptions with the autonomy of the organism, with that internal
interaction that makes the parts grow, and so do social organisms –
families, schools, and communities – whether we like it or not. We
are very poorly advised if, as we think about technology, as we walk
and sniff around that block, we do not take into account the presence of the multitudes of organisms that function according to their
own interactive, complex dynamics of which we have much less
knowledge than our knowledge of very fancy mechanisms. As we
walk we realize we have to worry about them because they are there.

As I prepared this lecture I was struggling to find an image. How
do we talk about something that is present but that is not seen? It is
as if it is not there but it is there, and so I suggest to you the image
of an eclipse. That's what we see on the moon. The moon doesn't
change, but there are times when we see only half the moon. It's not
necessarily the best image, but it allows me to say there has been
excess light, overattention, to prescriptive technologies as *the way
of doing things around here*. That emphasis has been eclipsing other
things, other ways in which things – organisms – live and react.

The fact that organisms are not in view, that their dynamics are
not being taken into account, makes it possible for us to do things
in a way that turns out to be quite deficient and inadequate. I think
that eclipse – the fact that essential parts of human and global existence are not in the light – is the reason why we hear so much now
about darkness. When Jane Jacobs writes about dark ages ahead,
when we hear Ronald Wright's Massey Lecture, *A Short History of
Progress* (2004), we get the feeling of darkness, of being stuck, that

people must have had when they saw a solar eclipse: that incredible sense of foreboding. But this eclipse now is not a cosmic one, it is manmade, and I hold that it is something one can think about, talk about, and do something about.

I will spend what remains of the time I have with you to ask, "What is it that is now incumbent for us to do?" Here we sit in the dimness of that eclipse, and we have the task of thinking about technology. James Ham very profoundly understood the difference between the mechanism and the organism. When he was president of the University of Toronto, he spent a great deal of time negotiating a memorandum of agreement among the different colleges that made this university. Now a more mechanically inclined person would not have done that, but this is precisely a response to an organism, to a university that had grown through the interplay of colleges, through that way of growing and learning from each other. Jim could have laid down the law as the president and said, "This is how this university will be run," yet he spent a great deal of time and patience to achieve understanding, a memorandum of agreement in which all parts saw how they could continue to grow together. That was a decision taken not by eclipsing the past but by looking into it and saying, "Yes, that's an organism; that's not a mechanism."

We may well ask, "What can we do as we sit in the dimness of this eclipse? We're faced with very genuine, practical tasks – these are not matters of the imagination." If we sniff around that block of technology there's an awful lot of very unpleasant smell, and it demands action. If you ask me what we can do, my first immediate dictum is always clarity. First and foremost as we try to shift that eclipse, let's think. Let's get some clarity – not images, but reality. Let's see what is there, discuss the appropriateness of models, and think not only of prescriptions. As we talk about the university we can say, "Is that a knowledge-production site, or is it a community in a very different sense? Performance measures that are fine for production may not be what are most needed here."

I also have a concern about language as a facet of clarity. Take, for instance, the issue of not misnaming things. In the search for clarity, in the attempt to pick up the scent of things that are there but not seen, we better name some of the organisms that have been left behind and look at what those prescriptions actually do. Do they do what they say? We all heard the promises of a paperless society, and we all live in the reality in which the prescriptive electronic technologies have grown together with the amount of paper that they were supposed to eliminate. There is a great deal to be said for thinking: thinking for the purpose of doing something. Some corrective steps may seem "minor," but a large number of small steps is, in fact, what changes a climate.

What do you do after you've taken a dim view? As I've said, for me the first step is clarity and thinking, without blaming, in the scientific tradition of evidence: describing what is there. Next examine behaviour – our actions. One of the things we all may want to do is to look at speed. Speed is an industrial production attribute. It's the assembly line that has to go fast. I think there is no merit, for instance, in accelerated speech. If you listen to the radio, there is no sense in getting more words per unit time. There's an awful lot to be said for clearer words and fewer of them.

Deescalate speed, and also deescalate vocabulary. Much of our vocabulary comes, again, out of production and advertising. I think we might make a pact with each other never to use the word "awesome." I think the world was fine without the word awesome. Deescalate vocabulary, deescalate hype. It's good enough if things work. Everything doesn't have to be "splendid," "cutting edge," "world class." Those are responses to production. See where those things come from. It's very poor practice to hurry on your plants in the winter; when we have fluorescent lights all our plants get spindly and look miserable. There is nothing to speed *per se.*

We could also think to deescalate email. There was a time when people felt it would be good for their soul if during Lent they would refrain from having coffee. How about for Christmas refraining from sending non-required email copies? I think it would be a tremendous contribution to sanity, of what we are as organisms, not to do things just because mechanically, electronically, they can be done. You can push the button of the mailing list with a joke nobody actually wants, but think of the eclipse. Think of what this *prevents* the receiver from thinking about, doing, or just being. Deescalate some of those things, and maybe deescalate expectations as we deescalate hype.

We then ought to very seriously rebalance. Remembering the eclipse, we ought to shine more attention, more light, more care, on some of those activities that involve organisms. That is often accomplished through knowledge and research. We know far more about sophisticated mechanisms than we know even about naïve organisms. If you think of the Human Genome Project, for example, you see that underlying it is the thought of parts that were assembled and that one can replace. It may be useful, but what about using research resources to understand how the body is nourished, how the body as an organism might have its parts interact so as to produce what the mechanical fixing of taking-out/putting-in is intended to do? You see why I say we need to rebalance our current activities. This doesn't mean stopping what we are doing, but it does mean increasing our efforts to think as organisms: emphasizing that parts grow through and with each other rather than focusing only on fixing a deficiency by making something nice, and then – presto! – it goes in and replaces what was wrong.

In that whole question of getting out of the eclipse, out of the dimness, we need to think of work: work as labour and income, work as atmosphere, and work as a contribution to society. The Atkinson Charitable Foundation has just published a report on how Europe handles shared work and shorter work. Such arrangements could perfectly well be made in a society like ours, and they would allow individuals more space and air to live and more to share.

We also need to think of work in terms of models. Are people human resources, or are they colleagues or co-workers? Are people people or are they pedestrians when you or I sit in a car? That rethinking is doable and absolutely urgent. Again I remind you of Jim Ham who, when he was the solo royal commissioner of the "Report of the Royal Commission on the Health and Safety in Mines" (1978), was eloquent and absolutely clear that people and their requirements – as members of families, as members of the community, as those who grow with and through each other – had priority and production had to be shaped accordingly.

We have to try to compensate for what caused the eclipse and to train ourselves not only to consider what is there and not seen but also to recognize, support, applaud, and put light on activities going on that take the organism's presence seriously: changes in agriculture, medicine, schooling, and social work, but most of all the activity of nonviolence. It's quite hard for me as a pacifist to discuss all this and not spend time on the worst, the most destructive, and most senseless prescriptive technology, and that is war.

We need to look at what is happening whenever there is a counter response that is *not* the senseless prescription for organized force but when that counter response is nonviolence. There's a lot more of it than one might think. One always thinks of war, but there are wars that didn't happen. There are genocides that didn't happen. When we think about Rwanda, we need to think about South Africa. Remember what could have happened there if other ways had not been found. Those other ways are ways in which people speak to others on their knees. They are not trivial. They are not simple. Those of us who were involved in the struggle around apartheid know how much we depended on those like Bishop Tutu who brought us back the response of those South Africans whom boycotts might hurt, to say, "Yes, go ahead, we are with you. In the end we may be hurt, but our children will not be killed."

The knowledge has to be brought that organisms – people's communities as well as the biosphere – are our resources. This very night we shudder to consider whether missile defence is being talked about in Ottawa: that tempting technology to protect somebody against nothing. We shudder and say, "See the darkness of the eclipse," but we also know that there are ways out. This is not cosmic. This is manmade. There are ways out, and the ways out are the big stuff but also the small stuff.

I want to end by talking about some really nice, small stuff right here in Toronto, as a prototype of development that may happen in other places: a series of artistic events including music, theatre, and shows, called Metamorphosis. Of course metamorphosis, after Ovid, is the way in which organisms change. Organisms don't get fixed, but there's an enormous amount of change – willing and unwilling – in organisms. That notion of looking at metamorphosis through the arts has been developed here in Toronto, and every one of you can be part of something like that. It isn't a big event to fix up our cultural identity, but it is artists working with each other as an organism, growing by being in each other's presence on a common task.

That cooperation is our hope for the future, a hope that compels us to keep on thinking about technology, but about a technology that encompasses and understands the difference between a mechanism and an organism: a hope that understands balance and appropriateness, and that provides to each one of us the conversation we need as we walk in our minds and thoughts and bodies around that block, so that we do it with respect, with competence, and with a sense of community. That's what Jim Ham would have done. Thank you.

NOTE

1   Sir William Petty's inquiry on growth in London was called "Another
    Essay in Political Arithmetick, Concerning the Growth of the City of Lon-
    don: With the Measures, Periods, Causes, and Consequences thereof"
    (1682).

8

The Holy and the Microscope: Conversations between Faith and Knowledge

(Guest lecture, given at the Newman Centre in the University of Toronto, Toronto, 2007[1])

My connection with this community has been a very strong and positive force in my own life, and I come back with great thanks and pleasure. I called this talk "The Holy and the Microscope" because I want to put to you something very different from what you would normally hear. It is a perspective nature brings us.

I would like to give you the thought that the increase in knowledge that undoubtedly has come to us – through science, through the world of learning, through the thinking that is as essential to people as every breath they take – that that collective increase in knowledge brings a corresponding increase in our awareness of the holy. I think it is quite wrong that more knowledge leads to a lesser depth and breadth of belief; all evidence points us to the fact that that is not so. In fact, it is the other way around. There is a partnership between our knowledge – our true and genuine knowledge of the world around us – and our consciousness of the holy.

By "the holy" I mean what is intrinsically unknowable. It is unknowable not because we are stupid, which indeed we are; it is unknowable because we are humans and because as humans, as for all other creatures in the universe, our ability to perceive is limited. We know in practical terms that there are animals who can hear frequencies we cannot hear. We know there are creatures who see parts of the spectrum the human eye cannot see. But, well beyond that, as humans our capacity is intrinsically limited.

I view the microscope both as my favourite tool and also as a symbol of the type of inquiry that looks below the surface, beyond the obvious, just as the telescope looks out. Our knowledge of the physical world increases the odds of our development of suitable tools, and as that wonderful array of scientific tools is developed the knowledge of the physical world increases. It increases tremendously, but what it brings, in fact, is the realization of the much greater realm of the intrinsically unknowable.

Let me give you an example of what I mean by that corresponding growth of knowledge and our awareness, our deep, profound awareness and respect for what is there but intrinsically unknowable to us as humans. It is that realm that I see as "the holy." Think of how much we know today about the human body, about human genetics. There's the Human Genome Project. There's more known in that whole area than has ever been known before. We can also count, and we know there are billions of people presently on this Earth. That's known. But what is in that realm of the intrinsically unknowable is the fact that of these billions of people, no two are the same.

Now if you think of cars, of stuff we make, you know you can pick a car somewhere and know exactly what's in it. It is more or less like the car you had. The components of people are profoundly different. Think just for a moment of the enormity of this fact. We seem to know more and more of the components that make a human being, and yet while one can go and find the blood type of the person in Outer Mongolia, or the blood type of the person who sits next to you, we know nothing of the profound plan of their assembly. All the millions of live human beings are supposedly made of corresponding components, and yet each and every one is totally unique. The plan of their assembly is beyond human comprehension. However we name the holy, if we can't see in that the limitation of our knowledge – the limitations of what is intrinsically knowable to us – then I think we do not do justice to what the human mind is.

I would say just don't go for the claim somebody might make that more knowledge and less ignorance will decrease our faith, because what is faith except the practical realization of that realm of the unknowable of what we are and in which we are part? Faith, to me, is the practical acknowledgement of the holy: our awareness that there is a domain of which we are part. We are in it the way fish are in the water, but it is not the domain of our knowledge. With every new tool, with every better microscope, we see more. As we increase our acquaintance with the very large and the very small that make up the universe in which we live, we see different things. We get a much more profound understanding, yet we have to realize that all we see *has always been there.*

I am a crystallographer. I use X-rays to know the positions of atoms, and when I look through the microscope I can say, "Look that one's missing. Some X-ray, some radiation must have knocked it out, and it has run away somewhere else." Nevertheless with all we do, we see *what has always been there.* We congratulate ourselves and give each other prizes for seeing something that hasn't been seen or understood before, yet it operated before. It *was there* before, and with the exception of artificial radioactivity, which is a subject one can separately discuss, all humanity has done essentially is to change the distribution of the atoms, but the atoms have always been there.

The knowledge we bring through the wonderful process of study, observation, and experimentation is what Newton so strongly felt, looking over the shoulder of the Creator, trying in a very small way to get a glimpse of what is actually going on. While we increasingly see the bits and pieces, this sort of knowledge gathering is only part of our work, and to this we have to add the realization of our profound ignorance. There are limits to human knowledge. How could we explain the fact that among billions of people now alive, made supposedly from the same components, no two are the same?

If we define "the holy" as what is intrinsically unknowable, we are in the wonderful position that the increase in knowledge, of which we as a contemporary civilization can be part, can allow us a much greater, deeper, and more profound appreciation of what, in fact, the holy is. That collective realization of the intrinsically unknowable in some ways becomes bigger as our knowledge and understanding of the physical world increases. Whether we look to the smallest of atoms or the largest system of stars, whether we look to a little insect or the complexity of the human body, we see to what extent our increased ability to comprehend their working opens up a realm that we see only by its effects.

This understanding is the foundation of faith: the acknowledgement of the existence of processes and activities that are totally outside and beyond our comprehension yet we are the beneficiary of them because our mind can see part of their working. If I'm right and the increase in knowledge also increases the realm of the intrinsically unknowable – if it is truly so as I claim that the more we know the more we know how much there is that is and will always be unknowable – then you may well ask, "Where does that leave us at the university? Here we are in a 'knowledge economy' trying to foster great minds and that crazy woman comes and says the more we know the more we realize how much unknowable is around. Where does that leave the university? Isn't that a bit of a mug's game?"

I would suggest to you that that is not so. We benefit immensely if we understand that our increase in knowledge, our development of better tools and deeper understanding, puts into view more and different realms of the holy as a gift for us to see, to appreciate, to reflect upon, and to learn from. Let us step back and look at what university activities have brought us in the last 200–300 years. There has been a vast increase in scientific information, codification, and application of the new knowledge. What have we learned from nature as a manifestation of the holy? What have we learned about the processes of nature from the largest to the smallest?

The number one thing that is abundantly clear is that *nature works*. There is functionality. It may not always work the way we like, speaking of climate change, but nature works. As we study the processes of nature we also find that *nature works extraordinarily frugally*. If you look at the growth of a plant or animal or if you study the soil, you will see how incredibly frugal the processes of nature are, how little waste there is, and how the waste becomes part of another cycle, of another manifestation. Nature works, nature works frugally with a minimum of waste, and in addition *the products of nature are beautiful*, whether they are beautiful to the eye or beautiful in their elegance.

Nature tells us, as a manifestation of the holy, that things can be functional, frugal, and beautiful. In the conversation between faith and practice, between faith and study, these lessons become crucial because they give us a yardstick to put on our own activities. Look at the works of our hands and minds. Do they actually work? It certainly doesn't take a great mind to answer the question of whether they are frugal. Do we do things as nature does frugally and with a minimum of waste? Are our works beautiful? Here we are with the collective gift of the development of the human mind that has given us an explosion of knowledge. It has given us the tools to look into the physical world and the intellectual discourse to grapple with the understanding of what it is that we see. It has given us clear evidence of the increased realm of the intrinsically unknowable and evidence that more knowledge inevitably drives us to the greater understanding of both the holy and of our own human limitations.

In addition to moral standards, nature has also given us some immensely practical standards that reflect the very fact that this world was not designed by humans. Nature works. Nature is frugal. Nature is beautiful. And how is it possible? To me that is the realm of the holy. That is the realm to which science and the microscope has one of the many keys that allows us to name the holy and to speak, think, and act accordingly. Thank you.

NOTE

1   Dr Franklin begins this talk by thanking the late Peter Sheen, an eminent member of the Newman Centre and one of the university's outstanding student chaplains, who first invited her to the Newman Centre. She also acknowledges his sister, Sister Tony Sheen, herself an eminent educator.

9

Reflecting on the Second Wave of Feminism: 1960–2010

(Taped at Massey College at the University of Toronto for a symposium in Ottawa on the History of the Canadian Women's Movement, 2008[1])

I'm grateful for the chance to share my views with you. There are three main strands in our common experience that I would like to emphasize. The first and main strand, that I cannot overemphasize, is the importance of the Royal Commission on the Status of Women in Canada (1970) for the overall shaping not only of the Canadian women's movement but also of the international women's movement.

This first strand consists of three components of the original call for the Royal Commission that are hard for our younger sisters now to see. I'd like to go back to Kay Macpherson's book,[2] in which there is a very brief and succinct account of the beginning. She describes the meeting held in 1966 at the call of Laura Sabia, who at that point had come to the end of her term as the president of the University Women's Club. She called for a meeting of representatives of women's organizations to discuss their common experience related to the status of women because all of them seemed to feel women were treated as second-class citizens.

As Kay writes, the meeting was held in the basement of The University Women's Club of Toronto. She found there about twenty women, as well as Laura, the chair, and Helen Tucker, the secretary. The women represented a broad range of organizations including the National Council of Women of Canada, University Women's Clubs, Business and Professional Women of Canada, United Church Women, the Catholic Women's League of Canada, The National

Council of Jewish Women of Canada, the Imperial Order Daughters
of the Empire (IODE), the Federation of Women Teachers' Associ-
ations of Ontario, Voice of Women, and women representing 4-H
Clubs. They became the core that later became the National Action
Committee on the Status of Women. Now imagine groups of women
from the IODE, to Catholic women, to the Canadian Women Voters'
Congress, to Jewish women, to teachers, to farm women meeting
and saying, "Something is wrong here, and we all have a piece of this
problem." Very quickly, as Kay writes, it became apparent that what
was needed was an overall inquiry.

The second component I want to emphasize is that while the
women who responded to the call acutely felt they were treated as
second-class citizens, they saw themselves as citizens, and they did
what Canadian citizens do, or "did," I should say. They assumed
they had a government and that the purpose of the government was,
together with the best input of their citizens, to work for what was
promised to Canadians, which was peace, order, and good government. They assumed there were civic instruments by which this goal
could be advanced if problems occurred in the course of time.

The call for the Royal Commission had these two components
that are of immense importance in the subsequent development and
hopefully the future development. First, women saw their issues as
common issues, not assuming there's one solution for all but that
because of their diversity – because common experience has different faces, different manifestations – they would come up with solutions that might be diverse but, nevertheless, just and equally useful
to all. Second, that there's a civic process of inquiry and examination of issues of national concern in which women have the rightful expectation (as all those who might think they are second-class
citizens) to participate: a process that affirms rather than diminishes
their participation in all institutions open to citizens. I wanted to
emphasize the spirit of that beginning because I still believe that
these roots, maybe extended to global citizenship, are the roots from
which our strength comes.

Having emphasized both the breadth of the core and the focus
of the core, the third component I would like to emphasize is the
community-building process, because the *process* of the Commission
is, in and of itself, so important. The fact that the Commission trav-
elled – that women in all localities got together because of the Commission, preparing submissions, looking at recommendations – meant

there was an opportunity of building a women's community that went well beyond the communities of the individual organizations that began the process. The women called for that meeting by Laura Sabia had very specific organizations. The Catholic women were concerned with issues of Catholic women. At the end of the process there were women's issues. There was a women's constituency, and the process of the Commission did a great deal to build it, which is a very Canadian achievement. Few other women we know internationally had that opportunity of getting to know their sisters locally.

The Commission facilitated the organic development of a pool of leadership that became available as the issues of feminism were percolating through the whole political process. Look where the leadership in the environmental movement came from. Look where the leadership in the equity movement came from. Nobody is born with a gene for running a meeting; it's developed. I've had the great privilege of having been part of that development.

I remember, for instance, in the early days of Voice of Women when we functioned bilingually without having translators. We would sit with those for whom we could translate, and everybody would speak in the language in which she was comfortable. I was sitting next to a young member of Voice of Women from Quebec in a meeting in Toronto that Kay Macpherson chaired, and chaired with skill and humour. That young delegate was just overwhelmed by the competence with which the meeting was chaired, and she said to me, "Where did she learn that? How did that come?" I described to her how Kay Macpherson, through being a member of the Association of Women Electors, through leading the Home and School Association, and through being a professional physiotherapist, had developed the competence that allowed her to run a rather controversial meeting efficiently and with a great sense of humour. The young woman from Quebec said, "Well, I'd better learn some of this." That woman was a young Solange Vincent, who became a moving force in the social movements for women, for the environment, and for justice in Quebec. I treasure that moment as being symbolic of how, out of a process of leadership and training, a seedbed developed that we would not have had if we had not had the Royal Commission.

The second strand I want to emphasize is that there was not only political breadth within Canada but also solidarity internationally and a component of peace. We should not forget that the Canadian's

women's movement and the international women's movement had
a strong component of anti-war: a component that said, as feminism says, that there is another way of living together. When my students and their students today ask me if I am a feminist and what
is feminism, I say, "Of course I'm a feminist. What else could I be?"
Feminism is not an employment agency for women: feminism is a
rightful social movement believing it is possible to have different,
non-patriarchal relationships between men, women, and children. It
is, in fact, the social relationship with respect to power and responsibility that women have developed that should be the norm of a
peaceful society, and that's a norm without violence. To me, an effort
to organize violence is patriarchal and unacceptable.

The objection to organized violence – which is usually violence
against women, against the helpless, against those second-class people
who seem to matter less – is very much at the core of much of the
women's movement. I don't forget that it was Voice of Women who
invited Soviet women, raised their own money, brought them across
the country when for many they looked like "the enemy," because we
were quite clear that in a world of equality "the enemy" so designated
by patriarchal authorities had no place. We wanted to demonstrate
there is nothing but the common cause of making a liveable world for
us and our children that will bring us from the patriarchal structures
under which we suffered to a world in which nobody would be dominated by structure: a world where there would be opportunity for
women, men, and children to take charge of their own destiny, not
individually, but together. I still believe very firmly that without that
peace component it is not possible to have equality.

I don't want to forget how people like Thérèse Casgrain, seen
by so many as an establishment figure, was willing to be part of a
women's peace presence that led her to be arrested in Paris in 1964,
to her great joy and being very good publicity. For women too there
are issues "up with which we will not put": issues of violence and
patriarchy. Whether it is domination of people, whether it is domination of the environment, whether it is nuclear testing, there is that
strand in our roots that understands clearly that justice is not possible if it is at the expense of others. That is my second strand.

My third strand is the strand of personal story, the stories our
young sisters will find quite unbelievable and the stuff of tall tales.
The sort of thing that happened to many in my generation when
they were trying to bring inclusive, non-sexist language into school
curriculum, when they brought thoughts of diversity, thoughts of

acceptance of differences, and also their own presence doing things differently into traditional workplaces. All those stories – about not going through the front door, not having women's washrooms, not being able to speak – those stories should not be lost because once change comes, really genuine and true change, the landscape so changes that the artifacts of the past look quaint and peculiar and seem to be figments of the imagination. The fact that those obstacles were real obstacles I think deserves recording.

Finally, I would ask whether you too were surprised, as I was, at the rise of lady patriarchs. I must admit it took me much too long to understand that women, once given the freedom to choose, could choose patriarchy as a mode of working. I have always held that the real issue is patriarchy, is dominance, and I really thought that once women had been given choices, and had understood what power does, they would not choose the instrumentality of patriarchy to assert their power and responsibility. I've been among those who agitated for giving women access to power. I wanted – and still want – feminists to be as effective as possible, but rank and power has always seemed to me akin to postal code. When I would congratulate a former student for becoming a professor, for becoming a dean, I thought of her new responsibility like having a larger postal code and a greater range to be useful, rather than three buttons on the shoulder and somebody saying "Madame Dean" to her.

The fact that there are women who enjoy patriarchy came somewhat as a surprise to me, and it shouldn't have. Historically we have had lady patriarchs, and we will have lady patriarchs in the future, and we will have to say to them, "Uh-uh. That won't do. There are other ways of doing it." Just as we find that, for many of our male colleagues and partners, the way in which women collaborate is a very enjoyable pattern. They fall into it with ease and grace. Nevertheless, patriarchy and dominance remain, and who occupies the seat of the great patriarch is probably more a matter of time and place than a matter of gender, but whoever it is we know where we stand.

NOTES

1 Dr Franklin was unable to attend and was asked by the organizers to record her perspectives on the symposium's theme for the symposium's website.
2 Kay Macpherson, *When in Doubt, Do Both: The Times of My Life* (Toronto: University of Toronto Press 1994).

10

Ursula Franklin Interviewed by
Mary Hynes*

(*Tapestry*, CBC Radio, 4 February 2007)

MH: Once there was a physicist. She worked very hard to gain her place in the world at a time when to be a woman in a laboratory was to be a rare specimen indeed. She was a great success. But this physicist came to realize something troubling about her work; simply put, it could be used in the cause of war – still a brilliant career, perhaps, but for this woman, no way. So she walked away. She applied herself instead to the physics of archaeological finds, becoming a pioneer in the field, and somewhere along the way she became something else: a walking example of the phrase "the courage of your convictions."

Dr Ursula Franklin, now eighty-five, is my guest today. If I were to read even a partial list of Ursula Franklin's accomplishments that would be the hour, we would be saying goodbye, so I'll try a very partial list: Ph.D. Experimental Physics, University professor, mentor to a generation of engineers, companion of the Order of Canada, Massey lecturer, fellow of the Royal Society of Canada, a Quaker, a peacemaker. There is a taste of her life and work in her new book, *The Ursula Franklin Reader: Pacifism as a Map*. Dr Franklin, welcome to *Tapestry*.

UF: Thank you, Mary. Thank you very much.

MH: You've said maps have always fascinated you. I look at the book. Here we have a map on the cover, we have your subtitle *Pacifism as a Map*. I'd like to start by asking you what's the fascination for you with maps?

---

* We gratefully acknowledge the CBC for permitting us to include this interview.

UF: Maps are two things to me: the helpfulness and the perspective of those who have gone before us. All people travel. There are journeys for all of us, and we all depend on the knowledge of others to get from here to there. The fascination for me with maps, new ones and old ones, is the relationship between the purpose of the travel and the choice of the map. In the book I describe my pleasure as a child at seeing for the first time a circumpolar map – that the reality can be pictured differently depending on where you stand and how and where you want to travel. The image of a map is such a nice, universal, collaborative image and it always has served me well.

MH: I love this idea. I have never thought of it in quite this way: that you are using the work – depending on the work – of others to get somewhere. That's what maps give you.

UF: Otherwise you could not and would not know how to travel. Even the earliest signs, the earliest pictures, paintings, cave paintings, are all to be interpreted as messages to a traveller. How do you get both the physical reality of where you are and the mental advice, "Go this way but not that" into a form that is helpful to others? The very purpose of a map is to be of help, to be of guidance.

MH: To show the way.

UF: To show the way. You may not be frightfully helpful when you put monsters in the sea, as you see in the old maps, but there's a message, and it's a message to somebody not known to the mapmaker, and I've always thought that was a nice thing.

MH: There's also the map as metaphor, which you deal with in your book when you say your maps are strange. They have no good guys and bad guys. Your maps have no "us and them," no winners and losers. You've said you sometimes feel lonely as a result, trying to navigate by your maps. What's lonely about that kind of map?

UF: Well, I want to respond in two ways. I don't think map is a metaphor. It's just as much a reality as the map that shows Highway 401 and the ramp to get there. There are real people who are helpful collaborators, and one can map where they are without saying they are good guys or bad guys, or without determining whether they stand on something green or red.

But by the same token if everybody around you has a roadmap with the ramp of the 401 and you want to navigate using a map made by others who have walked or used a canoe, you may feel lonely because you say, "Who else is walking here?" If you walk you feel pretty exposed with a roadmap. You may not even be allowed on the 401, yet you want to walk because you want to meet others who walk. The map is not a figment of the imagination but another way of recording what is there in reality.

MH: What an interesting choice of words you use: the walking map can make you feel exposed if you're on Highway 401. Does the pacifist map make you feel exposed in a world that is not necessarily a pacifist place?

UF: Certainly, it makes you exposed in a number of ways, like the person who's trying to walk on the 401. First of all you feel a fool. People say, "Well don't you know we *drive* here? Can't you *read*? That's not reality. That's not the hard-nosed world." You know there aren't many others. On the other hand it makes you exposed in a different way because, like on the 401, you see the inevitable carnage, and you say "Look guys, that may not be the way to get from here to there." So you are also vulnerable because you foresee the futility of doing something and you say, "There's a better way," and they whiz past you.

MH: You've heard so many of the arguments, arguments you're referring to, that pacifism as a way to be in the world is naïve, that it amounts to appeasement, that there is such a thing as "a just war." You know, "Hitler had to be stopped, and warfare was the way to stop him." Is there merit in any of those arguments in your mind?

UF: No. I think there is not. The reason I say so is that for me peace is not merely the absence of war, it's the presence of justice. If you work for the presence of justice then there are ways and means to deal with injustice that do not involve war, the threat of force, the building up of force, or the organized violence that military intervention entails. You see, if you ask me for a definition of violence, to me violence is resourcelessness.

MH: Resourcelessness.

UF: It's the resourcelessness of the powerful who choose not to use collaborative and other resources, but it's also the resourcelessness of the powerless who have been deprived of so many approaches that in the end what's left is throwing stones, figuratively and verbally. But nonviolence is resourcefulness; it is the opportunity to take a wide spectrum of appropriate resources to a problem.

Not all resources work. No war has ever worked, but why not try resourcefulness when one sees that the resourcelessness of violence doesn't work and hasn't worked? You know we don't beat our children anymore. People thought if you didn't have corporal punishment at school there would be no discipline, but we know we can have discipline at school. We can have respect between parents and children. It's against the law to beat your wife in this country, yet it doesn't mean that all marriages disintegrate. We have seen on the micro level that the recourse to violence is pointless, and my argument is *extend that*, and in many ways we have. Our schools are different, our families are different, our workplaces are different.

MH: I wasn't familiar with the work of Lewis Fry Richardson, a man whose work you admire. He was a British mathematician and a Quaker who suggested a new way of looking at war and a new way of appraising the statistics of war. Tell me about him.

UF: He's a most interesting person. He was the youngest member in his time to become a member of the British Royal Society. He was brilliant applied mathematician who worked for the Meteorological Office beginning just before the First World War but mainly between the wars, and he was a Quaker and a pacifist.

Being a conscientious objector in the First World War, he came into contact with Bertrand Russell's work, and he suddenly realized that the conflicting nations really weren't that different from the weather masses where the hot and cold air impinge on each other and you get thunderstorms. You get turbulence. He had been instrumental in the mathematics of weather prediction, and he thought, "Well surely one can see nations dealing with each other and coming to the point of conflict just as I see thunderstorms coming." He began to develop what is now known as "Richardson Processes," the basis of some peace research, and tried to publish what he called "Statistics of Deadly Quarrels." Nobody wanted to print it, but the most extraordinary thing at the time was that he made no distinction between friend and foe, between civilian and military. He counted all and said all are victims of war and all ought not to be in that position.

I've been fascinated by him. He did not see the publication of his own work. It was published by his son and others in 1950 after his death, but much conflict-resolution work has been based on this weather model, which I sometimes use to illustrate not only that it's inevitable that there are differences but also that one can deal with them. It's not the weather.

MH: When you see it on the page it's so striking because it's as blunt as this – those who are dead are dead, those who have suffered have suffered – and the loss and pain on the one side are no less meaningful and no less horrible than the loss and pain on the other side. It just completely takes the *us and them* right out of the equation. It comes down to "People are dying."

UF: Quite, and you see this is what has always brought women into the peace movement and has united women from the Women's International League for Peace and Freedom to Voice of Women, where I have had so much friendship and support. Women knew it wasn't "my suffering" or "their suffering"; it was everybody's suffering, and it was unnecessary and preventable. One had to do something to not let people suffer.

MH: But here's the question with no answer, perhaps. This narrative of good guys and bad guys seems to be inescapable in the world we live in today. It drives policy, it drives war, it shapes the way governments move. When this view of the world, when this us and them, seems so intractable, how do you get out from under it?

UF: I think you get out from under it when you see that *us and them* – that institution of the enemy – is a device for governance. It is a nice way to postpone listening to people, because the enemy is at the gate. The "public enemy" is a device. It's not a person, not a nation; it's a designated device of people management. It's very convenient to say we have to first deal with whatever – communism, terrorism, whatever is at hand – and then we might deal with homelessness, tuberculosis.

That doesn't mean there are not conflicts, but the resolution of conflict is not in the *us and them* but in dealing with issues. In no way do I deny either the issue of conflict or the thrust that people may have it in for other people. We don't live in a world of saints.

Given that, what I do say is that one needs means to deal with conflict that do not make the situation worse. If people suffer, their suffering is not alleviated by making others suffer. You have to deal with the suffering, but it's like contagious disease. With contagious diseases we have learned to separate: you deal with the illness, and you try to prevent its spread. There are similar ways of dealing with conflict. These ways are not painless, but war isn't painless. They are not cheap, but see how horribly, horribly expensive war is, and we could use the brains that are used for designing weapons, and strategies, and propaganda, and tactics. There could be a fair amount of spare brain and spare money, and there are better ways of using these resources.

MH: What do you think of the argument Tony Blair used to make quite elegantly that, in an age of terrorism, governments have to stand firm, they have to strike back, they have to show force – immediate force, deadly force – that anything else is giving in?

UF: Well, the elegance of Tony Blair might be there, but there is such a thing as reality recognition. He has been singularly unsuccessful, and so have others. One needs not only to say, "We stand firm – regardless of whether it works or not I am here cast in bronze." That doesn't solve anything. But what one would say to Tony Blair, and I hope he would be intelligent enough to know it, is that problems have been solved, except they have not been solved by war.

If you look at things that work, you see they work not by force but by a variety of means in which governments have a good deal to do – in regulation, in setting standards. Here we are two women in reasonably responsible positions. Our grandfathers would have thought the world would come to an end if the public broadcasting or the equivalent in an orderly country like Canada would let women talk to each other and the country. Now that changed – not by anybody shooting anybody, but by persistent argument including regulation and including a lot of demonstration that there are viable ways of including women. I remember a good friend of mine who began at a time when it was rare that women would read the news on CBC, and hers was always a weekend shift. She would say, "Well maybe the news doesn't have to be that reliable on a weekend. You can give it to a woman." Things change; why not let them change? Force and war *prevent* change; they don't bring it.

MH: My guest today is Ursula Franklin. Dr Franklin is professor emerita at the University of Toronto. She is also the author of more than 100 papers on the structure and properties of metals and alloys. Beyond the university, Dr Franklin once received an Order of Merit from the City of Toronto for work she did in neighbourhood planning. In 2001, she won the Pearson Peace Medal from the United Nations Association in Canada for her humanitarian work.

Dr Franklin also has a high school named after her. The Ursula Franklin Academy in Toronto is driven by Dr Franklin's belief that a good education blends the liberal arts and sciences with an emphasis on social justice. When it was time to plan the school colours, the academy went with navy blue, hunter green, and burgundy, and here's why: no country on Earth uses blue, green, and burgundy for the national flag. The colours tell students they are meant to be citizens of the world. Now we return to my conversation with Ursula Franklin.

A colleague of mine was very taken by something you said recently at Massey College: your idea that the eclipse can be a useful metaphor. When you look around you and think you've living in a dark time, in a dark age, the eclipse has something to say to you. Tell me more.

UF: Well, I have been quite troubled, not only by my own inability to make the case for pacifism but also by the fact that things seem to get worse rather than better and by the fact that very thoughtful people, including people I respect as much as I did the late Jane Jacobs, speak of dark times. I ask myself what happened to collaboration, to all the things that I and others have done? They don't suddenly disappear, and the world is full of jerks.

It came to me that it's really like an eclipse. What we've done is there, but there seems to be something between us and real enlightenment that takes that light of enlightenment away. It's an eclipse, and I think it's the eclipse of competitiveness, the eclipse of force – whether it is commercial, whether it is military – the eclipse of dominance. But it is an eclipse. The useful and constructive things have not gone away, but the light is not falling on them because it is deflected, in part, by the rhetoric of dominance and the practice of competitiveness.

As any mother who cuts up a pie knows, it is impossible for everybody to have the largest piece. The universe is there, and it's a limited, wonderful thing. It is impossible for any one group to constantly have the largest piece. It's just physically not doable, and that's the mirage: that's the thing that keeps from our direct sight the light of enlightenment and the inventory of useful things that could be brought to bear.

MH: I learned something just a few weeks ago about the Quaker path, something I hadn't been familiar with: that is the idea of the inner light, that there is a divine spark, a divine light in each person. I'd like to hear more about that from you, Dr Franklin, your understanding of the inner light, where it comes from, and what it means.

UF: It's actually quite simple. When you look back at the beginning of Quakerism, it came out of a time when people in England were very fed up with the difference between *word* and *deed*. What the church and the learned people said and what happened were so different, and for groups such as the Quakers or the Levellers it was a time of social ferment. They said, "That doesn't make sense."

Those who were Quakers realized eventually that they were perfectly capable of experiencing divine guidance without the help of ministers, church, incense, choir, and all the works. But they also realized that wisdom is not something that can be ordained or given. It is a gift of God, and that ability to discern – to know the difference between right and wrong – is inherent in a person. Their belief was that that was God's voice. It was the inner light: a light within, by which one can discern, that was given to all Christians, non-Christians, baptized, men, women, and children.

George Fox had a wonderful phrase to say to his colleagues and followers: "Walk cheerfully over the world answering to that of God in every person." He was among the first leadership of Quakers, and that "answering to that of God in every person" is a very valid thing because you appeal to what is good, right and divine in a person. That inner light may be buried under an awful lot of crud and prejudice, but it is there and there is a need to keep on trying. One may not be successful. Life may have distorted a person's mind to the extent that she has very little access to her inner light, but it doesn't mean it isn't there inherently.

MH: There's the eclipse again, right? How did you come to the Quaker faith? How did that journey begin for you?

UF: It began with pacifism. My father and his family had been Protestant German clergy, and I came from a long line of German Protestants. My mother's family was Jewish, and while I was very much in the mold of a Christian tradition I felt I could not live with a tradition that acknowledged war, that had "a just war." For me it was essential to combine pacifism and my basic Christian rules, and to me and others Quakerism is the place.

MH: Some of the most moving essays in the book, I think, are those in which you talk about Quakerism, Quaker meetings, and the place of silence in a Quaker meeting. You refer to collective silence as one of the most powerful spiritual forces: many people getting together to be silent. Tell me about that power. What happens when people come together in silence?

UF: It's really almost funny and indicative that you have to ask because it's such a rare and precious experience. What it does is that it protects you. It allows you to discard all the rattling and all the noise, and then you begin to be ready to hear. You see, the real treasure of silence – and I have a little essay in the book on it – is that it allows the unprogrammable to happen.

MH: The unprogrammable!

UF: There are things that happen that no one on Earth can predict or program. Many of those things go on, but so much in our lives is programmed there isn't a way to allow for the unprogrammed. You have to have silence to allow for the possibility of something that is not only unforeseen but also *unforeseeable* to happen. That collective silence, whether it leads to any insight or not, is the acknowledgement of the possibility of unforeseen insights, of unforeseen knowledge.

You had Richard Kearney here and he spoke about theology: God as a possibility. And I said, "Yes of course, but then you have to learn, and your own conduct has to be the witness for that possibility." It's not good enough to just sit there and say, "Wow." You then have to draw consequences from the learning.

MH: So you don't bask in this magical silence and then forget about it and go home.

UF: Or think Monday has nothing to do with what you experienced on Sunday.

MH: So what does that mean? What are you tangibly taking away from a moment of silence that feels almost sacred? What translates to Monday morning?

UF: A very different sense of proportion: what matters, what doesn't matter, and with that a matter-of-fact courage to do what one thinks is right and appropriate and just not to take part in a lot of things that are fluff and feather. That discernment of the inner light gives you a sense of proportion; it allows you to say what things really matter.

MH: Your essay on silence may have been my favourite in the book, but I also felt kind of sheepish because here we are on the radio making noise, talking and every time someone talks about silence on this program – and it happens a lot – you know how sacred it is, how enriching it is, how important it is, I feel like such a hypocrite. I think, "Okay, I should just shut up. I can't talk, talk, talk about silence." But I do want to get into this with you, Dr Franklin, because you've written so powerfully about what we lose when silence slips away.

UF: It's this openness to the unforeseen and unforeseeable. If one's openness to the unexpected, the unprogrammed, the unprogrammable is so reduced then creativity goes, calmness goes, and sense of proportion goes. What is lost is the realization that things can happen one doesn't foresee. Thoughts can come one hasn't anticipated. Doors can open one doesn't even know existed. The confidence that those things can occur, whether they are in one's own life or one's country's life, slips away as silence slips away.

MH: It's the stuff of news magazine cover stories these days: science versus religion, religion versus science. Have you ever felt there is some sort of inherent conflict as a woman of science and a person of belief? Has it ever felt as though the two are somehow at odds?

UF: No. I have actually always wondered why people get so excited about it. As I see it, all that science brings us – and I'm now not talking about the application of science but the inherently increased knowledge of the world around us – is to the realization of how little we know, and how much more there is. When you look at science in the broadest sense, from the cosmic to the molecular to the atomic, what has it told us? First of all, it tells us that nature works. Secondly it tells us that nature works frugally. The amount of energy that a natural process takes – I mean you and I couldn't design a dandelion. Nature works frugally with a minimum of waste, and the products of nature are beautiful.

Now why would anyone think that any belief of any form would be either threatened or contradicted by the accumulating results of scientific inquiry? You can argue with scientists about what they do with their knowledge. That's where I argue that my belief doesn't allow me to make an atomic bomb, but that's not science. To me that is the use for which a society, of which the scientists are an integral part, trains the scientists, pays for their work, imposes or encourages the application of their work. That's where I see the discussion.

MH: You write in your book, *The Ursula Franklin Reader*, "If you believe God is in every person then of course you don't shoot God, you don't starve, you don't belittle God. People have inherently the communality of their souls; they are part of a larger structure. If you are a physicist you know how difficult it is to maintain a single atom. To live a good life alone is as impossible as maintaining a single atom." Has faith been a constant for you? Have you known the dark night of the soul? Have you known periods of non-belief? Has it been there for you all through your life?

UF: No. I see the sense of your question. I just do not see faith as a sort of set of crutches that gets you through life. I see faith in the Bonhoeffer sense as the belief that strength will be given when it's needed. Now, I have certainly questioned that this would be so and been of little faith. I've probably acted with less courage and less kindness because I didn't believe I would have the resources to do what I would do or should do. For me this constitutes lack of belief: that I do not have the firmness of belief to do all I know I ought to do. In that Bonhoeffer sense I don't have enough faith to believe I will have the resources. That's how I see faith: that assurance of strength, the acting from strength even if what one does seems to be undoable.

MH: What if we substitute the word *belief*? Has your belief in a supreme being, in a creator, in a God, has that been there strongly for you through the years? Does that waver?

UF: I'm fairly unfussy about that. Whether regarding my own belief or other people's belief, I've always been you may say "sloppy" about the details of belief because I'm far more interested in the *consequences* of belief. I have had little patience in theological discussions because I am really not that concerned about the virgin birth, and I wouldn't lose sleep over some point that people feel very strongly about. But I am *very* interested in and meticulous about the *consequences* of belief, and of course the consequences of my beliefs have broadened. Now that I am old, I see far more things as moral questions: things I would have seen as a young person as practical decisions.

MH: What kinds of things are now moral questions?

UF: Shopping. I lived part of my life without having the luxury of shopping, so I got into shopping late in my life. I first shopped frugally to see that my budget was right. I only slowly began to learn that there is another standard, that I don't necessarily have to buy the cheapest; I should see how workers are paid, where things come from. The consequences of my faith have broadened as I grow old and have overridden my personal optimization in trying to do things right for me. In that sense I have had to learn a lot more about the consequences of my belief.

MH: So the consequences also mean how do you walk in the world as a result of what you believe?

UF: The consequences of belief only mean that. For me the consequences of my belief are *what I do* including how I deal, or try to deal, with people with whom I disagree. I have no other consequences of my belief except conduct, but my conduct certainly has changed in part through age and in part, I hope, through a more thorough understanding of my belief.

MH: Quakers are advised to live adventurously. What has that meant to you? I'm thinking perhaps apart from your career, your awards, your degrees. They all point to a life lived adventurously, but I'm wondering about the adventures that are not written down on paper. Where else in your life have you lived adventurously?

UF: Well, one can live adventurously by *not* doing certain things. I mean one of my somewhat unintended adventures has been to live without television. It wasn't just that I didn't need it. My husband agreed with that. We now find that we have lived without television, which was first mostly a time-saving thing for us, but the adventure of saying "I do not have to follow that road." The adventure is not only to go along a certain path; it's equally, or sometimes even more adventurous, not to go a certain path. So one of our adventures has been fifty years of marriage without television.

MH: Fifty years!

UF: I mean, we were married before television came into homes, but having no television means you talk to your partner. When you turn from the adventure of not doing something, the adventure is probably an ongoing conversation with your spouse that you would not have had had you spent your available time differently. You know one can live adventurously *by exclusion*, which allows you then to include very different things. I have cooked probably every meal with very limited exception for the last fifty years: three meals when we had children. If you add that up, it comes to thousands and thousands of meals, which for me is recreation and pleasure. It's a different adventure in a sense. It's not climbing the Himalayas, it isn't backpacking and spectacular, but it's life, and you live then adventurously maybe in very low key, in small print.

MH: I'm thrilled to hear about an adventure that takes place in the kitchen, in the family kitchen day after day at the stove, at the fridge, at the cutting board.

UF: Yes. It is an adventure. We never had a dishwasher, and when our kids were little they would help. I valued that time together because there are ages when kids don't with ease talk to their parents. When we did the dishes, they talked to each other, and I would hear things that I might not otherwise have heard. I remember my mother saying we should have a dishwasher and I said, "No, that's one thing I will not have." In fact, we moved into a house six years ago that was smaller because our family had all grown and that house had a dishwasher. I couldn't get it going and our oldest grandson, then at nursery school, had to show me. The thing had a safety catch so you had to both close and turn the handle, and I was unaware of that. My four-year-old grandson was in the kitchen as we moved in, and he had to show me how to work the dishwasher because at his daycare they helped and he knew how to do that.

MH: Was he thrilled to be doing this for his grandmother, the world-renowned engineer?

UF: He didn't see the profundity of it at all. He just thought, as he still does, that I'm a bit on the clumsy side and need instruction. But it's another adventure.

MH: Your collaborator on this book says something you don't often hear in a collection of essays and speeches. She finds it remarkable that you have such a loving perspective on the human condition. Is that how you see it? Is yours a loving perspective on who we all are, where we are, and what it all means?

UF: I'm not so sure. I think Michelle is kinder than I would be. I think it's an understanding perspective, in part because I know how very inadequate I am so why would I not allow others the level of frailty that I have to allow myself? I cannot expect of others more than I expect of myself, and I see what I do and how much it can be wanting. One needs at least to allow others the same level of excuses one allows oneself.

MH: Dr Franklin, it's an honour to share the studio with you. Thank you so much for coming in.

UF: Thank you. It's a pleasure for me and a very small way of saying thank you for all the work you are doing.

MH: *The Ursula Franklin Reader: Pacifism as a Map* is published by Between the Lines.[1]

NOTE

1 Mary Hynes concludes the broadcast by acknowledging that *Tapestry* is produced by Susan Mahoney and Marieke Meyer, with technical production by Dave Field.

11

In Conversation with Two Grade 10 Students at the Ursula Franklin Academy, 1997

This interview was conducted in preparation for a class project. Ursula was wearing a microphone, so her answers were audible on the tape, but the students' questions were not. We include this interview here as a prototype of the many informal interactions she had with young people throughout her life. The intimate setting of these conversations provided a mode of interaction that is not possible through public, formal appearances, and her responses to the students' questions regarding her early life and training include biographical material not available elsewhere.

One of the things I have to be forever grateful for is that I had very conscientious, very good parents who were committed to learning. They were both academics. My mother was an art historian and my father was an archaeologist, and neither of them had a particular bent to science. I was the only child, and I never felt there were any constraints on what I could do just because I was a girl. Many of my girlfriends had parents who felt a girl ought to get married and should learn how to sew and knit and be a good wife. My parents weren't like that at all.

I always had a great deal of pleasure in mathematics and in geometry. I was one of those children who loved puzzles and shapes and forms. My parents never said, "Oh well, you should learn languages," which I did, but mostly I had a great deal of pleasure in mathematics and a certain amount in the natural sciences. They were very clear that even if they didn't have too much knowledge of it, they would try to cultivate among their friends people who could help me and encourage me with my math. I've always been good at math.

I went to an all-girls' school, which was normal at the time. It was my parents' choice to send me to a public school, and it was a girls' school. As a kid I was very shy, and I hated to speak. Being an only child, I didn't have the sort of rough and tumble you have in a large family. Mine was a very gentle family where no voice was ever raised, so I was quite horrified by loud voices and people arguing. In our family there weren't loud arguments, and when I was with friends who had rambunctious families I would absolutely shrivel up.

In spite of my always having been interested in numbers and geometry and mathematics, when I was twelve or so, the equivalent of the guidance counsellor at school said to my mother that I was obviously such a shy and retiring personality she should encourage me to do something like gardening, as I wasn't cut out for the competitive life. Fortunately my mother just thought something rude and did what she felt was right. The guidance counsellor perhaps thought it was the good-girl syndrome – that I was just doing what was expected and had no initiative – but somehow I just wanted enough space to inquire. I learned to speak up in large part because I had an acute sense of feeling affronted when something unjust was done. I felt equally affronted when people were slipshod about mathematical arguments, and I learned to speak up largely on those issues. Of course like all things, once you practice it becomes less difficult.

I've always had an exceedingly keen sense of justice, whether it was with animals or with anything in school or at home. If I did something at school it was because I felt insulted that somebody was treated unjustly. This very keen sense of justice made it almost physically painful for me to be present when something wrong was being done, whether it was kicking a cat or pushing a kid around at school. If we had lived in another country at another time, I would probably have seriously considered going into law. It wasn't open to me because my mother was Jewish, and we were excluded from law, politics, and public affairs, but my daughter now is in law, and I would probably have seriously considered that.

It was fairly clear I would go to university and that I would go into the sciences. I had a lot of pleasure in the sciences and mathematics, in part because mathematics is one of the few things you can't manipulate by politics. When I was young, it was a great relief to me to be in a field in which politics had no place. It took me a long time to understand that there is a good deal of politics in the sciences – in who gets the education, in what sort of science is done – but when I was a kid, I thought the best escape from politics was to get into science.

When I went to university, it was fairly clear I had to do something more than mathematics. In my first term, I looked into chemistry, but then I heard undergraduate lectures in physics and when I heard that I knew, "That's for me. That's just the right mixture of the theoretical and the practical, of math and doing experiments." It became very apparent to me that what I was most interested in would be questions of structure – how things fit together – so I very naturally drifted into the area of crystallography.

It was a matter of luck that the first physics professor I had was such an inspiring teacher. I had the chance to work in the area of solid-state physics, which gave me very good training in structure and property. I did quite a lot of work in X-ray crystallography. My Ph.D., which I did at the Technical University of Berlin, was on questions of energy transfer in solids, which is related to how structures are formed, how they are stable, and how they work. The work we did was of sufficient quality that I was offered a postdoctoral scholarship and a postdoctoral position in the Department of Physics at the University of Toronto.

In 1949, with a fresh Ph.D., I came alone from Berlin to Toronto, not knowing anybody or anything, not knowing much about Canada, but knowing, I thought, a fair amount of solid-state physics. Having very much an academic command of English, I could speak English but I had no everyday English. I could talk about nuclear physics but I didn't have the right words for how to put out the garbage, or what to ask for in a grocery store, or when I needed stuff to wash my hair. When I got to Toronto it was very clear in my mind that I had to jump the barrier of a second language, which in many ways is a very lovely thing and a great discovery.

When you get another language it is as if you get another toolbox. It's a great gift, especially when my children grew up and I discovered children's poetry and children's stories in another language. It was also a great gift for me because when you get into a new language you begin to choose your words very carefully because you need to weigh them on another scale. At the beginning of learning another language, the language prevents you, or certainly prevented me, from being too rude or too critical. That's quite good for your survival, but it's also a very nice thing to be allowed to find your voice freshly as you turn around new words in a new language and say, "Does that really mean what I want to say?" I sort of learned what I meant to say for a second time in the second language and that was helpful.

I had a very small scholarship. The stipend was really intended for people who had a home here also. I didn't know that, and in many ways I also didn't care. I had a little room on the third floor of a house and cooked for myself and otherwise lived in the lab. I did some very nice work with Professor Edward Bullard in physics, primarily related to producing large single crystals that were used for radiation counters.

Professor Bullard was a geophysicist, and he was very interested in determining the age of the rocks in the Canadian Shield. That could be done by measuring the ratio of uranium to thorium in the rocks – not by grinding up the rocks and doing an analysis but by measuring the radiation: understanding that when these rocks were formed the naturally radioactive materials were in a sense frozen and encapsulated in them, and those materials would decay. The times were long enough to measure the decay times through the ratio of those two elements, and because they decayed at a different ratio, you could extrapolate to the point of formation.

This measuring was done by flying over the High Arctic. It required quite sensitive equipment, because we weren't crawling around on the ground but flying way above the ground. That was done for the first time, and it was the crystals I grew and the counters we built that were the first to determine the age of those rocks. That work grounded me very firmly in the areas of both structures and measuring radiation. I kept on with that work when the postdoc was renewed, and by 1952 that was finished. I also did other work primarily on the structure of metals and alloys with Professor Bruce Chalmers.

I was then hired by the Ontario Research Foundation, which is now ORTECH Inc. They did industrial research, and I then shifted gears and set up an X-ray laboratory for a variety of problems that were applied problems of Ontario industry. I had almost fifteen years there building up that department and working on a large variety of problems, such as determining conditions in which one could weld and repair in the High Arctic. People had begun working in the Arctic and had to do such things as welding, which is really melting metal and using it as a glue between two parts of metal at a temperature at which it's very difficult to maintain anything molten. We had to set up procedures determining how to do that and to test whether the procedures were effective. We did a fair amount of that type of work.

I also did a lot of work on the magnetic properties of materials in the practical sense of trying to determine the life or failure of ropes and cables on the cages that go down into the mines. They were heavy steel ropes. On the one hand, you cannot afford to let the little strands in them break and endanger the life of people; on the other hand, these are very expensive and you don't want to pull them out before it is necessary. We needed to develop methods that would not interfere with the workings and that could be non-destructive as well as non-interventional. You didn't want to stop the work, but at the same time you had to monitor safety continually. We developed magnetic methods – coils around those ropes to see how the magnetic properties would change with the deterioration and bending of the ropes.

It was also very interesting work theoretically, because there were so many things one needed to know and establish before one could entrust people's safety and lives to methods one developed. We also did a lot of corrosion work. I worked at the Ontario Research Foundation for almost fifteen years and enjoyed it very much.

During that time I got married, and both our children were born, which was a bit of a shock for the establishment. They had never had a female scientist before, and they had certainly never had a pregnant female scientist. They sort of went into shock when I first told them. The first time around I told them quite early that I was expecting a child and that, if they wanted to keep me on, I would want to shift to part-time. Since my parents were in Toronto then, it was possible for me to go to the lab on Tuesdays and Thursdays and Saturday mornings – at that time people still worked on Saturday mornings – and to take work home for the rest of the time. Not only did I want to continue working I also had to because both my husband and I had parents who depended on us. We needed two salaries because there were two sets of dependent parents.

I made it quite clear to the directors of research at the Ontario Research Foundation that they had to make a decision; if they didn't want to keep me on with that arrangement, they had to appoint somebody fairly soon, because I needed to train a successor. They went into endless committee meetings, because it had never happened before. If there's one thing that is not affected by committee meetings it is pregnancy: the baby comes when he or she comes. He came, and they had made no decision, so I just fell into that Tuesday/Thursday/Saturday/take-work-home mode. Nobody ever said anything at all, and two and a half years later our daughter was born. She was an easy baby, and I worked until the day before she was born and that was that. It's pretty tough when you try to keep a fairly demanding job with very young children. It's a time when one is permanently short of sleep. One survives, and I survived, having a fair amount of discipline as well as a very good and thoughtful husband.

By 1967, the Ontario Research Foundation had moved from Toronto to Mississauga, and it became quite difficult for me to commute. I also wanted to do more teaching. I had reached a stage at which I felt it was becoming important for me to teach and to get into another area of research, so I accepted an appointment as associate professor in the Faculty of Engineering. From 1967 until I retired in 1989 I taught in the Department of Metallurgy and Material Science. I developed two or three areas of work. I taught general material science to large groups of mechanical and electrical engineers who had to learn about materials and who had labs. I also taught courses on advanced X-ray techniques and on solid-state science to graduate students and began to develop my research in those two areas.

I then began to develop the application of engineering techniques to ancient materials, realizing that when testing how something was made – whether it's solid, whether there are faults in it and what they are – it really doesn't matter whether it was made yesterday or 2,000 years ago. I had done this sort of work at the Ontario Research Foundation, often for cases in court when determining whether something was to specification. The world of non-destructive techniques had progressed so one could find out how materials were fashioned without destroying them. That meant the techniques could be used in archaeology, for example, in which samples and objects are very precious. You want to know everything about a bronze arrowhead, but you don't want to destroy it in the process of learning about it. You want to have the thing *and* the knowledge.

In my researching, teaching, and working with archaeologists, I embarked on a field that is now called the science of ancient materials, or archaeometry, which takes stuff people make as evidence of what they knew and how they organized themselves. I taught courses and graduate courses to archaeologists. I've done lot of work on the casting of Chinese bronzes using the bronzes in the Royal Ontario Museum. My students and I have worked on metal artefacts of Native Peoples in the High Arctic, and we've also used these techniques on ancient textiles and on stone tools. We tried to replicate stone tools and looked at them under the microscope to see how they were worn and tried to use the made-up tools to get the same wear patterns. I spent *a lot* of my life doing that, and others continue to do that ongoing work.

Because of the combination of doing engineering work and historical work, I also became more and more interested in what technology is all about, and in how a society influences its own technology but is also influenced by it. I began both to research and to teach in the area of the social impact of technology: that it matters not only *what* we do but *how* we do it, and what the differences in technology have meant for our society and for other societies. I have written things, for example, on Chinese technologies. My work in this area has made me aware of the need to integrate all forms of learning and to be mindful that in understanding technology, both what is done and how it's done do make a difference.

12

Using Technology as if People Matter

(Opening plenary of SciMaTech 96, delivered at the
Cowichan Campus of Malaspina College, Duncan, BC,
1996, to teachers who were working to better integrate and
enhance the teaching of science, math, and technology in
their curricula)

Thank you for inviting me. I come to you as a colleague and a friend with no pretences to know either more or better how to deal with the problems we all need to address. Technology is a subject bigger than any of us, and it's worth considering together. The way we think about technology is fundamental because it reflects what we think about people, about society, and about the way in which people live together.

My aim is clarity. We live in a time in which many different words and ideas are used to try to describe complex situations, but not all is as complex as it appears. There are such things as "intentional befuddlements." There are such things as making things look more complicated than they actually are. My aim is clarity: to try to help us see and map what it is that we actually need to address.

I'll define technology so we know what we are discussing, and then I'd like to talk about some general and specific aspects of technology that relate to teaching and learning. I will have to switch between the general and specific because we are not only teachers but also parents and citizens, and many issues come to us on all those levels. Regardless of what and how we teach, the final integration of subject matter is in the person because we all both teach and learn as human beings. We don't teach and learn mathematics and become loving human beings when we teach or learn language. In the end we teach young people, and we try to be to them friends, teachers, and human beings. The final test of how well we integrate and how well they integrate is whether they and we come out as responsible people – as responsible citizens, who can switch from the specific to the general and integrate various components of knowledge and insight.

In all I have said and written, I have emphasized the definition of technology as practice. Technology is *the way we do things*. The way we do things involves devices, machinery. Today it involves computers, but to a very large extent it also involves organization, division of labour, and presupposed knowledge. Thinking of technology as practice tells us a number of things. One is that there has always been technology. There's always been a way to do things that defines the time and that changes – both deliberately from inside and by pressures from outside. Our technologies are not God-given. They are not there forever and ever, Amen. They change, and we can and must not only be aware of the forces that change the way we are doing things but also, if possible, both critique and modify them.

Many technologies, especially early technologies, are related to what I call "work-related technologies": ways of doing things so they become easier for those who do the work. Shovels, buckets, pumps, steam engines – these all have very profound work-related components. However, there are also what I call "control-related technologies," which do not really make the work easier, although they are sometimes advertised as doing so; instead, they make the *control of the work* easier. From the assembly line to the barcodes at the supermarket checkout, control-related technologies are not intended to make the cashiers' job easier as much as they are intended to control the stock, to keep track of what people do and how fast they do it, and to enhance bookkeeping. Barcodes in the library have similar functions. I'll leave it to you to look at your own administration to see whether the technologies into which you feed – including computer records, list-making, and recordkeeping – are really there to improve education or to enhance control.

As we think about technology in terms of practice there are two things we need to remember. One is that in this technological world, technology – the way we do things – increasingly feeds into a system. If one changes one thing in a system then all aspects of the system are affected. If one does a relatively trivial looking thing, such as introducing a fax machine into the process of communication, all aspects of the surrounding practices suddenly begin to be affected. The postal system, for example, has a very close relationship to the

introduction of the fax machine; there is a teeter-totter relationship between the new and old technology. The more the postal system declines, the more attractive the investment in a fax machine
becomes. In addition is the self-fulfilling prophecy that because "the
people who matter" have fax machines, the postal service becomes
less important to support because it is only there for "the people
who matter less." There's a *social justice component* in the system
aspect of technology.

There is also an *irreversible component*, and that's really important to keep in mind in teaching and learning. Once spellcheck is
available, the impetus for writing and spelling well is gone, and it's
very difficult to instil it back. When I am at the bank with a list of
cheques, there's almost a generation gap between the tellers who add
them up and the ones who rush to a calculator in order to add up
300, 400, and 250. I find myself smiling across to the teller, who is
somebody closer to my age, and we look at each other and say, "Yes,
we are probably the last ones who can add without calculators." As
we think about technology, the way we do things, we have to consider the irreversibility that technology and systems bring. It may not
be the end of the world as we know it if people can't add, but it may
just have to be considered.

How, then, should we think about technology? First of all, I'd say
we should think about it with care; we should think about why we
want to change practice, and who wants to change practice. In the
early Industrial Revolution we see an obvious impetus to change
practice in work-related technologies in an attempt to remove
labour, to lessen physical work. At the time, people were very mindful of the fact that machines replaced physical labour, and so they
ranked machines in terms of "horse power." Motors are still ranked
in terms of "horse power," but you don't find a computer being
ranked in "brain power" or "people power." There isn't a computer
that is "a quarter secretary," although computers replaced secretaries much more rapidly than motors replaced horses. We try to hide
the fact that there is a displacement, and we hide it by those simple
methods of ranking, rating, and classifying.

It's not the work-related technologies but the control-related technologies – those that pace and divide the work – that begin to be of
profound concern to us not only as teachers but also as citizens. There
is a shifting boundary between work-related and control-related
technologies. As typewriters developed into electric typewriters, and

later into computers with word-processing capabilities, we were still dealing with work-related technologies. When those computers are linked into work stations, however, and we begin to be able to count the input of an operator, we move into the realm of control-related technologies with very different dimensions. As we teach, we should be clear about the differences between work-related technologies and control-related technologies and also about the fact that many technologies intrinsically lead to deskilling.

You may still remember departmental secretaries who could type five carbon copies faultlessly, but you may also remember the awe and horror young staff had of them. You surely could not put in anything that needed correction. I recall submitting exam papers to a departmental secretary like that, and I proofread them with great care in order to leave Miss Bornock's office unscathed. Material submitted by computer, however, has not gone through that amount of care and editing, largely because it's so simple to change a 7 into a 7.7 if the calculation doesn't come out right. The deskilling is not just in the typing skills but in the editing skills; it is in the care.

Whether people can spell or do long division is marginal compared to their feeling of independence. Do we want to give students an everlasting dependence on devices? I have invigilated exams with engineering students from the time when it was a big deal that they were allowed to use slide rules to the time when they all had calculators. Dependence on calculators brings the inevitable moment of panic when, in the final exam, the calculator doesn't work, and the even greater panic when I would say as invigilator, "Well never mind. Write in your book the time when your calculator malfunctioned. You don't have to do the numerical work. Just do a back-of-the-envelope calculation and give an order of magnitude. I'm interested in whether it is 5 or 500; I'm not interested in whether it is 5.1073." I remember the look of panic on the faces of even the third-year engineering students who felt quite helpless to do that back-of-the-envelope calculation.

Those of us who teach with the help of sophisticated devices need to give time to those things that, in spite of the devices, remain the human task: the assessment, the estimate, the general overview. Precisely because the technology does, in fact, take on more and more of the intellectual human tasks, it really is essential to set aside time and exercises to do what the devices do. The goal is not to substitute for devices but to keep those parts of the task functional so one can do the back-of-the-envelope calculations, can express what needs to be said even if the spellcheck or the grammar check fails, and can read somebody else's handwriting. I used to do in-class assignments even with engineering students because I had no idea if they could write or spell. I would do that largely because I knew they would find themselves in situations where there is no substitute for either their hand or their mind. We cannot allow ourselves, because of the richness of devices, to leave students' hands and minds so undeveloped that they become dependent on devices to an extent that their own ingenuity and resourcefulness is undermined to the point of being dysfunctional.

Let me say something about the applications of new technologies – computers, the internet – to the teaching of math and science. First of all one has to see what's hype. Much of the hype regarding new technologies consists of the commercial interest that sits in the push for change, and that has to be considered. It's worth asking why we have to change practice. After all, humanity has learned and been taught for quite some time. If all teaching of the past had been as defective as it is sometimes argued, none of us would be able to spell or add or have an original thought.

First one has to look at the question of *why* to change practice, and then at the question of *how* to change practice. There are basically two ways to change practice. One is to do the old things in a new way: whether teaching French or Latin or geometry, to find new ways of teaching something that has been taught before. The second is to use the new technologies in order to teach new things. It is in that second area, in the enhanced capacity for integrating knowledge, where the real challenges and opportunities lie. Life is an integrated thing, and we live in an integrated manner. When you eat a steak that's too hard, it's not really a question of deciding whether that is a problem of chemistry or of the physics of a knife that doesn't properly work; it's a question of how you cope with an inadequate situation.

With the help of new technologies, there are more opportunities to teach in an integrated way without labelling things as being in particular fields of physics, chemistry, and math. What has to be brought into the lesson, however, is the discussion with young people on the nature of that integration. Students benefit from learning to look situationally at a task, at a question, and to walk around it to ask, "What is the knowledge, the information, the skill, the help that is needed to get from here to there?" Those questions apply whether you are counting birds, mending a birch bark canoe, or getting a car that's stuck out of a snow bank. The new technologies can make it easier to walk around the problem, but we must keep that human element: the definition of the question and the discussion of what's needed can only be done by humans who have learned to look situationally. As we think about technology, we need to think about it as assisting human endeavours, not driving them.

As we use new devices, new ways of doing things, two things emerge that have always been taken for granted as part of the landscape of learning without being labelled learning activities. One is that people work *with each other*. The other is that we must be ever mindful of the vital link between knowledge and understanding. Human and social skills developed through the process of doing something together are important forms of social learning.

When developing work-camp programs for people from very different backgrounds, for example, the people who have worked on reconciliation between either different races or different faith communities have found it easiest to stop talking and to *do something*, preferably for someone else. The great success of such programs has been that young people of very different backgrounds go out to do something to be of help to someone else, whether it's in an earthquake situation, a drought, or another emergency. In the process of doing something, the initial issue of how you get along, whether you are a Christian or Jew, black or white, man or woman, disappears because the skills developed of respecting and acknowledging both differences and similarities are not the *subject* but the *context* of the activity. From the schoolyard to the classroom a great deal of social learning – skills of tolerance, helpfulness, and seeing the common over the personal – comes out of doing things together.

The irony of technology as it relates to devices is that the more tasks one can shift from people to machines, the more attention and time one has to give to the development of human skills that were previously an automatic consequence of working together. If you and the kids have to shovel the snow, certain communication skills and other human skills develop because of that activity. When you have a contract for a snow blower, where is the helpfulness? Where is the tolerance? Where is the responsibility developed? As we joyfully utilize the advances given to us to help in our teaching, one of the things we need to do very consciously is to analyze the teaching situation and say, "We need both time and human capital to supple-ment device-supported learning so that the human skills learned as a consequence of previous ways of teaching and learning are not lost."

As we think about technology as practice, it is important to ask, "What are we practising? We can now try to replicate life and real-ity better through the integration of math, science, and technology, but what is the enterprise of education all about?" To my mind, the enterprise of education is to increase both knowledge and under-standing. Knowledge consists of the transfer of skills and informa-tion, and that part of education must be unbreakably linked to the component of understanding. Students must understand what their knowledge means – personally and socially, what is implied in what it means, and how it affects others – and bring that understanding into the whole process of acquiring an education. The new means of teaching and learning have to be supplemented by a much more sophisticated and enriched understanding of the limitations and responsibilities of knowledge. It may be a struggle not only to link knowledge and understanding in our teaching but also to convince others that the combination is essential.

That brings me to questions of means. Do you use a library? Do you use a CD-ROM? I'm absolutely partial to books and libraries, and particularly to librarians – to the effect of finding something you haven't looked for and the fellowship and communication that comes when you take somebody to the library. One has to discuss questions of means not only in terms of money but also in terms of the enterprise of education. The pursuit of skill and information can-not outrun the pursuit of understanding or you are in the most hor-rible three-legged race in which you have two highly skilful people tied together on their third leg of totally inappropriate and under-developed understanding. Finding means that enable students to link knowledge and understanding is in many ways the task.

It's a task in which students can very often be very helpful. I remem-ber years ago being asked by my department chair whether I could throw some light on a situation we had. A young new staff member from another department was asked to teach a course I also taught, and the chair got complaint after complaint, which all seemed to be rather trivial. It seemed as if there was something underneath those complaints, and he asked me if I could talk to the students to find out what was really going on so I did. The teacher was a bright young man, and it seemed there was nothing wrong, yet something wasn't working. In the end a student said to me, rather annoyed, "You know, you ask him a question, and he gives you a *book*."

That was *precisely* what was wrong. The students asked a question not only in order to get some information but also to have some human contact. There was something behind the question that the book didn't answer, and the young staff member was uneasy and uncertain. That was all that was wrong, but it is something very profound and it stayed with me. You cannot just give students a book, a computer program, or access to the internet when they come with a question. We really need to keep the complementarity of technologies in mind.

As we adapt to new ways of doing things, it is, of course, important to realize how much of the push for change is political and has nothing to do with teaching and learning but a great deal to with replacing people by machines and with supposed budgets. In response to such pressure, I think, there is absolutely no solution except solidarity and pigheadedness: a recognition that some things are negotiable and some things are not. In the field of education what is not negotiable in my mind is the primacy of human beings. The kids given into our care have to emerge from the educational system as functional citizens who can cope with the practical, political, and human aspects of life. If they don't learn coping skills through us, where will they learn them? That seems to me the non-negotiable part that one has to make public: that what is at stake here essentially comes down to the political and emotional sanity of the society – the need to see what matters.

Schumacher wrote a book, *Small Is Beautiful*, with the subtitle *Economics as If People Mattered*. We have to teach technology not *as if* but *because* people matter. We cannot use technology as a way to teach that people do not matter. There may be tasks, whether statistics or spelling, one can entrust to machines, but there are also the much more important *tasks of understanding* that cannot be delegated to technology and devices. The matter of clarity about which I'm so concerned is a matter of understanding – the analysis of where the push for automation comes from. Is that a way to save money? Are there other ways either to save or gain money? The better the devices we have, the greater the need for us to teach and practise understanding.

In the course of integrated teaching, a few things warrant particular attention right now, and one is numeracy. We have been able to teach our children an alertness to the meaning of words – not to fall for advertising. There's a level of sophistication among the young about the use of verbiage that veers away from the truth or is chosen deliberately in order to give an impression; however, there's no corresponding level of sophistication on numerical arguments. "X million was saved." Big number: compared to what? How many dollars or cents would it take from every citizen of North Bay to build a community centre? How much would it take from every citizen of Canada to keep the CBC or the international service? We are told we will save "x million" by cutting it, but what is that? As somebody on the international program of the CBC pointed out, it's a week's profit of the Bank of Nova Scotia. The yearly expenditure of the country for the CBC's international service is a week's profit for the Bank of Nova Scotia.

Now, your kids will not bring this up with the same ease with which they'll look at the advertising that claims something is whiter than white or worn by a great star. The level of numerical sophistication in the social sense is abysmal compared to the level of verbal sophistication. Right here and now and tomorrow, that's the task of the integrated curriculum; start on numeracy.

Start also by considering not only what a specific new technology *does* but also what that technology *prevents*. Because of that technology, what can no longer be done? Whether it's road and railway, fax and postal system, computer learning versus other ways of learning, or CD versus book, one has to look both at the *enabling* and at the *foreclosing* angle of any way in which things are done. When teaching through new technologies we must highlight not only the skills the new devices bring but also the skills that are not developed because of the use of those devices. It's often a very real trade-off. The advantages of the new technologies don't come for free, and the cost is not only in money.

The greatest cost is in the non-developed people skills that come with the new methods of teaching and learning, and those costs can be recognized and compensated for. The skill of cooperation, the skill of tolerance, which are essential social skills that develop slowly and painfully, are frequently short-circuited when you can just go back to the solitude of a computer screen. Again, considering what new technologies prevent is something all of us can do tomorrow morning.

I have always felt very strongly that as one teaches science and scientific processes – and particularly the application of science to specific problem-solving – one has to consider the notion of "side effects." The birth control pill supposedly has "side effects." Now the labelling of something as a side effect is purely a social judgment: that is, it is more important to prevent pregnancy than to have certain other health risks. A scientific application has only *effects*. These are equivalent in the first place. It is the social and commercial application that considers some effects unimportant and labels them as side effects rather than those who are affected. The slippery sidewalk is a "side effect" of a reduction of municipal budgets. It's a side effect until you break your hip; then it's a calamity. While one weighs the uses and the disadvantages, I think it's important that the implicit labelling of side effects be recognized by students as a social judgment rather than a scientific fact. Again, that's something one can do tomorrow morning.

In conclusion, if you ask me, "How should we think about technology?" I think we should think about it carefully, we should think about it analytically, and we should think about it with the conviction that in the end nothing matters except people. A friend of mine who was the director of education at one of the large boards outside Toronto once said that what parents and teachers hope is that the system will allow the students in the end to be personally happy and publicly useful. Whatever we do, whatever devices we apply, in the end that has to be our goal. Thank you.

13

Developing a *Li* of Massey

(Acceptance speech, Massey College's 40th Anniversary
Awards, University of Toronto, 2004)

It is a great privilege for me to speak on behalf of my fellow award winners and to thank all who have been part of conceiving of this honour. Probably the first reaction for each of us, when learning of this honour, was the question "Why me?" Certainly I can think of many within the Massey community who could rightfully stand in my place tonight, and my fellow award recipients assure me their response has been just the same.

We are thus here, not as much as "Exhibit A," but as a delegation that happened to be in town and that belongs to a much larger contingent. Members of such a contingent might be recognized, not so much by *what* they do, but *how* they do it: it is their *conduct* that would identify those who could stand in our place.

The term *conduct* is used here in the sense of the Chinese notion of *Li*. John Fraser and I share an interest in and respect for the philosophy of ancient China, and I would like to highlight a few elements of the very complex concept of *Li* so as to indicate the outline of a "*Li* of Massey." From its Confucian roots, *Li* draws on respect for tradition, an understanding of the importance of ritual, of doing things properly, as well as a conviction of the centrality of music and beauty in public life. But there are other roots of *Li*. From its Mohist tradition comes the knowledge that appropriate conduct is not a matter of prescription or of following meticulously a set of given rules; the right conduct is a matter of *discernment* – a process of ongoing weighing and assessment.

"Be aware" is a central and recurring dictum in the teachings, and being aware does not mean constantly looking out for mad dogs or terrorists. It means be aware of what is going on around you and respond to it with what the texts call "the standards of mutual concern." In today's parlance one would say, "Be forever mindful of the wider context within which you are called to live and work. Respond to it with knowledge, compassion and integrity."

The Chinese texts also speak of "mutual concern." This awareness of an essential reciprocity is vitally important in terms of proper conduct. Those who try to educate must be prepared to be educated; those who attempt to help have to accept help equally willingly. That is not easy for the likes of us, yet it is part of an emerging *Li*.

Vincent Del Buono reminded me of the title of Vincent Massey's autobiography *What's Past Is Prologue*. What a phrase! I do not know how Mr Massey would have responded to the question "Prologue to *what*?" but in terms of our experience at this, the fortieth anniversary of the College, the past is the prologue to the unforeseen, or even more so – to the unforeseeable.

This is where I want to close the circle I have tried to draw from this little gang of four [award recipients] to the ancient Chinese sages and back to Vincent Massey and the College. How is one to be ready for the unforeseen, the unforeseeable? Only, I think, by an emphasis on *conduct*. None of us knows what we may be called to do, but we may know that we will function within standards of mutual concern. If the work each of us has done, and the way we have tried to do it, can help to develop a *Li* for Massey, we will cherish these awards and the spirit they represent.

14

Three Lessons from the Natural World

(Convocation address, McGill University,
Montreal, 2006)

Friends, first and foremost, let me thank you for the singular honour you have extended to me. Congratulations to all of you who are graduating today, as well as to your families and teachers. I am very happy to speak to a Science convocation because the practice of science, the daily work in the lab, has been the source of so much pleasure and fulfillment in my own life. Allow me to speak about common insights that have come from the advances of science, both recent and traditional. These insights have come from all the diverse disciplines within the sciences.

If we accept, be it only for this discussion, the simple definition that research in the sciences attempts to understand and illuminate the working of the natural world – from the structure of galaxies to reactions on an atomic level – then there are some amazingly general, overarching insights that the sciences can bring to us, in spite of, or maybe because of, the great diversity of the various disciplines within the sciences.

Helped by modern imaging and communication techniques, scholars have been able to share these insights with the larger community and three attributes emerge. The natural world is incredibly *beautiful* – from the structure and arrangement of single molecules into an active cell, to the microstructure of crystalline surfaces, to the new complex nanomaterials, to the movement of the galaxies. Second, the natural world is incredibly *functional*. The more we learn about complexity, the greater is the marvel of functionality – whether it is the passage of a molecule through a membrane, the ultra-fast exchange of electrons in a chemical reaction triggered by light, or the formation of planetary materials over very long periods of time.

The natural world, the great biosphere of which we are such a small part, functions with an incredibly delicate complexity. Third, the natural world is extremely *frugal*. Thermodynamics, the great common yardstick of change, illuminates just how frugal are the workings of the natural world, how effectively energy is utilized, how symbiotically functions intertwine.

Yet, as each piece of newly revealed knowledge about the natural world elaborates just how beautiful, how functional, and how frugal the natural world is, it becomes equally clear, how many of our own human and social structures and processes are in fact *not* beautiful, functional, and frugal. They can be very ugly, dysfunctional, and wasteful. Ironically, many of these enterprises and processes have been designed or modified drawing on what was considered the latest and best scientific findings. Frequently – but let me stress emphatically by no means always – scientific information has been used to outsmart or outfox the natural world, to facilitate shortcuts or conduct end runs around the very processes studied. This approach has often resulted in increased efficiencies in one social or economic activity coupled with a great waste of other resources, or in the cumbersome ugliness of so-called economies of scale (not to mention the overall disregard of the dynamics of the biosphere in industrial and political planning).

While specific scientific findings may justify specific designs, the overarching insight of the study of the natural world brings counter evidence into the picture that should not be overlooked. Every scientific finding contains knowledge of beauty, frugality, and functionality. In fact, functionality, frugality, and beauty may be existentially so profoundly interrelated that nothing but an optimization of these attributes will work in the long run as a design principle for human society.

Why do I raise these issues with you here and at this moment in your lives? In the first place, I would like to highlight the great common insight that science has brought to our knowledge and understanding of the natural world, because this is sometimes overlooked in the great rush toward profitable applications of specific research. I would also like you to have these thoughts for use in your own work. As you apply and augment your own scientific knowledge, respect *the trio* of beauty, functionality, and frugality, and check for their simultaneous presence in all you undertake. It would not

surprise me if, within your lifetime, it will become common knowledge that what makes and maintains a liveable world is the simultaneous presence of beauty, functionality, and frugality.

I wish you well.

15

The Place of Knowledge in Our Personal and Collective Lives

(Convocation address, Ryerson University,
Toronto, 2012)

Let me give you my thanks for the honour and great privilege of receiving this citation and degree from a university that is so true to its own mission. Let me congratulate the graduates and their families. I would so much like to tell you how much I want to rejoice with you in your achievement.

Over and above the privilege of receiving this Honorary Degree, to be part of the convocation of this School of Continuing Education is something I profoundly value. We all are on the same journey, but to be with you knowing you have sought out this path, coming to learning in the context of the mandate of the University already as practitioners who work trying to resolve problems in the community, that is a great privilege for me. I applaud the discipline, the friendship, the search, and the persistence that brought you to this moment. I know you will make good use of what you have learned and of the friendships you have established here. The wide range of subjects you have taken during your time here is an indication of the breadth of the contributions you will make, but you also have something profoundly in common, however different your fields of endeavour will be.

The first thing you have in common is your achievement that brought you here tonight. That achievement, that graduation attests to, means you have increased your knowledge and your professional competence. I would like to spend the few minutes I have with you to share some thoughts on the place of knowledge in the endeavours we undertake both personally and collectively.

Knowledge as I use the term here is not merely a collection of facts. Knowledge is the sum of two major components: information and understanding. Throughout your studies there will have been moments in which you were totally consumed to generate, accumulate, and assess information. You may also have experienced periods in which you were preoccupied by an overwhelming need to understand that information in its broadest context. At times it may have been easier to amass data than to struggle to clarify their understanding, meaning, and context. You may have felt that knowledge is a bit like a communal teeter-totter in which information is on one end of the bar and understanding is on the other and it is rather difficult to keep them in balance. If you so felt, you were right.

As you return to the world of work you may be asked to bring your new knowledge to a particular situation very much in agreement with the aims of your university. You may find that task requires more and better information, but you may also discover that what is needed most is a better, different, and possibly more sophisticated level of understanding. I would urge you to remember that your role should be to provide *both* information and understanding. In other words, don't let anybody tell you, "Just give me the facts never mind what they mean." Conversely, don't accept an assignment when one says, "Never mind if the facts aren't complete or totally correct, just write a moving summary." Don't let yourself be pushed to disconnect information and understanding.

That's one of the thoughts I'd so much like to leave with you. Part of what you take from your time here is the awareness that information and understanding should not be separated. Search for both, and knowledge is the sum of these two components.

You may, on this festive day, also look at yourself and take cognizance of how you as a human being have changed during the time you have been here. You realize you know more. You know a lot more, but you may ask yourself, do you know better? The difference between knowing more and knowing better gets us back to the components of knowledge – understanding and information.

How does one keep and maintain that balance on the teeter-totter between information and understanding? None of us can do that alone. That's where other people come in. That's where one has to be so keenly aware that knowledge is collective and it is cumulative. We all sometimes feel overwhelmed, if not drowned, in more and more information. That's painfully evident and has been so for some time. There are people who coined the term "data smog," and it is the light of understanding that helps us – you and me and everyone – to find our way through that data smog.

The collective aspect of knowledge might be a little bit more difficult to remember because you've gone through umpteen individual tests to test *your* knowledge, but in fact we deal with *our* knowledge. The pooling of information, its validation, assessment, and understanding are all human, collective, and collaborative processes. It is by working together, by interaction, by response and reply, that we create and transmit that light of understanding.

It is because of my realization, after a long life, of how central that part of our knowledge is that comes out of working with each other, that I am convinced in my belief that knowledge is a common good. It is not a piece of private property. I firmly believe that no one of us, in that sense, owns what we know. We hold our knowledge in trust and therefore have some responsibility for the integrity of its use. I've many times been uncomfortable with the notion of intellectual property because I'm so keenly aware how frequently contributions of knowledge arise from the life of ordinary people living and working together and trying to cope with things rather than from solitary inquiry. Whenever you retrieve data, whether you find things on Google or discover a secret code, the starting places of all that knowledge are human hearts, human hands, and human minds trying collectively to cope with life.

As I wish you well and every success, I hope you will retain these thoughts: the teeter-totter that is knowledge; the need to balance understanding and information; and the contribution of living, of others, to our knowledge. However fancy our systems of transmitting, collecting, and manipulating knowledge may become, its roots are human. It's people – it's their hearts, their hands, and their minds – that together produce the knowledge the world needs for its betterment, and in the end whatever we do has to be caring and respectful of all people in all places.

I wish you well: enjoy, rejoice, and be grateful. Thank you.

16

Interview with Dr Tarah Brookfield

(Interview conducted at Wilfrid Laurier University in
Waterloo, 2010[1])

TB: I'm interested in your involvement in the early 1960s in rela-
tion to the studies about fallout, and your role with Voice of
Women (VOW).
UF: You see the crucial role of fallout in the development and coa-
lescence of VOW: a group of women who came together in response
to the editorial Lotta Dempsey wrote in *The Toronto Star* about
the difficulty of getting an atmospheric test ban and the likelihood
of even more fallout from testing that was being done in the fear
of another war. It was very clear at the time that this was not a private problem or a national problem. One of the things the atom
bomb made clear was that in the modern world there is no neutrality. You cannot opt out of fallout, even if you're in Sweden or Swit-
zerland. The implications that slowly emerged from that fact was
that fallout was a different form of pollution. Fallout meant that
materials with incredibly long half-lives were being incorporated
into food chains in the living world, and these were absolutely irreversible processes. No peace treaty, no change of government could
ever, for anyone, reverse that.

This awareness percolated through to ordinary people, and particularly to women, who saw how a growing human body would
grow from nourishment that contained radioactive material for no
reason except the boys wanted to play war games and test their
toys. The hypocrisy around the discussion of the Partial Test Ban
Treaty, which was again and again delayed or obscured, brought
Lotta Dempsey to the point where, after another failure, she said,
"Uh-uh. That's not something we can leave to others. This is a
common problem. It's not my problem. It's not your problem. It's

our problem. It's not my children. It's not your children. It's *every* child." If we cannot get together and say, "This has to stop," God help us, and why should She?

Out of this awareness came the understanding that to make the argument – not only philosophically and politically, but also personally and practically – one has to say what's going on in direct terms. Is that a drop in the ocean or a major problem? What do we know and what we do not know? I'm a physicist, and I'm also a Quaker, a pacifist, and a feminist. It was very clear that as a scientist, a mother, and a pacifist, I could be useful in this discussion in two ways. First, to explain to my sisters and the general public what is so special and important about fallout. Second, to say to the government, "You are supposed to stand on guard for us. What on Earth are you doing?"

Because of the general ignorance and inattentiveness to fallout, there was very little known and even less published on the uptake of radioisotopes in a growing human body. On the other hand, fallout had happened, and how would we ever know how much we had lived with? There were some people in the United States who began to think the only piece of evidence that existed were the milk teeth of young children who were born before the first atmospheric fallout, whose teeth were formed from milk, from nourishment that had not been contaminated. Those one had to compare to teeth or bone that would later be tested, and those one had to get. The baseline wasn't there. The people in the US had begun to ask dentists, but dentists, of course, don't usually get baby teeth, and when they do it's because there are complications. The dentists didn't get normal baby teeth, so it was through the mothers one could collect the teeth and at the same time collect information, such as where they lived and whether their children were breastfed or bottle-fed.

The process of gathering baby teeth from the mothers also spread the message of what was at stake, so it produced a baseline, and it was also very much an educational thing. It produced the material that went into the briefs to go to the government about the inadequacy of testing. It was an enormous community building and a political education. There was absolutely nothing like funding; this was totally self-generated. The women who got together did what they could – bake sales for this and that, dealing with practicalities of room rental. There was a decision to make the little buttons and the offering of that lovely cartoon of the kid who said, "I gave my tooth to science."

The process generated its own funds, its own educational material, its own scientific background, and its own critique of the monitoring systems – both provincial for food and federal for atmosphere. It educated the women, the teachers, the children, and then the government, the schools, and the review boards.

TB: Had you already been involved with the peace movement when you came to Canada?

UF: No, I came to Canada as a postdoctoral fellow, but I've been a Quaker. I became very interested in the responsibility of scientists and was active in the area of the social responsibility of science. I also became interested in peace research, which was the first project externally for which VOW raised funds. They raised funds for the Canadian Peace Research Institute. Our acquaintance with peace research was so helpful – not only personally but percolating through the organization. In debates one was able not only to say what one was against but also to be practical, functional, and organizational about the things that could be done.

When VOW formed it became almost like an extended family to me. I was so much in tune with what motivated other women, and so comfortable in working with women, which was a relief from being always the only woman in a totally male environment. Through the years I have considered VOW like an extended family for which I had some responsibility but which also gave me an enormous amount of support and friendship. It was a milieu in which I could build the position that I took as a scientist and as a pacifist without being totally isolated.

TB: How did you get involved with Murray Hunt?

UF: Well, you know how it goes, one conversation leads to another. We were both at the university and it was a fairly obvious linkage.

TB: What was your exact role with the teeth in terms of the testing and the sorting?

UF: I had no part in dealing with the teeth once they were handed over to Murray Hunt. We wanted to be absolutely clear that the handling of the teeth was not done by people who had any interest in the results; while we collected the teeth and agreed on the information to be provided, we very deliberately did not want to have, or to be seen as having had, any impact on the study. Murray Hunt then handed the material over to Chalk River. That distance was

not from a lack of caring but from a wish to create a baseline for
all future studies that was clear and impeccably beyond the notion
of any personal interference.

TB: When the results of the study were announced, you made a
comment that perhaps we should have gone back earlier in time to
the biggest year of testing.

UF: I don't recall that because, you know, these were the only stock
we had. It would have been wonderful if medical authorities or
governments had done that, but within the realm of responsibility
and authority it was the best we could do. In many ways, people
had generally been very cavalier about radiation.

All the work on the effect of X-rays was only coming out then:
the stuff Dr Alice Stewart and others did on fetal X-rays in England, where they cheerfully X-rayed pregnant women. She followed
through on what that did in terms of the health of the babies. All
this came up in the scientific literature only around that time. There
was a very cavalier attitude in the medical and scientific professions to radiation damage.

TB: Are you familiar with the activism of Rosalie Bertell?

UF: Very much so. We have been good friends over all these years.
I'm familiar with Rosalie's work on the effects of low-level radiation, both her original analysis of the Hiroshima data and the
work she did with uranium miners. Our work comes out of a similar wish to make it clear that in the modern world nobody has
the right to put a burden on the health of innocent people because
there is no opting out.

Rosalie started work on the long-term effects of fallout, just like
Ella Stewart who looked at the X-raying of pregnant women and
had the time and patience in the long haul to use records of the
British medical system to see what actually happened to those children compared to children whose mothers were not X-rayed. By
the same token, Rosalie was able to look at low-level radiation: not
the immediate "bang and run," but what happens with low-level
radiation. What happened in Samoa? What happens to fish and to
wildlife? What happens to plant mutation? These questions feed
into the work of Vandana Shiva and others who see how only by
attending to peace, to conditions for all, can individual conditions
be optimized.

TB: What would you say the public response was to women's activism in this era?

UF: I would separate public response into the male and female response. There was a real supportiveness among women, from active doing to quiet facilitating. The men were generally very annoyed. Their reactions were somewhere between hostility and annoyance, and they rarely gave support. It's not without good reason that much of the women's liberation leadership came out of the women's peace organization, as did the human rights and anti-discrimination leadership. At one point, I realized that every provincial Human Rights Commissioner had been a very active member of VOW before. Some of the most prominent human-rights officials, the people to whom the governments turned to enact and oversee some of the antidiscrimination clauses – particularly the Human Rights Complaints Commissioners – were VOW members.

Voice of Women had an incredible role as a training ground and seedbed, because there was genuine room and appreciation for all talents: those who could run a bake sale, who could keep the books in balance, who could read or write foreign press, who had the skill to draw cartoons, to lay out the fliers, to find somebody to print them cheaply. There was the need and opportunity for apprenticeship. Nobody was paid so people did things very efficiently and delegated as much as they could. There was on-the-spot learning that produced a variety of leadership skills that then went into the National Action Committee on the Status of Women (NAC), into the women's movement, into the legal profession, into the Women's Legal Education and Action Fund (LEAF), into work with women's pensions – the women lawyers who set up a feminist practice.

VOW was a feminist organization, and among its very earliest activities it supported strikes of women textile workers. It strongly supported the women's-led unions in the labour movement, the fair wages for women. Leadership and organizational support came from these things just as there was support for peace research.

These were elements, in a sense, in the general tapestry of a peaceful society. You couldn't have a peaceful society if some people were systematically underpaid and undervalued. You couldn't have a peaceful society when all the best minds were paid to think about war. Peace research was immensely important even if there wasn't a particular VOW outcome. The structural conditions that made it difficult or impossible to have a peaceful society contained a knowledge base.

The first visit of the Soviet women was around textbooks. How do we educate our children? Again, it's *all* children. It's not how *I* see the world, but how *we* see the world, and how the world sees us. The collective context brings us back to the teeth: there is a common base, not depending on status, on political opinion of parents, but on economic conditions, on regional conditions. As with many of the vow projects, the attention to textbooks was in many ways implicitly a teach-in: teaching us and those with whom we worked about the practicalities, as well as the collective state of mind that peace requires.

TB: There seems to be a transition from momentum very much centred around the fallout, to the Vietnam War, and then to NAC, and then to Status of Women, and they're all interconnected.

UF: A lot of other things went on simultaneously. There was interest in Aboriginal women, in women overseas, in Soviet women, in textbooks. It wasn't one project leading to the next; it was a network of projects, which all together, like a real fishing net, tried to capture the essentials of peace. All the nodes in that net were practical things, were the teaching of *doing*. Whether it's a strike, fallout, textbooks, cadet training, or war toys, they were the nodes in that net that tried to capture and advance the conditions of a peaceful world and leave outside the competitiveness, the "me first," and the notion of "an enemy."

TB: In reading about Muriel Duckworth's ideas about her faith and her pacifism, she is quoted as saying that her beliefs were really shaken in World War II with the idea that fascism needed to be stopped. I'm not sure if she would go so far as to say there is such thing as a "just war" in certain circumstances. Can you talk a little bit about that?

UF: Muriel was a very good friend. When you look at her writings you will see that quite early, in spite of the tradition from which she came, through the losses in her own family, she felt that while evil had to be confronted and overcome, the use of killing as an instrument was unacceptable. She was very clear that the need to confront evil when it occurs as forcefully as possible did not include the right to kill. The necessity is that evil be overcome by other means. As in the subtitle of Marion Douglas Kerans's book, she was "A Very Active Pacifist," and a wonderful person.

TB: You went together to protest against NATO.

UF: Oh, we did millions of things together. The most impressive
one for me was when we were together in Suffield. VOW had a very
strong objection, and I was one of the people who articulated it,
to chemical and biological warfare, and particularly to the secrecy
of the research. We eventually even argued that before the Defence
Research Board. They said, "We need defensive research. We have
to have means to protect people from other people's attacks." We
said, "Then that is public health. There is no one to be protected
in preference to anyone else. That is not a reason for doing secret
research."

TB: Something like 90 percent of their files were censored and not
available?

UF: Yes, but we didn't really want the results. We wanted to talk
about principles. For instance, if the necessity arises to develop
antidotes to supposed poisons, and that research is funded by public money, then the results have to become public knowledge. To
play around with designating deserving recipients is not the purpose of a publicly funded agency. We argued that, and then there
was a vigil and a visit to Suffield. As a consequence, Muriel and I
saw the chief of the Defence Research Board in Ottawa. We both
went. I made the scientific point, and Mariel took the general pacifist and VOW approach. He was a well-known chemist, and he was
there with his colleagues. I'm sure Muriel made the much greater
impression than I did. She was wonderful and absolutely steadfast in her position as a citizen. She did not question the need for
research into protection from anticipated dangers but was unwilling to grant priority of protection to the military. She was incredibly impressive.

TB: ... Were you involved at all with Hanna Newcombe's work?

UF: Yes, very much so. Hannah and I and Hannah's late husband,
Alan, knew each other from square one, from the start of the Peace
Research Institute when many of the VOW members wrote and
compiled abstracts and did that work with no external funding but
with the understanding that we are in this together and each would
free the other to do what she can do best.

TB: Many of the women had children. Did children come along to
the meetings, the marches, or were there childcare volunteers?

UF: Yes, you sort of said, "Can I dump the baby?" "You go to that
meeting and I'll do that." Kids often came, whether they wanted

to or not, but much of this was kitchen-table work. There was the odd demonstration, but behind those was probably twenty times more work done at the kitchen table between moments of quiet. I remember once talking to a group of women and saying how your life changes in these involvements. Your housekeeping standards change. You have boxes with clippings that you shove under the couch, and there was a sort of ripple going through the room. You knew many of those had stopped being fussy about ironing sheets.

Another notable aspect of VOW was that right from the beginning it had been a bilingual organization. People were encouraged to speak in the language in which they were comfortable. At meetings you would try to seat those who were not comfortable or experienced in one of your official languages with somebody could quickly translate what was said. We've always operated bilingually without ever having any money to do so. Such are the practices of what I consider a peaceful society; people's needs must be met, and all require respect.

TB: There's no point being hypocritical about how you organize yourselves.

UF: Or even specific about organizing. You organize at the moment, as the moment needs it. This is why we have such poor records: because there was nobody ever in charge of anything. Sure, we have records – I still think Kay Macpherson's book is one of the best records – but the "Records" in big capital letters that you lock up in a vault, for that you need an organization. It wasn't by choice but by necessity. A general secretary was the best we ever did.

You have to remember that this was before email. There was a very fine system of consultation based on the night rates of the phone and the time change. You start on the East Coast when it's six o'clock, and you get cheap rates when you phone people in Ontario. They consult locally, then when it's six o'clock there they phone Manitoba; then the West Coast can phone back in the morning and you had a tab of what happened nationally on the cheapest of phone rates, giving each an hour, going and then reporting.

TB: It takes a lot of energy and organization to make that work.

UF: It does, but it works. Of course, it also means a good deal of local autonomy. We didn't micromanage and copy everybody over everything. There was a good deal of variation both in the temperament of local groups and in their task, what they did and what they felt comfortable with.

TB: ... It seems the momentum starts falling a bit in 1975. People move on to different projects, or they're tired.

UF: It may not be that they are tired. Look when the Royal Commission started. There began to be a very different structural framework with the Royal Commission and then the NAC: a structure that was only possible because of the work that was done before. The Royal Commission was an enormous community-building effort. I don't think the notion of being tired is as good a description as the notion of being refocused.

There was a great deal of energy in the NAC and in all the moves to bring equality into the law, and that energy would not have been there had it not been the same energy. It may not have been the same people because they were fifteen years older, but the Royal Commission could not have happened had there not been that broad community of women of very diverse background, all feeling they were second-class citizens. They felt something needed to be done, and it was done: they got the Royal Commission. The Commission's recommendations, however, had to be translated into law. Equality had to be obligatory and not a matter of grace and favour that depended on the government of the day.

TB: Do you think it also had to do with a calmer international presence at the time?

UF: I really doubt it. It looks calm to us now, but the end of the Vietnam War in 1975 left a lot of open questions. You have a point about calmness in the sense that the Americans were exhausted after the Vietnam War. The next fear of confrontation was not as acute as it was fifteen years earlier, but it was because one confrontation had ended with so much anguish. It is that anguish of the situation that now looks like a calm, but it wasn't a calm as much as a searching and reconfiguring.

TB: ... What would you say the legacy of the 1960s–70s activism is for today?

UF: The legacy I see is the understanding of the collectivity. The notion that comes strongly into the political discourse during that time is the notion of privatization, and all the women's movement did was very much the other side of that coin. Things can be personal, and they are political. The women I worked with understood the link between the personal and political, but they rejected the private. They regarded the tearing of the social fabric very much as a collective problem and rejected the notion that everything can be privatized. Peace cannot be privatized. Justice cannot be privatized. The legacy, I think, is the awareness that there are ways to work for peace and justice that are neither competitive nor private. The great enemy we did not understand was lurking around, was the virus of privatization: the notion that something can be my business but not yours beyond individual issues.

It seems to me the two central points are the understanding of the collective as the opposite of the private, and the real danger of the virus of privatization getting into areas that are intrinsically collective and indivisible. It's not a matter of taste, or liking, or political policy: there is historical evidence that justice is indivisible. It's either for all or for nobody. Peace is indivisible.

The indivisibility of peace brings us back to the fallout. There's just no argument. It doesn't matter who's in charge of what. There was a time when people could have war in one place and not know anything about it in another. China could go on when there was a Thirty Years' War in Europe. But that's not where *we* are. It's a reality that has to be faced. One of the legacies we talked about is facing that reality on the ground level, in the here and now, in the nitty gritty, in the children's teeth. There is that indivisibility of peace, then is the need to find structures through which one can work – from the textbooks, to the war toys, to the alternatives to war production – to build a peaceful society.

TB: That's wonderful! Thank you so much.

NOTE

1   The work for which this interview was conducted was published in Tarah Brookfield's book *Cold War Comforts: Canadian Women, Child Safety, and Global Insecurity* (Waterloo: Wilfrid Laurier University Press 2012).

17

Peace: A Necessity for an Equal Society

(The closing speech of An Equal Society: Into the Year 2000 –
a conference presented by the Ontario Advisory Council on
Women's Issues with the Provincial, Federal, and Territorial
Status of Women Councils, Toronto, 4 November 1986)

There are advantages and disadvantages to being the last speaker of
a conference. The disadvantage is that most things that need to be
said have already been said; the advantage is that one has accumulated a list of comments that may not have come to mind had one
been speaking at the beginning of the conference. In that category
are two things I want to mention that relate to my main theme.

The first item is the problem of social structures. We work in social
and political structures that are very often not of our making. We
have to understand more about how these structures operate and
ask ourselves, "Do we want to be in these structures? Do they themselves so determine not only *what* is being done but *how* it is being
done, that the things that need doing cannot be done within them?"
The second item is the question of technology. Not only do we live
with other people and with institutions, but increasingly we live with
technology: technology that takes the place of people, replaces the
work of people, and makes human relationships and social structures profoundly different. I want to illustrate these two ideas as we
talk about peace.

I felt it was necessary to talk about peace as the absolute necessity to have an equal society. I also thought about how I would
define "equality" as we go from the Canadian background to the
larger background of a very much more unequal world. One definition of equality that is operationally helpful is to say that when we
talk about an equal society we mean a society in which all members
"matter" equally. The wellbeing of women and children, of black

people and people in small countries must matter as much as the wellbeing of the powerful and must enter with equal weight into the decision-making.

In an equal society, everybody matters. We may want to keep that in mind because the needs of people are different, their stations in life are different, and their perspectives are different. Long before we have equality in the true political and material sense, we can have equality of caring. The real bridge that makes inequality temporary is that assurance of caring and that assurance that people "matter." You may remember Fritz Schumacher, who wrote a book, *Small Is Beautiful: Economics as If People Mattered.* I used that phrase once and was corrected because I said "because people matter." Somebody pulled out the Schumacher copy and said Schumacher was much more cautious. I assume that people matter, and I approach my government, my university, my students, and my life not *as if* people matter but in the belief that the prime platform of all activity is that people matter and that we want a society in which people matter equally.

Such a society, of course, has two requirements. One is peace, and one is justice. There is no way in which those two can be divided. At home we have a sign that says, "If you want peace, work for justice." Peace is a commitment to the future. There is no future without peace. In more specific terms, peace is not so much the absence of war as it is the absence of fear. That joins us with our sisters and brothers who have to fear the very survival of their children, who have to fear hunger or unemployment, who fear their children will never get a fair share, who fear for their land – people who have reason to be afraid of the next day. Not everyone has the luxury to worry about nuclear war, but all of us know there is fear, and fear means being afraid of things one has no power to change. An equal society is a society in which people have control over their own lives. For that reason I consider that freedom from fear is the very definition of peace.

If we talk about equality and technology, we realize that in a peculiar way the greatest equality that exists across this Earth today is the equality of destruction. The technology of war has made the distinction between those who are combatant and those who are bystanders less and less discernible. Nuclear war involves the globe, and it does not matter anymore that 94 percent of the people who live on this Earth are neither citizens of the Soviet Union nor of the

United States. There is a horrible equality that means everybody is going to be a victim. There is no way to have a special status except if you are a member of the military who sits somewhere in a bunker. It is that knowledge of the equality of being victimized that is at the base of the peace movement. Anyone who is concerned about equality and about the future must realize that the most urgent agenda item is peace.

Working for peace does not mean everybody has to participate in a demonstration against cruise missile testing, although I wish they would, but it does mean we have to refuse the use of threats and the instilling of fear as means to achieve a peaceful future. We cannot be less fearful if others, as a result of our individual or corporate action, become more fearful. Just as in the workplace, some people cannot be secure while others are being threatened. We know it is counterproductive to be part of a scene in which workers, clients, or different parts of the population are played against each other. We know that every measure presented to us as assuring the future and assuring peace that entails making others fearful is a measure toward war, is a step toward destruction.

Every day as we work for equality, we have to keep in mind that one of the great barriers to achieving justice and equality is the inappropriate use of our resources: our national, fiscal, human, and technical resources. When my students cannot find jobs except in the military or in doing research on things that kill, although I know they can build devices to monitor pollution and do other good and constructive work, then I am afraid.

I would like to put to you a number of tasks that each one of us has to do if we have a commitment to the future. Some may not look as much like peace work as others. The first task is very easy for women: to consider the practice of equality. People should not be labelled but be judged as human beings. We know from the discrimination we see and experience in our own lives that being labelled a "woman" already presupposes the course of the interview, the job you get, the pay. Because we know what labelling entails, we must object to the practice whenever it occurs.

One of the most persistent labels is the label of "the enemy." I want to dwell for a moment on what "having an enemy" as a social institution does to a society. Not only can that society never be an equal society but "having an enemy" means the enemy has to be dealt with. One has to put in the money to deal with the enemy.

Whether one builds prisons or maintains an army, as a social institution one has to produce the enemy in its daily manifestation – to produce the crime, to produce the disloyalty – in order to justify the resources used to combat the enemy. Having "an enemy" also takes up a good deal of time and money and prevents many social changes because "We cannot do it now, we have to battle the enemy." Both the Soviet Union and the United States have been served very well by the enemy concept. It provided the glue that held together a society that otherwise would have had to reform itself quite drastically. Avoiding the label of "the enemy" does not mean there are not people with whom we fundamentally and strongly disagree, or countries between which there are conflicts, but none of these disagreements is permanent. On both social and religious grounds, one should refuse the premise that things cannot be changed, that people cannot be redeemed, or that any enemy is there permanently.

Every year Ruth Savard prepares a comparison of the military and social budgets of the world for publication by the United Nations. Her figures compare what is spent on schools, on health care, and on the military. The emerging picture is dismal. In Canada we are pointing up the same comparisons in yet another way. Our Quebec brothers and sisters have engaged in a disarmament campaign by asking the prime minister to spend the cost of one fully equipped F–18 fighter plane (about $62 million) on socially useful work such as daycare centres, health care, and the opportunity for young men and women to work constructively for and in their country.

To put this amount into perspective, the total amount of money the University of New Brunswick gets from both federal and provincial governments is $60 million. The great upset at the National Research Council about cutbacks in basic science research deals with something that is less than the price of one F–18 fighter. Is the future really served by such military expenditures or are there better ways to assure an equal society and a future for all? These are questions we should ask and must ask if we believe that preparations for war are incompatible with striving and working for an equal society.

I want to use the last few minutes to comment on structure and feminism. I am very frequently asked, "Is there something so special about women that we need equity and equality and everything will automatically be better? What about Margaret Thatcher and similar symbols of peace, equality, and kindness?" I usually reply that there are essentially two ways in which our society organizes itself. There are the hierarchical structures we have inherited from the church and the army in which there is always somebody on top of the ladder or pyramid-type structure. All these structures have certain things in common, regardless of whether they are the army, the church, the university, or other hierarchical institutions. For instance, they always equate rank with competence in spite of the obvious experience to the contrary. If you have two buttons on your shoulder or a larger rug on the floor you are considered to be more competent.

The much more insidious part of the hierarchical system is that people are ranked with respect to each other. Everybody is either above or below somebody and consequently that system has no place for equality, and with that, little place for friendship. It took me so long to understand why it is that there is so little friendship among men and so much friendship among women – but I will come back to that.

Then there is the system that is non-hierarchical. It is cooperative and comes out of places that are mostly in the women's realm – the family, the farm, the school – in which rank is really pretty pointless. When your kid screams at two o'clock in the morning it is fairly useless to put on a uniform and say, "Salute!" You try to find out what is the matter, and even in that great inequality between an adult and a small child there is communication on which the next step is based. When somebody has brought up twins, or coped with an alcoholic boss, you know she can cope. If you have a difficult job you turn to her and say, "Okay, she will manage. She has experience in coping."

Women value experience and consider it transferable. That transferability of experience on which women build much of their strength is often missing in a hierarchical system. It is also the equality in a cooperative situation that makes for friendship. Women know that what each contributes may be different, but that there are very few people who have nothing at all to contribute in a given situation.

In the hierarchical system – and the highest positions are often occupied by men – people look at everyone else as potential threats, as potential competitors for their place; however, women in a non-hierarchical situation tend to look at other women as sources of support unless proven otherwise. You only have to look at a typing pool or an office where women, who initially may have nothing in common, can work well together. They work on the basis of an equality that comes from knowing there is hardly anyone who does not have something to contribute. Skill and wisdom are needed to make each contribution count. We should be quite clear that it is the values and practices of the non-hierarchical structures that hold the key to equality and peace, and the experiences of working and adapting non-hierarchical structures are found among many women.

If you look at my two models you will see that there are women, such as Margaret Thatcher and others, who opt into the hierarchical system and find it possible to work in what is essentially a male mode. There are also men who find it more interesting and stimulating to work in the cooperative mode. Outside the cooperative mode there is no way of dealing with the impending destruction. If the world does not get away from the mode in which private or national gain is the main motivation and adopt the strategy of the women's world, which is mostly aimed to minimize the disaster, there is no way to the future.

I say to you, consider all that you do in the light of your commitment to the future. Consider that the achievements women must make have to be attained by means that assure others do not suffer from our success. Keep in mind that there is a component of caring in the notion of equality and that, as we move toward a practical, social, and economic equality and toward our own decision-making, we must make sure at all times that people matter, and that all people matter equally. As we so proceed, we have to refuse to condone activities, expenditures, and structures that are basically anti-people, that are destructive, and that misapply the very resources women and men bring to the future. Thank you.

18

Educating Engineers for the Modern World

(The Seventh Annual J.W. Hodgins Memorial Lecture,
McMaster University, Hamilton, 1990[1])

I would like to begin by saying how very honoured I feel to give this lecture, and how very much I hope that what I say will be acceptable in the spirit of the work Dean Hodgins did. Discussions on future directions in engineering – both engineering practice and engineering research – build historically on Dean Hodgins's work and on the approach that the best of engineers took in the 1970s and 1980s when they wrestled with how the young in this field ought to be trained.

We all know the world has changed, and that dimensions of the social and technical fabric of this world have emerged and possibly necessitated a very different approach both to the practice of engineering and to the training of engineers. Essentially, I would like to put before you a bit of a review of what engineering is, of what engineers do, and of the link to the hard sciences that Dr Hodgins found so essential to include in the education of engineers. I will then make some suggestions on how a change of approach might be accomplished, taking us from where we are toward where I think the profession and its contributions ought to be.

Engineering, of course, means a number of separate things: it means a body of knowledge, a group of practitioners, and a profession that is very closely and tightly governed. It's a self-governing profession with its own codes of ethics and standards that stands as an encompassed territory within the larger social fabric. The nature of engineering, and of engineering faculties, which are called faculties of Applied Science and Engineering, have been very much influenced by the growth of science, but in many ways engineering has preceded and interlaced its own work with that of science. Much of the drive for more knowledge has, in fact, *come out of the practice.*

I have never subscribed to the idea that science is there first and then there's application, then there's technology, then there's engineering. To me, science is not the mother of engineering or technology but, at best, a younger sister. It is only on doing that one can ask the next question of knowledge, and that dynamic of *both knowing and doing* is profoundly related both to the practice of engineering and to the relationship between science and engineering. Some people used to say "Scientists want to know; engineers want to do." It is the limits of knowing – and also the limits of knowledge that the doing exposes – that very often determines the relationship between applied science and engineering. I see this relationship as a spectrum rather than as a hierarchical structure where one is first and the other is derivative. In this day and age, I do not think one can separate science from engineering.

The permeation of mathematics into engineering was more than just measuring and comparing numbers as the engineers of the Renaissance did. There was a change in the structure of knowledge that mathematics brought to engineering. In both the practice and the education of engineers there has been an increased link to the sciences, and science separates knowledge from experience. That is what science is all about. The very nature of science is that it provides the methodology and shortens the technique. It is a coordinate system that separates knowledge from experience, and consequently, people today can go to university and learn the building of bridges from somebody who has never built a bridge.

The separation of knowledge and experience has led to an enormous rise in information, the spread of science, but it has a dark side because of the discounting of experience. The very process that separates knowledge from experience – a process that concentrates knowledge in books as well as in experts – has led to the fact that people find their own experience occasionally untrustworthy and very often not required. If you go into a hearing on environmental assessment for instance, the neighbours who say "It stinks around here, and I don't want to put up with it" are looked upon as if they are lesser beings than those who come and say, "The level of hydrogen sulphide is unacceptable within fifteen square kilometres of the plant." The common sense that comes from experience is very frequently put down as being not as valuable as the data that is

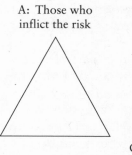

A: Those who
inflict the risk

B: Those who
regulate the risk

C: Those who
bear the risk

Figure 1

The triangle used here is from Jerome (Jerry) Ravetz, "Risks and Their Regulation," *The Merger of Knowledge and Power: Essays in Critical Science* (London: Mansell, 1990).

separated from the experience. We have arrived at a time when it is absolutely essential to rehabilitate experience because most of the things the world now has to deal with are problems in which knowledge cannot be separated from experience.

Let me give you a conceptual map of the social territory in which engineering functions. It is a very primitive map, but it will help me share some of my thoughts. We remember the early employers of engineers: the state needed engineers as surveyors; the army needed a corps of engineers. Engineers are normally employed. Their skills are used and rewarded by others. Even those we consider "self-employed" are those who choose their employers case by case. Very few engineers do engineering for themselves beyond building a doghouse or a boat. Most need employers, and those who train engineers are fully aware that the product of that education must be *people who are employable.* For many years, the activities of engineering practice and engineering schools were located very much along the A–B axis in figure 1: between those who utilized the skills of engineers and those who assembled and augmented those skills.

The increased sophistication of employers of technology, whether in the public or private sector, has led to the development of engineering as an academic discipline as well as to its links to the hard sciences that Dr Hodgins so emphasized. In modern times employers and engineers have developed increased dependence on each other, whether the employers were manufacturers, nation-states, or other public authorities. There is a historical benchmark in the history of

technology that marks the much tighter and more profound relationship between engineering and the employer, and that is the arrival
of electricity.

As electricity became a part of life, for the first time there was
a source of energy that could not be stored. You could not pile up
electricity for next winter the way coal or wood could be piled up.
One needed a distribution system before the new form of energy
could be used. The public sector provided the distribution networks
and required people who could design, build, maintain, and run
these systems and do so in cooperation with citizens who may have
had different priorities. There's a very fine book by Thomas Parke
Hughes called *Networks of Power*[2] describing that relationship and
how the planning of electricity became a political as well as a technical issue. If you look at the history of Ontario Hydro, you will
understand why.

As technology encompassed more and more of normal life, a lot
of things happened on the A–B axis between engineers as the pro-
viders of knowledge – as the doers of things – and those, either com-
mercially or publicly, who want to see certain things done in terms
of their own interests. What has been almost forgotten is the corner
of the triangle that becomes so important in modern society, that
third corner, which I will call "the recipients": those who are on the
receiving end of engineering endeavours and technologies whether
they want these changes or whether they don't.

I would suggest that what is required now is increased attention
to the recipient corner. The recipients (those who are at the receiving
end of technology) are becoming important factors in the social fabric
because technology is now so all-encompassing. There are more and
more recipients. They are the workers: those who drive automobiles
rather than manufacture or sell them; those who work with technology – the machine and telephone operators; those who are actively or
passively recipients of engineering endeavours. Of course one of the
recipients is nature. We need to look at that recipient corner.

From the receiving end, we can very clearly see a number of differentiations we can make about technology. We know that technical and technological innovations can be quite usefully divided
into work-related technologies and control-related technologies.
Work-related technologies are those fruits of engineering applications that make work easier for the worker: the mechanized shovel
that takes the place of somebody having to dig a hole; the typewriter

that relieves the person from writing things longhand. However, there is also something appropriately called control-related technologies: technologies that allow somebody other than the worker to have control over the process.

A good deal of technology, even if it looks like work-related technology, is in fact control-related technology. If you look back at the great debates about the introduction of machines into the workplace during the Industrial Revolution, you will see that many of the work-related inventions and innovations came from the master craftsmen themselves – from the doers. What produced the great upheaval and unsettledness was the control-related aspect. It was the factory owners who began to be in charge of the work and not the craftsmen who had been in that position previously.

It's very worthwhile to read a book by a woman historian, Maxine Berg, called *The Machinery Question*,[3] that examines the politics of the early-middle nineteenth century in England, including the parliamentary debate on the question of introducing mechanical looms. It brought forward the voice of the people who were the recipients and showed how in many cases the view from their end of the work looked very different from the view of the regulators.

One reason why there is such an assertion of the voices on the recipient side of this triangle is because of the increase in control-related technology. The skills engineers and inventors bring to the task make it possible today to do what already in the Industrial Revolution was a great dream: to have a factory without workers – just to dispose of those people who may have demands or get sick or not come. The Victorians always thought they would get drunk. Drunkenness, disorder, lack of skills, unpredictability, upishness would all vanish once you got people out of the way and put some dependable, if expensive, machines into their place. That debate in the public sphere was foremost in the British mind in the 1830s and 1840s, and it's well worth reading about.

But there is more to consider in that recipient corner. One factor that has not been considered with sufficient weight and severity, although it is often articulated, is that in that recipient corner sits nature. I am reluctant to speak about "the environment" because I find it such an egocentred, technocentred term that implies there is nothing much more to creation than giving the backdrop for us. It's *our* environment, not that we are in the environment of the bullfrogs. I think the too-frequent use of the term "environment" makes us forget that human beings are not the only occupants of this planet, and everything is not there to be adjusted the way one adjusts an infrastructure or a taxation system. I prefer to separate issues based in the environment – one can call it the "manmade environment" in the very intentional sense of the word because it was mostly men who made that environment – and issues that are based in nature.

Nature is a force, a participant. Nature is not our backdrop on the stage of which we may say, "Oh well, it's getting a bit dirty; we'd better have another backdrop." If one thinks workers have rebelled, one now has to see that in the most profound sense of the word, nature rebels. There's unrest in that recipient corner, and part of that unrest is nature feeling the impact of technology, feeling the impact of those practices in which engineers had a large part.

When we talk, as Fritz Schumacher did, about "appropriate technology," then we speak about activities along the A–C axis. Then we say, "Are there practices of engineering that are appropriate for the recipients rather than for the employers? Are there cars designed for the drivers rather than for the assembly line? Is there a way to devise work, or roads, or traffic with the end users in mind?" I think the most profound question is, "Are there ways of doing engineering in which nature need not to be objecting, in which nature need not deteriorate under the impact of these activities?" We need to look at this diagram with some care even if it is vastly oversimplified.

The employer domain, both private and public, overlaps quite significantly with the domain of engineering practice and education. Engineers consider economics as part of their concern, and in the training and the practice there is a realization of that overlap. But engineering also interacts significantly, and in a much less recognized way, with the recipient community – either directly, or through the intervention of the employer, or through the intervention of the state through regulation. There is a clear area of interaction between the recipient and what I call here the employer: those who do or finance the doing of things that impact technically and technologically the constituency of the recipients. My major concern is the area in which the three domains overlap. I think what now needs to happen is to integrate both engineering practice and engineering training into the real world of multifaceted demands.

At the moment engineering education and even more so engineering practice in North America are poorly prepared for dealing with the profession's impact on social issues. What do I mean by that? Let me first remind you that engineering as a profession has developed its own standards and norms just as medicine and law have done. When you look at time and motion studies, you see engineering as a normative profession that declares, "There is a right way of doing it, and we worked it out." It was worked out around the capabilities and limitations of machines: the machine was the norm. When one talks about man-machine interface, the intention has usually been to adjust the human being to the machine. People are "helped" to adjust, and studies in earlier as well as later engineering show that very clearly.

As long as a machine is the norm, it is exceedingly difficult for engineers trained in the traditional way to identify with the recipient sector, to feel themselves impacted. When I teach the social impact of technology, I do not find it difficult to make it clear to engineers that technology has a social impact; however, it is almost impossible for me to make it clear to them that *they* are being impacted. Just as it is easy to teach people management in the sense of their imagining themselves being managers, it is exceedingly difficult to teach somebody what it means to be managed – to be part of a large choreographed organization – and it's something people have to know when they make career choices. Do you work in a small outfit? Do you work in a large outfit? What does one undertake when one works in a tightly managed structure? By the same token, it is at present easy for engineers to understand that others are impacted by their work. It is exceedingly difficult, at least for me, to help them place themselves in the shoes of others: to let them understand what it is to be impacted and to understand that they are severely impacted by forces outside their own making.

To make that link between engineering and those who are at the receiving end of engineering activities is very difficult, so I welcome, for instance, a proposal before this university to create a course on engineering and society. But what we need is a lot more, and it relates in a way to the social climate. The social climate of engineering is still the climate of a separate profession there to be hired with very little understanding of what the work or behaviour of engineers does to others. That realization brings us to the question of where engineers stand with respect to the whole of society, and especially with respect to women.

Women in engineering are not, of course, only those who study or practise. The world of engineering is full of women at the university and otherwise: they are secretaries, they are technicians, they are librarians working in that engineering corner. One of the barometers of the degree to which engineers and engineering education can move into that sphere of the participants, of the recipients, is the way in which women are treated in the social environment of engineering.

I take a very dim view of sexist behaviour in undergraduate engineering, articles in journals that put down women and "art-scis" as people who are different. I find it objectionable not only as something that offends others, but also as something that is tolerated although it is known to offend others. The Toronto engineers had a vote just a year ago to decide whether they would continue the student newspaper *The Toike* after there had been massive protests against its sexism and racism. The students voted 80 percent to continue *The Toike*. Now it seems to me totally inappropriate that those who offend vote on whether they wish to continue to offend.

To me, it is an indication of where engineering education stands at a time in which it's very clear that what matters is what happens when engineers interact with their larger community, what happens in the environment, and what happens to people. In my opinion, one cannot continue to educate those who will operate much of the machinery of a technological society and not see to it that it is being done with a sense of profound respect for others: be the others women, be the others non-machines, be it nature, be it people in other parts of the world.

I find it very sad that while normative professions other than engineering have career options for those who wish to look at the recipient area in their particular professional world, that is not yet the case in engineering. If you are at law school, you can specialize in advocacy and poverty law. You can say, "Yes, I put my professional skills into the needs of this area rather than into the needs of that, and I am recognized as a professional. My practice may not be as lucrative as if I had specialized in corporate law, but I am a respected lawyer if I deal with human rights, with poverty law, with advocacy." If you are in medicine, which is as normative as engineering, as a professional you can legitimately specialize in public health; you can specialize in health and safety as it relates to pollution, to allergy, to the work place. In the medical sense you can become a voice for the recipient community.

No one in engineering at any university can legitimately specialize to become a voice for either nature or people in that recipient
community. When engineers and physicists work for Energy Probe,
they are the opposition; they are not respected professionals. When
Ralph Nader or others hire engineers to examine safety and cars,
they are consumer advocates. When Greenpeace needs to deal with
chemical engineers, they are barely considered people in the profession. I think there has to be an option for engineers – both in their
education and in the use of their specialized skills – to deal with the
area of the impact of engineering on recipients.

It is in the area that deals primarily with people rather than
machine design, with making things happen within the recipient sector, that the future of engineering is located. The norm must become
the living world. If engineering doesn't wish to leave to medicine,
law, and architecture the dealing with this sector and become essentially irrelevant, then it has to take cognisance of the fact that the
norm on this planet is the living world, not the world of machines.
In addition to people, there is nature, and if the knowledge and the
doing of engineers cannot address the very profound problems that
people and nature experience in a technological society that engineers have helped to build, then that society, if it can rectify itself, will
rectify itself without engineers. I think it's a profound crisis in the
profession to see where as a profession engineering goes: becoming
more and more hired hands or recognizing that a new dimension is
opening in which the skills that engineers have, and can augment,
will be vitally needed.

I think that is what is before us. The barometer of change I will
follow will be to what extent women, and those who may have a
worldview different from engineers, are being welcomed into engineering: not in order to be made over to become one of the tribe, but
to be recognized as partners and possibly as teachers to bring a different perspective into engineering. Thank you.

NOTES

1   This lecture was given in honour of Dean Hodgins in the year when
    McMaster University was offering, for the first time, an option for engin-
    eering students to study Engineering and Society. President Lee introduced

Ursula Franklin as the first woman speaking in the series, and Mrs Hodgins was in the audience.

2   Thomas Parke Hughes, *Networks of Power: Electrification in Western Society, 1880–1930* (Baltimore: John Hopkins University Press 1993).

3   The full title of Maxine Berg's book is *The Machinery Question and the Making of Political Economy, 1815–1848.*

19

Monocultures of the Soil, Monocultures of the Mind: Cautionary Tales from the Mechanization of Agriculture

(Keynote address, 8th Wendy Michener Symposium for The Canadian Association of Fine Arts Deans, York University, Toronto, 21 October 1994)

Thank you, friends. I'm always amazed at these introductions and wonder two things: "Is that really me?" and "Am I alive, or is that an obituary type of thing that one only says for people who are dead or nearly dying?" I am alive, I assure you. Whether I live up to the billing will be up to you.

I want to emphasize a point made in the introduction. My base discipline is physics. I'm basically a crystallographer, and one of the things that has always interested me, and that is in a sense the red thread through most of the things I'm doing, is the notion of *the concept of structure.* Whether it's atoms, or groups, or social groups, the whole is shaped not only by what is there in terms of the parts but also by how the parts themselves are interconnected. How do the parts relate? How does the structure between the parts and the whole make a difference in the properties, in the functioning, in the usefulness? These questions are as relevant to social structures as to physical ones. I've always been interested in how a change in structure changes properties – makes certain things possible, makes other things unlikely – whether these are chemical reactions or the interplay of people. What holds together the interests that I have, and have had, is that red thread of structure.

I would urge you to take what I say critically. I don't ask you to believe what I say, but for this morning we are together I ask you to take in what I say like a visitor into your own home. Ask about

what sort of thought that is, and what sort of usefulness there might
be to ask that visitor back into your own landscape. The title of
the symposium is Art, Technology, and Responsibility, and I leave
the art entirely to you. I want to talk about what is more my area;
I want to talk about technology. I hope to leave you considering
how what I say about technology might influence your view of your
responsibility with respect to your students, your profession, and
your institution.

First, I would like to define technology and look at what technology is all about. Then, as more or less the centre of our considerations, I want to show why I think a great deal of care is needed in
the use, assessment, and value we place on technology – why this is
not something we can uncritically apply or reject. Finally, I would
like to say a few things about what I think can be done to enhance
our critical and informed views on technology, and where we might
look for the unexpected, the "unprogrammed."

Technology is neither new nor is it an unknown. For that reason
I say, "Handle with care." I will define technology, as I always have
done, as *practice*: the way we do things around here. That definition
includes devices, it implies systems, but it also very strongly implies
that there may be other ways of doing things. In that sense, technology defines both the content and the practitioner, and I'd like to stay
with that definition of technology in its entirety as practice. It's new
practice. It's ways of doing things, neither inevitable, nor necessarily
good or bad, but incredibly powerful. I want to stress not only what
technologies do but also what technologies prevent.

One of the really interesting things for me is how people predict what technologies might bring. Because you are deans of fine
art, and I know this is a visual society and people like to see things
on the screen, I've brought two overheads. Both are copies from a
rather nice and fairly unknown book. Keeping in tune with the sort
of millennial feeling that comes at us now, one can look at what
was said at the turn of the last century. There's a lovely book called
Futuredays: A Nineteenth-Century Vision of the Year 2000[1] that was
reissued about ten years ago with an introduction by Isaac Asimov.
It is, in fact, a set of postcards that were commissioned by a French
publisher in 1898 to publish in 1900 suggesting what life would be
like in the year 2000. These are commercial illustrations of French
artist Jean Marc Côté at the turn of the century, and the illustrations are extremely preoccupied with the use of technology. What

The Rural Postman

A Very Busy Farmer

would the insights of science bring to the betterment of human life? I want to show you just two of those postcards that were published in 1900.

One is a lovely image of postal delivery. You will see a nice postie, a man arriving on a contraption that looks like a hovercraft or something similar, bringing the morning mail to an eager citizen on a balcony, and I like it. I think it's really nice. You see the rustic setting, and you think, "Well there is flight. We can fly, and why don't we fly to each other and bring each other the morning mail?" The second one I'll show you imagines the farmer in the year 2000. The caption says with an obvious touch of irony, "A Very Busy Farmer." There sits a portly French farmer on a nice stool on his porch, shifting gears on a machine with several levers – harvesting, bundling, and storing. This is very much "Agriculture with the Help of Electricity." The farmer is surrounded by a rustic setting and is sitting there the way French farmers, I'm sure, dreamt they would sit benefitting from technology.

Now we know what has happened to the mail, and I don't think any of us dreams of a nice postman in a mini-helicopter coming to our balcony in the morning to deliver the mail. We know what happened to agriculture, and we know the farmer doesn't sit in the corner of his field shifting gears with no blood, sweat, and tears and getting his farm in fine shape with the help of electricity.

I show these to demonstrate how difficult it is to understand that *when one thing changes all things change.* The way we do one thing affects inevitably, and very often decisively, many other things. The fact the mail can be delivered by airplane doesn't mean the mail is delivered to a person by airplane but that you get a total disruption of the mail system. The fact that it becomes easy to harvest an acreage doesn't mean the farmer has leisure but that somebody says, "Then I can plant ten times as much," and you get not into ten farms but into agribusiness.

It's important to realize that, while a great many of the changes technology is advertised to do do in fact happen, they also open the door for much more significant structural changes that often affect the development of a society in a completely opposite way. The immense enthusiasm we find at the turn of the twentieth century for the application of science – for thinking that it is equated with betterment, that it is equated with progress – is illustrated in these postcards in a very nice, direct, and unpretentious way. But one has to ask both what does that technology do and what does that technology *prevent?*

Because we have so very much experience with the application of technology in terms of mechanization in agriculture, I want to look a little bit at what happened in agriculture in order to give you a feeling of what might happen in culture. I would like to suggest that it is not just a facile analogy to look at what happens in the soil and what happens in the mind. It's basically an ecofeminist approach that denies, both collectively and individually, the split between body and mind. There is a link between the soil in which we as a human community live and the mind with which we collectively view our lives and organize our affairs. One cannot be holistic in one's mind and mechanistic in one's agriculture. That's a sort of schizophrenia that modern societies try to have and very often find almost impossible to live with.

The Blakes and the artists of this world try to find a language that can explain the impossibility of separating forever either mind and body or collectively nature and collective intellect. Take this idea with as much criticism as you can muster, but take it seriously for the hour we are together. I want to leave with two thoughts: that technology changes the total context, and that the way in which we do things very often shapes the task.

Five or six years ago, my friends at *Ideas* wrote and presented a lovely paper to the Learned Societies called "War, Peace, and the Evening News." It was an analysis of CBC National News over a period of years during which the time allotted for each item shrunk from something like five minutes to one minute. The content analysis revealed that there are certain problems, questions, and news items that cannot be dealt with satisfactorily in one minute. In the course of one minute one can usually only deal with conflict. Who did it? Who shot whom? What happened? War in its broadest definition of the word is much favoured over peace. The black and white, the football analogy of conflict, the good guys/bad guys depiction, all benefit from the short clip. The things that say "however," "notwithstanding," "in the background yet there is" are impossible to present if you don't have a bit of time and an audience with an attention span. That paper reveals that what looks like a fairly trivial decision – to change the length of time given to a news item – is in fact an extremely powerful filter to the content of what can be transmitted.

The tools we use can shape the task, and can shape the task in a way that is not always very transparent. For that reason one has to ask again and again not only what does the technology do but also what does the technology prevent? How is the continuation of a particular way of doing something going to affect the issue, and what is the reason why one has done that in the first place?

Those questions bring me to agriculture. At the very beginning, the mechanization and intensification of agriculture had the rightful and noble object to see that people wouldn't go hungry: that there would be more food for more people at affordable prices. It was a task intended to meet real needs. Now we know very well that whether it is agriculture or the mechanization of clothing and weaving, once needs are met in the local community there arises the necessity to create needs, to create wants that in fact were not there or were not part of hunger. We know from the analogy of food how much malnutrition can exist in the presence of an abundance of food.

One thing the increase in agriculture brought was a dependence on both transportation and distribution. The mechanization in agriculture was successful to such an extent largely because it gave rise to a network for distribution and a network for transport, and there's an analogy in the field of communication. The fact that food would be transported and distributed introduced variables into the relationship between producer and consumer that had nothing to do with either one of them. There are questions of shelf life, questions of preserving things, questions regarding what can be shipped. We have a pear tree in the back of our garden. It's a very old pear tree of a lovely sweet variety that nobody grows because the fruit bruises. Lots of stuff that isn't robust enough to allow shipping is not grown. The increase in the production of food required and brought about at the same time as a co-requisite an increase in both transportation and distribution. Of course you know the next step – the step of treating the soil, of fertilizers, of pesticides, of "efficiency" that leads us to monocultures. Once somebody is able to produce one product in a large acreage, the soil is conditioned to be good for that product: the atmosphere, the food, the medication of soil, crop, and animals are conditioned for that monoculture.

In the case of agriculture we know where monocultures led: they led to an enormous dependence on fertilizer, a depletion of the soil, and the realization that pesticides are not just beneficial and that soil erodes. The enormous management of soil for drainage gives rise to equally enormous floods, as seen in the Midwest. The soil is not able to absorb water any more because it's full of culverts. The water has been *managed*, and you get these colossal floods and disasters that already a decade ago led to the notion that one had to question the carrying capacity of the Earth, the atmosphere, and the soil. One had to question what is in the food we eat and the air we breathe, and why it is there.

The notion of sustainability that has come through the mechanization of industry in general, but agriculture in particular, is very much in people's minds. There's a sense of extreme vulnerability. One knows that crops in monoculture are very vulnerable to disease, to particular insects. One also begins to see what the introduction of these cash crops has done particularly to rural communities, whether in Canada or the Third World. I suggest you take very seriously work that comes out of the Third World, such as the work by Vandana Shiva, who gave the Bertrand Russell Peace Lectures at McMaster last year: her work on staying alive, on the violence of the green revolution. Those things are important not only for those in the Third World but also for us.

I want to draw some analogies and say what it is we need to look at when we think in terms of *culture* rather than *agriculture*. What is it that one sees not in the body of our society as much as in its mind? I would suggest you think of that soil erosion, of the break up of community, of the lack of cohesion, and of what is happening to our social fabric.

We know all about pollution. We know of the pollution of the body, but we also know about pollution of the mind starting from the lack of silence, the pollution of noise, of unwanted random information. I would suggest that the junk food on the shelf is very well paralleled by junk food for the mind. We educate children now about junk food and about nutritional snacks, but there is not yet a parallel of making people aware of the junk food for the mind, which is as important a topic as junk food for the body. The malnutrition one finds among the affluent in the physical sense has very much a parallel in the malnutrition of the mind.

You may well look at fertilizers again and think, "There's a soil that cannot live anymore without fertilizer." Particularly when you fill out the next grant application say, "Are the grants the fertilizers for that monocultural crop? Would our crop grow without fertilizers or are we in the position of the farmers that our soil, our resourcefulness, our imagination, is so depleted that it needs the fertilization of support and grants before anything will grow?"

Think for a moment of what happens on a store shelf when people begin to be picky about their apples – not for what they taste like but for what they look like – and think again when you get applications and things you're asked to evaluate. To what extent are we affected by the outward form? I find myself being faced with lovely, desktop-printed stuff. I read it and think, "That's nice," and then I say, "That's very attractively done, but actually it says absolutely nothing." That is a bit like the strawberries we get that look so nice and taste of nothing. We need to examine – and if necessary articulate – our views on perfection. What is it that we want? A perfect content, a good taste, something that's nice and possibly juicy, or do we really just want something to put on the table that looks nice at a reception?

I think we should look particularly strongly at the vulnerability of monocultures, and recognize that it is neither efficient nor appropriate to concentrate on one crop only. The vulnerability of the monocultures in the field, the fact they are so totally unprotected from sudden invasions of insects, should give us a lot of cause to think about violence. Why is our society so susceptible to violence? Why is it that we have every reason to be apprehensive about moves toward fascism, toward hate, toward violence? I think to a large extent it has a something to do with our moving toward a monoculture of the mind.

What is the defence? In agriculture, of course, it is diversity; it is having other things grow. Any good gardener knows there is such a thing as companion planting: some crops, even if they are not all as yielding as a monoculture might be, protect each other. There are plants that may not yield a great deal but they attract the bees that pollinate the trees. The great defence against vulnerability toward one pest, toward one insect, is diversity. Some crops remain immune when others are attacked. In a field that has a healthy diversity the vulnerability is vastly reduced not because others are not vulnerable, but because they are vulnerable to other things. The uniform vulnerability a monoculture has is best – and possibly solely – combated and healed by diversity. I think we have to ask ourselves, "What about diversity? How can we see that we don't fall into that monoculture trap that was begun with noble intentions, with the wish to feed, with the wish to eliminate hunger and poverty?"

That brings me to the third part of our theme: responsibility. Having become aware of the links among art, technology, and responsibility, what is it we might do in terms of responsibility? First, I think that awareness of what happened in agriculture, of what technology can do in terms of changing context, *has to be cultivated*. It has to come foremost into our conscience, into our critical mind.

All technologies have to be handled with care and a good deal of thoughtfulness.

The second thing one must do is to be as clear as one can about structural relationships. When you look at the producers and consumers of food, for example, what happened in the mechanization of agriculture was the creation of a new caste of people who distribute, and the distributors then began to have an incredibly large steering affect on the producers and the consumers. It is no more the consumers who say, "I like that sort of tomatoes" to the farmer, it's Loblaws. It is the distributors who begin to be the real power that determine both what is grown and what is available on the shelf.

That's the situation I would suggest you find yourself in when you discuss the information superhighway. Watch the power of the distributors. The farmers aren't any better off than they were at the turn of the century, and the consumers may or may not be dramatically better off. Those who are better off are the distributors: the shareholders in Loblaws, the trucking firms, and the refrigeration plants. That whole layer of structure is where the efficiency produced an enormous return and structural change, though not necessarily for the clerks at Loblaws.

I would suggest to you: "Watch it. That can happen to the products of the mind." That can happen to the food for thought, and it isn't inevitable just as it hasn't been inevitable with food. In agriculture you see the beginning of countercurrents. You see the beginning of initiatives and reactions of the consumers. You see the popularity of farmers' markets – attempts to link producer and consumer directly. You may feel there is already a similar trend in the cultural sphere. I find it almost ironic and amazing that among all the rhetoric we hear about the joys of the information superhighway and the 500-channel universe, what do people do? They go to readings: they pay money to sit in a stuffy hall on hard chairs to hear one person read from a book. Look at the incredible popularity of readings over the last five years. That's well worth thinking about because it's not inevitable that one goes into mass distribution. There's a lot to be said for farmers' markets.

After being aware, after seeing the structural relationships and the antidotes, my third point would be – and this is particularly for those of you who teach – resist monoculture. Create seedbeds for varieties that at this point in time may not look as if they are desired by the majority of consumers. There are varieties of food, and varieties of food for thought, in forms that may not be mass-producible or desirable by large numbers. It may be incumbent upon you to produce the seedbeds and the little local markets for those things that cannot be obtained by the Loblaws of the intellect, and that, I think, is very much on your doorstep.

It is also a good idea to not fall for euphemisms. Label and name things for what they are. You deal with intellectual property. Farmers deal with expropriation. One may want to forgo the nice and lovely words when one talks, for instance, about what I consider a very real problem: the privatization of knowledge. I'm still of a generation that believes knowledge is a common good. Now we live in a time, including in my own faculty, in which knowledge is considered in very many ways a private property in terms of procurement: somebody gives you a grant, and you do what they say you should do and grow that crop for their personal use.

It's important to be clear in one's thought and teaching whether one thinks in terms of expropriation rather than private or intellectual property. It may be good to remember C.B. Macpherson's definition of the distinction between private and public property. He said that private property is *the right to exclude people from the use and benefit of something.* Public property in fact is *the right of everybody not to be excluded from the use and benefit of something.* In the arts you may ask yourself, are you dealing with a piece of intellectual work from which somebody can be excluded the use and benefit of? The question of intellectual property is very important not only as a factual device but also as a social force.

Finally, when we talk about naming, we have to talk about language. How do we talk about culture? I was very impressed by a paper by Richard Madsen, who was one of the team who some years ago wrote the book *The Habits of the Heart.*[2] Madsen published a paper in *Social Research* called "Global Monoculture, Multiculture, and Polyculture," in which he pointed out that at present cultural discourse is carried on in three languages simultaneously, and "culture" is used here in the broadest sense of the word, of social discourse. The main language in which cultural discourse is carried on is the language of the market. Does it pay? If not, why not? Who pays? The second language is the language of behavioural science, of institutional structures motivating people, arranging people to do what they may or may not want to do. There's only in a rather mute voice the third language, which is the language of tradition: the language of going back to reasons and values for which particular things were done or not done.

There is nothing holy about those three languages. In fact, I would suggest it is really important for people in the arts to shun the dominant language of social discourse, which is the language of the market, and name it and say, "Yes, this is how it looks if you address this problem in the language of the market." Maybe there are also other languages we should talk about and in which we should speak. There's the language of joy, pleasure, satisfaction, human relations. There is, heaven help us, at the university also the language of scholarship. One can say does that contribute to scholarship, does that contribute to knowledge, just as we may say does that contribute to joy, to enjoyment, to the betterment of the community. There's the language of justice. There's the language of peace. Don't confine yourself in your discourse to the current languages of markets, social sciences, and behavioural sciences. Define your own language and use it. Use it deliberately, and give notice that you use it. The discourse need not be carried on solely in the language of the current dominant politics.

While still discussing language, and this is my last point relating back to technology, let's be very clear whether we talk about people or whether we talk about devices. I have a sort of private feud going on with language that blurs the distinction between people and devices. When people say, "I didn't have any input into that report," I say, "Why on Earth don't you say 'Nobody asked me'?" There are human terms, and there are machine terms. I get mad when somebody says, "I need to interface more with my students." Why don't you say, "I must find the time to talk to my students?" It's perfectly possible to use a human language when one talks about human beings. I get equally mad when I see human language used when one talks about devices. My computer doesn't have a virus. My computer has a malfunctioning disc. It may happen that my chairman catches a virus, but my computer has a malfunctioning disc. Whatever the jargon of the trade, I really don't believe my computer has a memory. It has a storage device. I have nightmares and memories. My computer just stores stuff and sometimes messes it up.

I think my concern with clear language is more than just a personal idiosyncrasy. If we want to be a humane and human society we have to see that our language as well as our action focuses on what we have in common, and what we have in common are human values not an internet. We may use that communication system but not think that it is what binds us together.

For whatever it's worth. I would suggest you think of the information superhighway essentially as an extension of the Star Wars system: as a social device to support advanced technology. "At one point there was an evil empire against which a great shield had to be built so all of us could live happily ever after and the communication and space technologies would equally live happily ever after." I would suggest you look very critically at the information highway, whether it is not as inappropriate as the Star Wars system was. The existence of that great basin of human ignorance that is waiting to be entertained and educated is as elusive as the evil empire, and what one might be sucked into is essentially a high-tech make-work system that is not for the benefit of either the producer or the consumer, and I leave you with that. Thank you.

NOTES

1   *Futuredays: A Nineteenth-Century Vision of the Year 2000*, text by Issac Asimov, illustrations by Jean Marc Côté (London: Virgin Books 1986).
2   The full title of Richard Madsen's book is *The Habits of the Heart: Individualism and Commitment in American Life*.

20

The How and Why of Communication: Orienteering in Cyberspace

(The Southam Lecture, given to The Canadian
Communication Association, McMaster University,
Hamilton, 1996)

My talk today is entitled "The How and Why of Communication: Orienteering in Cyberspace." If you were to look up "orienteering," the dictionary would tell you it is a sport that combines cross-country running with navigation by map and compass. Now if it is your mind rather than your legs that do the cross-country running, in this day and age you may still very badly need navigation by map and compass to know what's front and back, and possibly even why it is that you are running. It's those questions of the how and why of communication that I would like to address.

As somebody who has an interest in the social impact of technology, as well as a physicist trained to look at things in a structural sense, I have had always a great deal of pleasure in looking at structures and in understanding the role of the part in the whole. In considering that how and why of communication, I would like to go back to what I think are the basic cultural and historical tasks of communication. I'd like to go with you through what technology, from the very beginning, has done to the task of communication – how it has structured it – because it is that terrain in which you and I are running. Finally, I'd like to consider with you how new maps, roads, and obstacles have arisen because of the interventions of technology.

I'm often asked to define technology, and I define technology as *practice*: the way we do things. That definition of technology includes all the devices, the systems of control, the management, and the planning, but it also includes the social acceptance that "That's the way things are done around here." The way things are done changes; it has changed and will continue to change. So technology is practice, and what is being practised in this case is communication.

Communication in its non-mediated form is essentially concerned with, and will always be concerned with, the sending and receiving of messages. That's what you do when you communicate. In the most simple case we can define, there's a sender and a receiver. There can, of course, be large numbers of senders and receivers. There is a messenger, a receiver, and a message, and a message has both content and sound.

We may want to distinguish three basic cases of communication. There is the case of the individual sender addressing the individual receiver, the ever-lasting one-to-one communication. Whether someone says, "I love you," or someone says, "You still owe me five bucks," the message takes that form of communication. There is also the case in which one sender addresses a large number of receivers, such as a sermon from a pulpit or a royal proclamation. Finally, there is the much rarer case, in which a large number of senders sends the same message to one receiver, such as the scriptural case that happened at the time of the crucifixion, when the people were asked, "Whom should I set free?" and they said, "Barrabus." These three cases are not mediated; they are direct, unmediated communication.

When technology intervenes, it changes the human relationship in terms of time and space, time and distance, and duration and space. The great and enormous first technology that came into communication was writing. Writing separated the message from the sound, and consequently it separated the message from the messenger. It meant the message could outlast the sound of those who proclaimed it. You could speak of the Laws of Moses long after Moses was dead, and you could write them down and carry them to other places. Because one did not see or hear the sender anymore, there emerged a question of the authority of the message. Was that Moses speaking? The authority of the message depended very heavily on the authority of the sender; the more authority the sender had, the more authority the message had. Here we come to the point at which we have a sort of three-star sender, such as the king or the pope, who sends three-star messages to a large number of receivers. That's where the law, the Holy Writ, gets its historical roots and its historical manifestation.

It is worth reflecting for a moment on what it has done to civilization that in some civilizations the law could be written down and carried along both in space and in time, while other civilizations chose not to separate the message from the messenger. On one side you have what history calls "the People of the Book": those of Jewish or Islamic roots who write it down and in which subsequent generations spend a great deal of time interpreting the Holy Writ. On the other hand, you have many Aboriginal cultures that never felt it was right to separate the knowledge from those who transferred the knowledge, in which elders have taught future elders to interpret the knowledge of the tribe. I would suggest there are very profound lessons to be dug out on the origins and practice of fundamentalism as it relates to that first technology of writing. Does one interpret the law in the current or the past context? Is the book or the elder the authority?

The next enormously important technological invention was printing. Printing essentially enlarged the circle of receivers and the community of senders, and as a consequence a number of interesting things happened to what we call "the authentication." In the case of writing the burden is on the sender to give authority to the message through sign and seal. Printing put an additional complexity into the community of senders. The sender function split into that of the author and the publisher. Those who printed were not necessarily subservient to those who wrote. Independent publishers began to make a living by the activity of publishing. You remember Stillman Drake's insightful discussion of the influence of the printers in the early Renaissance. When they began to republish Euclid's *Geometry* the great classics of knowledge suddenly became available to people who did not go to the university.

At the stage when the sender split into publisher and author, the question of the truthfulness and veracity of the message became more urgent and the authentication of the message became much more a part of communication. Then came the need to quote, to give footnotes, to name sources in order to say very clearly from whom and how the authors knew what they were stating.

The need to authenticate a message got another twist during the Scientific Revolution because now science put in another dimension. Science began to produce new sources of evidence. There was the experiment, through which something could be demonstrated as true through a form of proof not available before. There were facts – something established that could be observed by others – and those became important because now one had the task of ranking the information. Through the increased discourse of activity and printing, reading and dissemination, many more facts entered the public sphere, and it was the people in law who had to say, "Look, we need to rank that information in terms of its credibility, in terms of its veracity."

It's not by chance that the modern development of evidence and law are both parallel with the development of science. Three categories arose that are distinct in the court of law and treated differently by anyone who deals with communication. There's evidence – the sort of thing on which people in court take an oath and say "We have seen it." There is hearsay: "We heard about it, but we haven't seen it." Then there's a category of gossip that is in a sense partial and purposely collected information that begins to be transferred for a purpose.

At that point in the evolution of communication technologies information began to be ranked both by the source – where did it come from? – and by the method of transmission – how did you learn it? There's a difference from the direct experimental having seen it, to having heard it, to having collected it possibly for a particular purpose. It is that double thread of where it comes from and how you learned it that gets us then into the realm of books, broadsheets, and newspapers in all of which *content* as well *intent* is important. The sender has at his or her disposal a variety of sources from which to choose something that goes to a large number of receivers.

Now because we have books, newspapers, and broadsheets, the public realm begins to come into the process of communication both as a receiver and a source of information. The orienteering, the looking at who does what where, begins to be influenced by the fact that the public realm is both a source and a receiver of information. At this stage, the sender no longer knows whether her message is received, whether anybody reads the book, or what he gets out of that. That is a new and different situation socially because communication, both in terms of receiving and of sending, begins to be a public affair and not just something for the select few. As the books and broadsheets reach the public realm, one begins to see messages sent out waiting and looking for receivers; we begin to see senders with only hypothetical or no receivers. Arthur Koestler called his autobiography *Arrow in the Blue*. That time is at the middle of the Scientific Revolution, the beginning of the Industrial Revolution. The time of the great civil wars in England is the beginning of the time of messages looking for receivers.

Now we have to take a jump and look at the advent of modern technologies. The use of electricity brought electric and electronic technologies that fundamentally changed the relationship between senders and receivers by changing the way in which the message was transferred. There are three profound effects we have to think about as we think of the impact of electric and electronic technologies. While telephone and telegraph could still be explained somewhat on the printing and distribution model, now we get into a profoundly new thing that is equivalent to the impact of writing, and that is that electronic recording allows for the first time the separation of a sound from its source. Prior to that, if you were annoyed by the sound of somebody playing the bagpipes across from you, for example, you could wait it out. You can't play the bagpipes beyond a certain length of time. On the other hand, if that person has a tape of someone playing the bagpipes, you've lost. You can have twenty-four hours of bagpipes.

One cannot overemphasize the fundamental importance in terms of communication to the separation of sound and source. Such separation not only allows you to transcend time and space in the same manner as writing had done but also allows you to preserve sound. You can record and replay the words of people who are not with us anymore. You can play them in Puna. It has also allowed the changing and mixing of sound. You may not recognize somebody's voice anymore. Because of the laborious development of writing, the question of the authenticity of the written word never came to the crunch that has come with the use of electronic media. Remember the Watergate tapes. Remember the hesitance of courts of law to accept electronic evidence, wiretapping.

The possibility of falsifying the message *through the conduit of the means of transmission* is much greater on electronic tape than it was on clay tablets. That is the absolute crux of the new problems and the new opportunities. Add to that the speed of transmission of electricity and of fibre-optics: add the lack of reliability of electricity, and the possibility of combining text and image. All this leads us to where we are now.

The internet provides a situation in which a very large pool of senders and a very large pool of receivers flow into each other to such an extent that messages and information have to be extracted by a variety of processes that are not really transparent. Think back to the beginning of communication, to a time when, if you heard a message, you knew what was said and who said it, to that simple writing it down with sign and seal over the printing, to the authentication, the quote, the differentiations one learned to make between evidence and speculation. Think of the skill that the community of those who communicated, printed, wrote, and dealt with text developed in text and in critical tools to check and verify.

Now we go into the pool of information on the internet and we say, "Where on Earth is that from? Who on Earth is sending the message? Is it original? Is it complete?" You all know the incredible problems of copyright. Who can print what? Who can quote? Many of these questions become quite meaningless because at the moment the pool is such that anybody can fish in it as well as drop their own dead fish into it. Out of the multitude of senders and receivers, one isn't really clear anymore what is an authentic message and what is what one would call a reprint. You can say now, "Here I am in the sport of orienteering, running around like a mad rabbit, and where is my compass if I want information? If I want to check whether something is correct, how do I navigate?"

There are a few things I would like to suggest. It may turn out that we have reached the end of the process I laid out as being the task of communication: to send and receive a message. Information may now have become so much of an environment that the area in which we run is full of thick underbrush and we may have to have other maps. At the moment the maps we have look pretty inadequate. When we look at our email, for example, we find there the old map of the mail system into which we add duplicate copies to various people. We get the round-robin note out of the mail system, in which somebody adds something to the letter of somebody else. We get the newsgroups, which in fact break open that mail system and work as if one could read everybody's mail. We get discussion groups in which the sender need not be identified so there is a lack of real clarity.

We may never return to the notion that communication is essentially the sending of messages from a sender to a receiver. Still there remains the need for somebody to say to somebody else in the privacy of their lives or in a sealed letter, "I love you" or "You owe me five bucks." The world hasn't changed so that need doesn't exist anymore.

Some things have very profoundly changed, however, and one of the things that has changed, or increased immensely, is the sending of messages in search of receivers. In addition to purposeful communication, even those as books hoping for a receiver, other kinds of messages seem to appear not only on the internet but in printed media and the radio. I characterize these by the notion of "landfill": stuff that clutters the mind without any possibility of being of consequence to people. When I listen to the radio there is maybe a weekly, daily, hourly report on business, and the radio station says, "Be the first to know!" I say, "Why?" I have never found why I ought to know the price of gold fixing for July in the London Stock Market or the decrease in the Nikkei Index or on the Toronto Stock Exchange before I go to lunch. If that is a message, what do I do as a receiver? Do I feed my family meatloaf all week because Nikkei Index dropped an astounding 0.1 percent? What do I do with that stuff, with those fifteen pages of stock quotes in the paper? That's landfill, landfill for the mind, and it's a very difficult thing to deal with when, in fact, you want to communicate, when you expect some messages that have meaning for you and all you get is landfill.

I want to suggest that such "landfill" might have two particular cultural purposes. One is to acculturate people, to say, "Guys, you may not understand this at all, but it is vitally important." Every hour on the hour you'll get something on the stock market, something on the Nikkei Index. This is acculturation in the same sense in which the morning prayer at school was acculturation. It wasn't that one expected each child to commune with God. It was meant to say, "Look that's important. That's what we pray to around here." You need to look at the quotes on the stock exchange as a reassertion of a particular branch of our culture.

Another point I would like to make regarding electronic landfill is that one has to look not only at what a particular technology *does* but also at what a particular technology *prevents*. Historically there has always been censorship. There has always been the attempt by certain powers to prevent a message from reaching a receiver. This has been done by eliminating the messenger, discrediting the message, or discrediting the receiver. I would like to suggest that there is also the *censorship of stuffing*: not of jamming the frequency but of putting in so many inconsequential and irrelevant messages that the receivers can't cope. As a result, messages that have been sent, or might be sent, are not reaching the receiver purely because of overload, swamping, and stuffing. One of the profound tasks those who are interested in communication have to deal with at the moment is not only to *authenticate* information but also to develop the critical faculties that allow receivers to *discern* what is relevant information and what is landfill.

Before closing I would like to say something about the development of websites. In developing a website, somebody institutionally or personally takes the role of author, editor, or publisher, by identifying themselves and saying, "Yes, that's us. If you doubt the information you doubt us." The completely unattached message flow is intercepted by messages that now come through sources that want to be identified. Websites may very well be the electronic equivalent of the broadsheets we saw in the 1600s and 1700s. There remains that enormous need of *discerning*: of developing of the critical tools to assess what is relevant in that whole vegetation through which we try to find our way in cyberspace. To continue the soil analogy, what can grow and what should go on the trash heap? That's not an easy task. It's a task at which we all need to work, and it's a task that relates very much to power and control.

In conclusion, I would like to suggest that one of the ways in which we can develop discernment is to go back to the absolute square one of communication – a sender and a receiver – and increase it into a circle by thinking of reciprocity: by preparing for the receiver to talk back to the sender, and consequently providing an opportunity for the sender to modify the message because of the response from the receiver. As you work to discern the difference between information that is "intentional landfill," that stuffs up the place so other messages don't get through, and information that has the potential for creating new movements, fresh ideas, some human change, I would suggest that you ask yourselves these questions. Can the receiver – in any way shape or form – utilize that information? Is it possible to develop a reciprocity so the sender can be influenced by the response of the receiver? Is this message participating in the problem of censorship through overload? It is with those questions that I'd like to open the discussion. I'm interested in your comments, and I in no way think you have to believe what I say as long as it stimulated you to some thought. Thank you.

21

Technology as Social Instruction

(Conference keynote address, Saint Mary's University,
Halifax, 23 March 1998)

Thank you very much for coming. What I hope to do tonight is to help increase our discernment, our critical assessment, of what is going on around us – be it from a political, personal, or ecological perspective – and I want to do that by talking about technology. I have always been interested in technology because I think it is important what people *do*. Be it historically or contemporarily, I have always found it much more interesting to find out what people *do* rather than what they *say*, and most things people *do* are done together. While every one of us does things alone, we function in a social setting. It has been so historically. What people have done together and how they have done it is worth a good deal of attention because that describes past and present: the communities we have built, and the communities we wish to build.

I define technology as practice: *the way we do things around here*. This definition incorporates not only machines and devices, the new and the old, but also social organization, division of labour, management or mismanagement. Technology also means the use of knowledge, both ancient and modern, and that is what I mean by technology as "social instruction." Future times will judge us not only by *what* this society has done but also by *how* it has been done.

From a historical perspective, the tasks of civilization have changed very little. Societies have always needed to find ways to nourish, to raise food, to find shelter, to build shelter, to provide livelihood for their members, ways to deal with health and sickness, with the transmission of knowledge and tradition, with means of getting from here to there, and ways of communicating within and outside. What has changed immensely is *how* these things were done – how the food was grown, how the shelter was built, how the livelihood was obtained, how the health was measured and furthered, how tradition and knowledge was transferred, and how one communicated. That *how* – the technology, the way we go around collectively doing things – in and of itself immensely restructures a society, even in our time. It's worth remembering how the single shift from the technologies of the railway to the technologies of vehicle transport changed the structure of our society.

Every tool shapes the task. We know that from the simple and trivial tools in the kitchen. When you suddenly get a wonderful device that slices and dices, your menus change. You begin to slice and dice and serve things you never served before. Anyone who has ever worked in a department that got an electron microscope after a long struggle knows that the problems of the universe suddenly begin to translate themselves into things that require very large magnification. The way in which a tool shapes the task should never quite leave our consciousness.

When we look historically at changes in technology and in the incorporation of new knowledge, we find that attempts to change things have often been the result of the wish to manipulate the dimensions of time and of distance in space. Most technologies attempt to make the conquering of distance easier – be it in communication, be it in transportation – and as a consequence have profoundly affected the dimensions of time.

A colleague and I recently had an interesting conversation on the impact of one of the very early technologies: writing. What writing did – the fact that one could separate the message from the messenger – was a tremendous opening up of both the availability of distance and the possibility of conquering time. When Moses wrote down the Ten Commandments, it meant they could be carried to places where Moses was not and could be read at times long after the death of Moses. One needs to reflect quite profoundly on what it means when a society chooses to separate knowledge from the knower. In an oral tradition, such as in our Aboriginal cultures, those who know are the keepers of knowledge, but what happens when a society lets knowledge become independent from knower and interpreter?

That separation should lead us, I think, to some reflection on the relationship between fundamentalism and orthodoxy and writing. The People of the Book, whether they are Christians, Jews, or

Muslims, can be pretty intolerant and pretty fundamentalist and go back to the book and say, "There it is," compared to those who entrust the most important knowledge of their culture to individuals who then pass it on in a way in which it remains relevant to the situation of their time. We may want to remember how long certain parts of knowledge – even in literate societies – were not committed to paper, how long women hesitated to put on paper their experience and to divorce that knowledge from themselves. Technology disconnects knowledge from its social context.

I want to consider the ways modern technologies restructure what we do. Electrical and electronic technologies are tools that very much transcend and modify both time and physical distance. I'd like to talk in terms of their application on a narrow spectrum around specific questions: How do we communicate? How do we work? How do we teach?

Before doing that I need to mention briefly the benchmark of the Industrial Revolution because between the mid-eighteenth and mid-nineteenth centuries, something really important happened in Western society. Through the introduction of machinery, the process of work and the division of labour changed in a very fundamental way. It was a time when one began to divide the process of working on something – the classical example is the assembly of a watch – from one person doing everything and maybe specializing in watches for particular classes or occasions, to the process William Petty described in which one person made all the springs and one did all the dials, one did all the cases, and then the parts were assembled. The productivity – the number of watches being made – went up considerably. Of course the skill went down. You only needed to know how to make the spring or the dial, not everything. The whole notion – that there is production that is organized, managed, and planned, in which tasks are divided into fragments related to the process of later assembly – that production notion is a product of the Industrial Revolution.

It was a very great success in terms of its economic impact, so much so that the principle of production became increasingly applied to areas for which it initially was most certainly not intended: administration, governance, and many other activities began to be organized around that technology of production. The production mentality is frequently not appropriate to the task, particularly to the task of education; nevertheless, we basically work in a production mentality that permeates all activities. Whatever doesn't produce is not counted: it's not of value, not worth noticing.

In the current social instruction, the end product of production is *money*. This society is intent on instructing its citizens that what matters is the production of money. I don't have to elaborate on the structures set up solely to let money produce more money. We now see a whole investment economy on the globe that is feeding back into governance through agreements such as NAFTA. This investment economy hangs over the world as a sort of clasp for the production mentality that structures the world into a production site of money. The production mentality sees all social relations as relations of production. It sees people as consumers and producers and talks of "input" rather than seeing that the end of producing is only one of many social activities, and that other activities – such as caring, non-economic, non-monetary, ecological, cultural activities – have a place, though nothing tangible is produced. It is in the climate of that production mentality that we need to look at the way in which we do things.

In terms of electronic technologies, I particularly want to talk about communication: how we talk or do not talk to each other, how we know and transfer knowledge. Here the manipulation of space and time is incredibly important because what the electronic technologies allow for the first time is to break a historic pattern of what the German psychiatrist Carl Jung named "synchronicity" – the fact that people do things in a certain rhythm.

I don't have to remind you our society is bound on a certain rhythm from the past of a religious rhythm: from the bells that divided the day, to the three meals a day that we tell our children are the basis of a sane and healthy life, to a division of time and a rhythm of work during the week day. There's an enormous amount of synchronicity in our lives, and it is out of this that many of us derive a sense of meaning and community. Even if we do not work side by side with people, we know of those who gather for worship at a certain time. We are aware of those who put their children to bed at a certain hour. There's work, there's play, there's synchronicity.

Electronic technologies cut and fragment synchronicity and introduce an asynchronicity that is very profound. We can, for example, be part of a communal experience without being there. We watch a ballgame on television, and my colleagues talk about it as if they had been there together. They say, "Did you see that guy kicking the other guy?" as if they had been there, and nobody had been there. You have the feeling of being present without being present. You can be present at a political debate in another jurisdiction, and you can all be there without leaving your houses. You can tape a game and look at it at your convenience, and then you can talk to people about it and they may not be home, so you put the message on their answering machine. You have a lively exchange of political views without anybody ever talking to anybody; you can have a dialogue without ever looking anybody in the eye or connecting in person.

You can also work on a common project without ever knowing your co-workers. Many people may never see or know the people with whom they work. That asynchronicity, that fragmentation of communication, that sort of phantom idea of community, has very profound social effects because it rules out those processes that people can only engage in when they are, in fact, together. As one of the prototype examples of this genre of impact, I have an example I call "the fax machine in the band office."

Imagine you are friendly with a group of Aboriginal people who pride themselves on the fact that all their really important decisions are made collectively. They work by consensus, they get together, they hash things through and come to a considered and accepted decision. In between they go off to their business and somebody looks after the band office. You put a fax machine into the band office and the great "I-Ams," whether they are in Ottawa or else-where, begin to send faxes. *We want your approval of the agenda.* They look at it and say, "Okay," or "Too much," and it goes back. Another fax comes: *We want your comment on this agenda item.* Likely it is a somewhat junior and less weighty person who sends the faxes back and forth, and three weeks later when the elders actually meet, there is a stack of reports or faxes which *de facto* have made all the decisions. The real consensus-based decisions – Do we do it? Do we not do it? Why? Why not? What would we do if we didn't do it? – all those things for which real thought, wisdom, and con-sensus are needed are eliminated through the exchange of a dozen seemingly irrelevant fax messages. The whole process is distorted if not destroyed by the presence of what looks like an extremely help-ful device to bridge the isolation of a community out of normal com-munication reach.

That's one of the structuring effects that comes out of the asyn-chronous nature of electronic communications. You can chop up things to your liking and by doing so eliminate the macro picture by making everything into a micro issue. While the micro issue – do you approve of the agenda? – may be neither here nor there, a decision on it hides or eliminates the decision and the discussion of the macro issue. Those are what I would call "unintended social instructions." I'm sure the people who approved of putting the fax machine into the band office did not want to eliminate consensus in searching for wisdom among the elders. They wanted to make it easier. In our collective searching, we have to be mindful that technologies can have unintended implications that can change basic social functions, and those functions are pretty important.

I would like to elaborate on those likely unintended but very serious implications that occur when one uses asynchronistic technologies in teaching. I see as the purpose of education the growth in knowledge and understanding. Whether at grade school or at university, the process of instruction includes much more than the transfer of information. An enormous amount of social learning goes on in a classroom – learning that is not explicitly called for in a math class or a French class. It is what I call implicit learning: what one learns while learning.

A great deal is learned while learning, such as the realization of the difficulties or ease of others who learn at the same time, but at different paces. There is a need to learn tolerance, discipline. There's a need to learn context. There's learning from questions asked, from joint exploration. There's a need to manage anger and frustration, either when you don't get it when everybody else does or visa versa – when nobody seems to get it, and you – snap! – can multiply by twenty-seven in five seconds flat. There's a need for tolerance, ingenuity, anger management, understanding, and knowing how to recognize the needs of others. All this is learned implicitly while certain subjects are explicitly pursued.

Now when one finds a way of pursuing these other subjects by putting single students in front of single computers, or one doesn't teach at all but has spellchecks or calculators, then one has to say, what is happening to that implicit, "by the way" learning? Can we afford not to teach tolerance? If we don't teach it when we teach arithmetic or geography, do we have to teach it somewhere else in some other way?

To help this concept of implicit learning stay in your mind, I want to give you an example of something that struck me when I first came to this country. I was not acquainted with the institution of the ski lift. I came as a postdoctoral fellow, and in the winter I saw several colleagues with rather grievous sports injuries. I saw healthy young men hobbling around on crutches as a result of skiing injuries. I was not a great skier but a reasonably competent skier. I had always lived in a world in which you learned enough about falling and ice and skiing by getting up the slope that you really couldn't injure yourself a great deal on going down. Once you got up, you knew enough to go down. It took me a while to understand what the ski lift was doing. By removing the simple need to get up the hill, the ski lift was also removing the learning that took place *while climbing the hill*: learning how to assess the snow, how to fall.

I recalled this lesson about implicit learning when I began to think of what a spellcheck or a calculator was doing. Now it's not an argument against ski lifts or spellchecks, but it is an argument for analysis. It is an argument for clarity, to say do we know what we are doing? Do we know what actually happens in a classroom or in a seminar setting? Do we know what we do when we separate synchronous classroom learning into asynchronous activities of acquiring the knowledge and writing it down and take out that component of being together – of the interaction? If I have anything to say to you, it is to please *really think* about what is going on in your community, in your classroom. What is actually happening as we use the answering machine, the fax machine?

Some of you may say, "Isn't that what women have always been wanting, to be able to do more than one thing at a time or to be able to do something at a time when it is right for her and not for anyone else? It is wonderful to have an answering machine. It is wonderful to be able to go on the internet at 11:00 at night." But it isn't everything. I remind those who think of the easing of women's lives that very often women engaged in asynchronous activities in order to remain in the rhythm of their family, of their work, of their children. They didn't do it because it was quick or easy or sexy; they did it because the asynchronicity was the only way to preserve their own authenticity. It was the overriding, more important rhythm that allowed them to cope as well as they did with the asynchronicity. The overriding rhythm for us is citizenship: it's our community. If ways of teaching, learning, and working preclude the building, maintaining, and enriching of the larger collectivity then I think they are destructive. If, on the other hand, they add to that collectivity then we can work around those areas that the new ways of doing leave either unattended or poorly served.

Finally, I think all these problems pale over the profound problem that these technologies interpreted as social instructions reveal. Presently, "modern technology" gives no instruction but production, and that leaves us the problem of work, of meaningful work. If as a society we wish to utilize the new technologies that allow the conquering of distance and time, then it is my private opinion that it is not possible to do so if one solely pursues the production of money. If, on the other hand, one pursues the presence of community, and an ecology of activity in which material production is one but not the only social activity, then we have to find public funding for those novel technologies. I'm a great supporter of the bit tax, which taxes electronic transactions. From such revenues, novel developments could be supported, while guaranteeing an annual income to citizens whether they are involved in material production or not.

That's what I look forward to: when we truly interpret technology as social instruction, but we say *we* give the instruction and for us what matters is community and our country.

22

Research, Policy, and Action: Working for Justice through Integrated Research

(Research in Women's Health Conference, Ottawa;
Dr Franklin's keynote recorded at Massey College,
University of Toronto, 1999)

Good morning, friends. I consider it a real privilege to be slated for the beginning of this conference, and I'm particularly happy that the focus of the conference is women's health in the broadest possible sense of the word, meaning not only physical or economic health but also the social, political, and spiritual health and wellbeing of women, both individually and collectively. While the conference will focus on equity and gender issues, the suggested designs and measures that come forward must be applicable to all forms of injustice, to all manifestations of inequality.

Health for me is both an individual and a collective parameter. I would define health as the ability to function harmoniously and creatively without either experiencing or inflicting pain. Of course we all know ill health, both the experiencing and the inflicting of pain, is part of life, but it should be an exception not a norm. It should be the very thing we work on so ill health happens as little and as temporarily as possible.

The advancement for all of both individual and collective health is a very important issue, and to me it is basically an issue of justice. You will be looking at the pathways one can take in order to improve health for all – health for women and health for the community – and for you those pathways will basically be research and policy. I want to talk first about policy and then about the meaning, the usefulness, and the traps around the notion of research, having spent a good deal of my life doing research as well as trying to influence policy.

Policy consists of the rules and practices, the regulations, activities, and interactions that govern how people live and work with each other. Many policies do not work well for women, but, in fact, they don't work well for anybody else either. There used to be a slogan my friend Maggie Benston liked that said, "What isn't appropriate for women isn't appropriate, period."

We have to remember that in many ways the social and political changes that have been possible for women have changed and benefitted the whole community. We are not talking as much about changes *for* women as changes *through* women. Just remember in your own lives how frequently the changes we have fought for to allow advances for women have in fact changed the atmosphere for everybody. I'm surely not the only one who remembers that change of scenery. I've been in meetings, for instance, in which, at around 4:45 the only woman would quietly get up, gather her papers, and mutter, "I'm sorry but I have to go. I have to pick up my boy at daycare." Five years later you sit at a meeting with a bright and bushy-tailed young man who, at 4:45 rustles and makes a great production and says, "Sorry, I need to pick up my son at daycare. It's my turn at parenting." Sometimes I think, "My boy, I wish you knew and could feel what it took to allow you to shine and get a merit point for parenting." So while changes in policy may look as if they are *for* women, they are usually changes *through* women and toward justice for the betterment of all.

Some of these changes may be permanent, but others have to be renegotiated again and again because often we address the manifestations and not necessarily the justice issues. I will give you one example before I talk about research. I was on the first committee at the University of Toronto charged with the equalization of women's salaries, attempting to see that women staff members would get paid the same for the same work. It was a difficult task. The methodology had to be developed. It was done, and the results were just incredible. The gap was much larger than women had expected. At that time it could be equalized because the university was able to set aside money so it didn't come through departmental budgets. When it was equalized we thought that had changed. Uh uh. Don't kid yourself. Five years later, we looked at new hires. The women were hired at the bottom of the obligatory scale; the men were hired at the top. Many of these policy changes, as they addressed manifestations, had to be renegotiated. Never think you've done something until you have dealt with the issue of justice. Very often one can only deal with manifestations, and that is often only the repainting of an existing structure.

Having a policy is not good enough. One has to monitor the genuine compliance, not only with the letter but also with the spirit, and the spirit – and I can't say this often enough – is *the advancement of justice*. In the end, you cannot have improvement for some at the expense of the improvement of others. If there is betterment, that betterment is indivisible. The betterment of those who need it most will be felt as the betterment of those who need it least.

The monitoring of policy very often involves the gathering of facts, the compiling of evidence, and, with that, what we call research. Research, in this society, is frequently something that has the status of Holy Writ. It is written in black gothic letters, and something appears more credible when it is labelled research. I am sure you all are sufficiently sophisticated to know that nonsense plotted on graph paper remains nonsense. It doesn't get any more valid by being put in bar graphs or in technicolour, but the temptation to believe it exists, and it exists because research has often given us very good insights. I've been a member of the National Research Council and of the Science Council of Canada. I've done research all my life. There's nothing wrong with good research, but there's an awful lot wrong with bad research: slipshod proof of prejudices that are riding on the good name of research. One has to develop a very good critical ability of assessing what indeed is research, and what is good research.

If you ask me what is research, I would define research as the systematic and transparent pursuit of answers to a question. It is a human and social activity as much as it is a scientific, scholarly, professional activity. I would add that it's important to understand that the really important decision in research is the asking of the question. It is the human, social, and political setting that poses the question, and this is why women have so often suffered from pseudo-research.

Remember all the measurements of brain size, of IQ. Now why would that be done? What's the question? The question is not whether people have different sized brains. People have different sized heads. So what? The question is *the attempt to rank*. Are the big brains better than the small brains? Are there more male, white, upper-class brains that are big? Are there more female, lower-class heads that are small? It is the ranking that propels the research because otherwise it would be a "So what?" issue. Sure, some people are more apt to answer questions quickly. When you do IQ tests some people will be quicker than others, more thorough, more responsive, just as some kids learn faster than others. It's the ranking and the attempt to correlate that makes all these measurements useful, or in fact needed. Who needs brain size? You need hat size. You don't need brain size, except if one wants to use these rankings.

The really important question in research is, what motivates? What is the beginning of the research? Whose question are we dealing with? Who asks the question? Why is that question important to them? The next question is something that used to drive my graduate students around the bend. When they came with research proposals, I would ask them, "What will you know when you know it? When you have found whatever it is you're spending a year or two to find out, how will that advance the question and the consideration?" As you talk about research, keep in mind that the thing that matters most is the question. One can ask different questions, and women have asked different questions. I hope you will see that video from the National Film Board, in which I had a hand. It's called *Asking Different Questions: Women and Science* (1996). Asking different questions matters.[1]

I would ask you to keep in mind a few things that relate to both research and policy. Number 1: keep the question clear. Be clear what is being asked, why it's being asked, what will be known when it's finished, and who will have that knowledge. Think with equal clarity of the context. What is the setting of your research? Make sure you consult and involve the subjects. I will never forget a lesson that my then very young daughter taught me. We went to the market together one Saturday morning early, which we enjoy. The market began to get a bit more crowded, and she suddenly tugged at me and said, "I want to go home; there are too many legs where I am." We have to listen to those who say, "There are too many legs where I am," or there may be too many potholes where they are. So keep the context clear. Ask the subjects.

Please also keep clear the link among research, action, and policy. Is the research and the action going to advance betterment or delay it? I am sure I'm not the only one who has been frustrated by delays in policy and official action because more research is needed. Don't overlook the role that research and its sponsoring can take as a shock absorber and dirt reflector. I'm sure Elizabeth May will have a bagful of stories on this.

In addition, give good care to the process of research. Judge *how* you do it, not only *what* is being done. Be exceeding critical on *how* it's being done. Good research by women for women, good feminist research, is horizontal; it's interactive and it's not hierarchal. Consider also the need for retrospective research. The world has always been full of good intentions expressed in policy. We give little time to looking at what indeed then happened to all those good intentions. Did we solve the problems and are now really dealing with phantom problems, as I think math education for girls is, or do we have perpetuated problems that have to be dealt with again and again as in the case of the salary differential?

Finally, if you suggest new structures, make sure these structures are appropriate for women. Don't forget your feminism. Don't forget that feminism is not an employment agency for women but a structure for social, human interaction that is different from patriarchy. Feminism is another way of living together, for women, men, and children. I personally have no use for patriarchy, even when there are lady patriarchs, and I hope that applies to you, too. I thank you all.

NOTE

1 At this point Dr Franklin refers to the historical example of Dr Alice Hamilton's work with typhoid, an example explained in more detail in this book in the speech "Research as a Social Enterprise: Are We Asking the Right Questions?"

23

What Is at Stake?: Universities in Context

(Canadian Association of University Teachers,
Ottawa, 1999)

I have worked in and around universities long enough to appreciate their context and complexities. I know too that they are important parts of every society, and that we are here because we are deeply concerned about the changes we witness in Canada's social fabric and in the university's place within it.

There are things that are easier to do and say when one is old and no longer has job or reputation to lose, and this certainly holds true for those associated with universities. Throughout the years, the vision of tenure has been a contribution to self-censorship as well as to academic freedom. I want, therefore, to use the gift of my independence, and my persistent love for and belief in the importance of the work of universities, to consider with you the social function of universities and colleges. I want to indicate how these institutions have grown, evolved, and mutated within our social ecology and put to you some thoughts on how to respond to the commercial threats to higher education in Canada.

Allow me first to share a turn of phrase I learned from my husband. Sometimes he characterizes reports or pronouncements as "awfulizing," indicating the piling of one horror story upon the next with no analysis or resolution in sight. I do not want to awfulize. I want to address the question, "What is at stake?" because I believe Canadian universities and colleges must continue to operate in the public interest and that this operation cannot be taken for granted.

Let me start from the premise that to remain silent on crucial issues is to make a conscious decision. It is therefore pointless to remain silent in order to avoid accountability. We will be held responsible for our silence, as well as for our activities, just as the university teachers of the Germany of my childhood were held responsible –

morally and fraternally – for their silence and collaboration with an evil system. We need to think clearly and to speak out together with insights coming from the collective knowledge, experience, and conviction of our community.

Historically, the social function of the university has remained basically the same: it is the place or institution where the ruling apparatus of the time transfers to the next generation the attitudes, skills, and knowledge needed to cope with the future. Changes in social relations, beliefs, or power structures have always impacted universities because questions of what is most needed to cope with the future had to be constantly revisited. Was it still Latin, law, science, or management knowledge that was needed? Who needed and deserved this vital coping knowledge? The sons of the rich? Their daughters? The children of workers? Of Aboriginal peoples? Of new immigrants? Every change in society has resonated through university communities, and the communities have usually responded well, though often slowly. In the end, universal literacy and public education, including public postsecondary education, has to be regarded as one of the major social achievements of the past century.

From this history emerged the concept of *knowledge as a common good* and the modern understanding of universities as *major national resources*: resources that include not only physical facilities such as laboratories, libraries, and hospitals but also staff with valuable expertise and skills. The potential of universities to generate new knowledge on request was realized by modern nations mainly, though not exclusively, as it relates to war and its conduct. The activity of research itself – the focused and concerted pursuit of a scientific or technical question so treasured in contemporary society – was greatly perfected during wartime. You will remember the rise of operations research and systems analysis in the Second World War.

The growing importance of research as a university-based activity changed the nature and function of colleges and universities drastically. Beyond the training of knowledgeable people, the research function – i.e., the creation and assessment of new knowledge – began to define the economic and political role of the institution itself. The increased emphasis that occurred during my academic life on the selection and promotion of faculty on the basis of research success, including success in attracting research funding, is as much a social and political development as it is an intellectual one.[1]

Today one needs to think of universities and colleges basically as knowledge-production sites, or maybe more appropriately as

information-production sites in the full meaning of industrial production. Yet, even with this image in mind, two open questions
remain: what kind of knowledge is being produced, and who receives
the products? After all, universities and colleges are publicly funded
institutions and knowledge is a public good rather than a private
possession. The wartime experience demonstrated to national governments the potential of focused research in the pursuit of national
objectives; at the same time, universities and colleges began to count
on research funding as sources of income. The gradual shift within
academic communities from doing "interesting" research to looking for "fundable" research topics was subtle, but very important,
signalling the increasingly obvious steering effect of research finan-
cing upon university policies such as hiring and promotion, and thus
upon teaching and curricular choices.

These developments affected individual faculty members as well
as their institutions and raised a number of fundamental questions.
For instance, in times of peace should individual scholars engage
in secret or classified research? Should universities and colleges, as
public institutions, permit the use of their facilities for such endeavours? In the immediate postwar period, a number of my colleagues
and I struggled to persuade our respective universities to refuse the
approval of classified research contracts. In some instances our
actions were successful, in others, camouflage manoeuvres allowed
compliance with the letter of regulations, yet negated their spirit.

Much, of course, was left to the decisions of the individual faculty
member. I remember I was the only member of my department who,
as a matter of conviction, did not seek support from sources such
as the Defence Research Board (though they often offered unclassi-
fied research funding), Atomic Energy of Canada Limited (AECL), or
Ontario Hydro. I also remember some not too friendly discussions
with my dean, who pointed out that my views not only impacted
my own research career but also deprived students of "relevant"
research training and the department of much needed contributions to equipment and supplies. His understanding of the university
as a production site meant that as long as the funding source was
respectable, and the project within the law, faculty members should
compete for all appropriate research funds to bring in business and
put the faculty on the map, so to speak.

I have delineated these relatively recent changes in the social and
political role of our universities and colleges in order to put the current problems in an appropriate context. Yet, I need to mention one

more significant sea change that occurred in the mid to late 1970s. Up to that time, grants in aid of research, usually called operating grants, were awarded by the federal granting agencies on the basis of a researcher's merit and reputation. The quality of past research, judged mainly by peer assessment, publication record, etc., rather than the subject matter of the research itself, determined the access to public funds. This changed, first for the sciences and engineering sector, then for the social sciences, the humanities, and medicine, when strategic or thematic grants began to be awarded. Suddenly, the subject matter of the research proposal became a factor in its adjudication: was the problem relevant and worthy of public support? This became a decision to be made by those providing the funds, not by researchers.

A similar development had occurred earlier in the United States, where significant public research funds were tied to end uses of national priority. My colleagues in the States would call it "nose-cone research" when their grant applications for crystallographic studies had to be justified by hopes of finding materials resistant to thermal shock and thus suitable for the nose cones of rockets. We Canadians felt quite superior, since we did not have to engage in such packaging techniques. When Canada began to award strategic grants, the changes did not occur at the insistence of the granting agencies or the Federal Government but in response to pressures from the universities and from university-based researchers who were hoping for access to new funds. In my view, this development shifted the decision on the nature of the knowledge to be produced at the university even more toward outside influences.

Let me return now to the questions I asked earlier. If universities and colleges have turned into publicly equipped knowledge-production sites, what kind of knowledge is being produced and who will receive it? In other words, who can ask questions, and who gets answers? Elementary, dear Watson. The funders ask or approve of the research questions and will receive the results. The results may become publicly available through publications and reports, although the research strategies and the context of the questions may limit the general usefulness of the findings. Worse still, many significant problems remain unresearched or underexplored because of lack of recognition and funding; just compare the fate of peace research at Canadian universities over the past decades to the growth of business schools in the same time span and at the same institutions.

Where does this leave us as teachers and as citizens? Our long and hard fought for public investment into higher education has yielded industrial-scale sites that are essentially assembly plants for economically useful knowledge and training facilities for skilled practitioners. They are profitable plants but not universities or colleges in terms of the definitions offered earlier. These plants are not places to transmit to the young values, knowledge, insights, skills, and critical abilities to cope with the future – unless one believes the global future is solely profitable commerce and business as usual. Those of us who consider teaching and research a form of stewardship for the future find that the essential academic decision-making is taken out of our hands. What we are to teach and how we are to teach it no longer appear subjects of academic and social discourse, but have become "market decisions."

What then can we do if we want to retain Canadian universities and colleges as institutions serving the public interest? Let me urge a concerted response on three levels. The first level is clarity. We need to analyze, discuss, and be clear on the new economic and political structures imposed today on universities and colleges. Much of this work is being done, though it needs to reach wider circles. Second is solidarity. What we are discussing here is not so much a university problem, but the university manifestation of a general, technologically facilitated shift of power and accountability. The impact of this new misdistribution of power is also felt in many other public institutions in Canada. Solidarity with them should be part of our response. The third level is politics. We are citizens of Canada and have the legitimate right to be *governed* rather than to be *administered on behalf of global commerce.* The protection of public institutions from interference is in the end a matter of governance: a matter of establishing and safeguarding public/private boundaries. As history has shown over and over again, there is no substitute for good government. It has to be part of the present response, so that it can be part of the future.

NOTE

1   In November 1986, Dr Franklin wrote a guest editorial in *Canadian Research* entitled "The Seedless Harvest" on the topic of the government's changing relationship with the National Research Council.

24

Research as a Social Enterprise: Are We Asking the Right Questions?

(The Royal Society Lecture, sponsored by the Royal Society of Canada's Women in Scholarship Committee and the Office of the Vice-President (Research), Carleton University, Ottawa, 6 November 2002)

Thank you all. I'm happy to see all of you, and as it is becoming I hope the younger ones will give their seats to the older ones. Although this isn't the subway, I'm afraid it will be a bit of a ride. I'd like to thank you all for coming because I know that time is the ultimate of nonrenewable resources; no one can give you back the hour or two that you are giving me in trust. I can only assure you that I will try not to misuse your trust and see to it that this hour is both a conversation between us and an opportunity to foster more conversations among all of you.

Our society is faced with grave problems. Nothing seems to me more urgent than that people get together in an atmosphere of trust and respect to share their knowledge, their thoughts, and their ignorance in the hope of a better conduct of the world's affairs. It is this notion – that there are ways to better the human condition through the application of thought, knowledge, observation, and sharing of insights – that has been at the root of the Royal Society. When the institution began in Britain, there was sharing of knowledge among not only academics but also lay practitioners of "the new science." There was a prevailing belief that education, in the broadest sense of the word, is both a common good and an instrument for the collective pursuit of social betterment.

If you were to ask me, "What is education?" I would say education is an enterprise that attempts to increase both knowledge and under-

standing, and I am quite insistent about linking the two components. We all know people who know it all and understand absolutely
nothing; we also know people who have a profound understanding of their problems, as well as of the human and social situation
around them, yet lack either the knowledge or the access to useful knowledge, to do anything about the situation. I would like to
talk about research, which is our main social enterprise to increase
knowledge and understanding, and I will try to pay particular attention to the linkage between the two components.

The case I want to make to you is based on the central role
of research in our society. At the beginning of all inquiry, of all
research, stands a question. Somebody wants to know something
that either they don't know or can't ask anybody about. After all,
there are things that are unknown. Research is the organized process of attempting to access, gain, and evaluate knowledge. I want
to convince you that the most important part of this endeavour is
not the answer; the most important part is the question. I want to
illustrate this view both historically and in terms of different disciplines. Often, the most creative, the intellectually most demanding
and noteworthy parts of research are the questions. Asking different
questions can open far more windows than elaborating on answers
to already obvious questions.

Why do I use our precious time together pondering the asking
of questions rather than struggling to find answers? I choose to do
this because I believe, with Virginia Woolf, that we all see the same
world, but we see it through different eyes. To all of you I say, pay
a great deal of attention to the questions and don't necessarily be
dazzled by more and more elaborate, spectacular, or highly dressed-
up answers. I want to say this to my senior academic colleagues,
who have to adjudicate, evaluate, promote, and fund research, just
as much as I want to say it to my young colleagues who will com-
mit a good deal of their lives to doing research. To both I say, *do* pay
attention to the question. Cultivate the different eyes that Virginia
Woolf mentions. Try and look at the world differently and ask different questions. Realize that it is in the different questions that new
intellectual contributions may lie. Treasure different eyes and different questions and shun what I call "the extension of the obvious."

Allow me to state how I want to proceed. First of all, I want
to give you some illustrations of what I mean by asking different
questions, of looking at the enterprise of gathering knowledge and

understanding with different eyes, or from a different point of view. I will choose my examples from what we call the "hard sciences" because I'd like to convince you that even in physics, chemistry, and mathematics, where the research tools might be considered objective, there are different questions to be asked of the same evidence: different questions because of a different point of view of the researchers, because of their different eyes. Having done this, I think I owe it to you to say what questions I would wish to ask, were I to begin a career in research now. Finally, I hope I can show the extent to which the scientific disciplines and their interactions – so well represented by the Royal Society – have benefited from the work of those asking different questions.

You will find the examples I choose, and others I could give, are primarily based on the work of women scholars. I am drawing on their experience, not only because this is a "Women in Scholarship" lecture but also because history has made it clear that those from the margin – and women in scholarship have frequently found themselves on the margin – are exactly those who ask the different questions. It does not really matter whether this different questioning is consciously chosen or whether life has put them through experiences that just made their eyes see things differently.

I will begin with an example from my own work – not because I think it's more important than other examples but because it's what I know best experimentally. I worked for a number of years as a senior research scientist at the Ontario Research Foundation (ORF), an institution that did research on behalf of Ontario's industry. One of the projects in which I became very involved related to the development of copper based alloys. Very briefly, its aim was to develop what was then called "stainless copper" – an alloy comparable to stainless steel (i.e., a corrosion-resistant material that could be used in external applications). Exposed to the atmosphere, the alloy would weather uniformly so as to be covered by a lovely green patination – like the patina on old copper roofs – but at the same time would provide the corrosion protection of stainless steel. Stainless copper could open a big market in the construction industry for the copper suppliers.

I was able to develop what looked like promising prototype alloys, and the Ontario Research Foundation took out a patent on them. Among its industrial clients, Noranda was interested and opted for a year's trial of the best of these alloys. In such tests, small coupons of

the alloy are exposed for a year to representative or harsher environmental conditions and then evaluated regarding the state of their
exposed surfaces. This procedure was followed. One exposure site
was in Quebec, in East End Montreal close to the Noranda plant.
The other was around Noranda's headquarters in Birmingham. A
year later we looked at the coupons. East End Montreal looked
pretty good, or, as one says around here, "not too bad." On the other
hand, the coupons in Birmingham were awful. The stuff looked as if
it had chicken pox. There were heavy localized corrosive attacks on
the coupons and no lovely green patina at all.

The end of the tests coincided with a big corrosion conference in
Birmingham to which I was invited. There was great conclave about
the tests. This was in the mid-1960s and I was quite young at the
time. All the others participants were men, and they were all much
older than I. After they looked at the results and tut-tutted about
them, they said, "Well, you know, it's a beginning. Please go back to
it. We will give you another year to develop a better alloy, one that
will withstand the conditions we have here in Birmingham." I looked
at the coupons and could only say, "No way. What is on those coupons is in the lungs of your children. You don't need better alloys;
what you need is better air."

That was in 1967, and they really thought I was mad. I mean, they
weren't even angry. They just thought I was quite deranged. But the
eyes of somebody like me, who had young children, saw very clearly
that what was on those coupons was exactly the stuff that would be
in the lungs of Birmingham children, and that it would be irrespon-
sible to camouflage that evidence under the guise of research into
better alloys. It was necessary to say to Noranda, "This is as good as
your copper alloys will get, and if you want to use them, you better
do something about your air quality." Personally, I could not accept
Noranda's offer of further alloy development. The issue resolved
itself on two levels. From Noranda's point of view, the Vietnam
War took care of the copper market, and I left the Ontario Research
Foundation to teach at the University of Toronto.

That was how I first learned that one could look at the same piece
of science with very different eyes. A scientist with one set of eyes
could say "Go," and a colleague with a different set of eyes could
say "No way." Years later I was able to utilize my knowledge of the
effects of the environment on copper alloys in my technical studies of ancient Chinese bronzes. Indeed, much of the work I've done

since with archaeologists involved, if I may use this phrase, looking through the other end of the telescope. I could learn something about ancient environments by looking at the state of the surface of artefacts excavated at various sites. Such observations, together with study of the objects' methods of fabrication, allowed me – of course, not alone but with other colleagues – to open a new area of interactions between the sciences and archaeology, a field that is now called "archaeometry."

When the Royal Society awarded me the Sir John William Dawson Medal in 1991 for my contributions to interdisciplinary scholarship, I felt particularly happy. But this is what happens very often: a new field of research emerges when someone looks with different eyes at a given situation. I would like to give you now two examples of major fields having been opened because somebody looked at the world with different eyes. The first is a historical case, dating back 100 years.

Alice Hamilton was one of the early woman physicians, graduating in the States at the turn of the past century, who worked in Chicago in the settlement movement with Jane Addams. Alice Hamilton was a paediatrician who worked in the immigrant districts of Chicago. She was practising there when, in 1902, Chicago was struck with a horrible outbreak of typhoid. It resulted in a great deal of illness and suffering, but it was also accompanied by a horrendous public rage that had a strong anti-immigrant theme. Many of the typhoid cases had occurred in the poor districts of Chicago, and, of course, those were the districts where many of the new immigrants lived. The press and much of the public pointed to these horrible immigrants, whether they came from Poland or the American South, and asserted that the newcomers seemed to know nothing about hygiene or public heath: that their habits were making the whole community sick and the outbreak was their fault.

Alice Hamilton, living and working in the immigrant community, had a very good grasp of the situation, and she did something nobody else had done before. She plotted the incidents of typhoid on a city map and overlaid this plot with a map of the repairs of the city's sewage system. Lo and behold, the highest incidence of typhoid occurred in districts where the city had not obeyed its regular maintenance and repair schedules of the sewage system, which consequently had deteriorated badly. Based on this evidence, it was quite clear that it was conditions for which the city was responsible

that had led to the concentration of typhoid in certain districts: it
was in the poor districts that the city didn't repair the sewage system; it was in these districts that the incidents of typhoid were high;
and it was in these districts that new immigrants had settled.

The evidence brought down the city administration, but more
important in the long run, it launched Alice Hamilton and others
into an area we now call "environmental medicine." In 1910, Alice
Hamilton became the first person to publish papers on the effect
of lead paint in tenement houses on the health and development of
young children. The warnings about the effects of lead ingestion on
the developing nervous system of young children go back to Alice
Hamilton. In fact, the study of the impact of the environment on
human health goes back to Alice Hamilton's looking at that typhoid
data with different eyes.

One more closing remark on Alice Hamilton. It took till about the
end of the First World War, to make the Harvard School of Medicine
realize (in 1919) that it would be necessary for medical students to
study the role of the environment in health and illness. Harvard created a chair for what was then called "Industrial Hygiene," which
we now call "Environmental Medicine." A search committee con-
cluded that the best person for the new teaching position would
be Alice Hamilton – but a woman was considered unacceptable.
Another search committee came to the same conclusion. Eventually
Alice Hamilton was appointed to the Harvard School of Medicine,
but it's interesting to note that there were a number of caveats that
the Board of Governors found necessary to put to the appointment
notice:

(1) The appointment of Alice Hamilton should not be considered
a precedent regarding the appointment of women.

(2) Professor Hamilton, though a member of the faculty, was not
entitled to apply for football tickets. (Alice Hamilton at that point
was a single woman of forty-nine, so I don't quite know what privilege was removed from her.)

(3) She also could not become a member of the Faculty Club.
(Again, I do not think she felt this caveat imposed horrible hard-
ships on her.)

(4) Finally, she would not be entitled to walk in the commence-
ment procession. (As I see it, this constraint was to remind her and
her colleagues that, while Harvard might need women's knowledge,
the university did not wish to draw public attention to this fact.)

Happily she survived quite well in spite of these constraints and so did the field of environmental medicine, which is now a major field of teaching and research. But again, the root of that discipline, its bedrock, came from the fact that somebody asked different questions.

My closing illustration is about a colleague of ours at the University of Alberta. Think back to the early 1980s, when chemotherapy had become one of the much used and trusted instruments in the fight against cancer. During this period the Alberta authorities decided that, in terms of cancer treatment, the medication should come to the patient rather than the patient to the medication. Thus chemotherapy treatment should be administered, whenever possible, in local hospitals and nursing stations – many of them in the far north. The Chemistry Department at the University of Alberta was heavily engaged in the development of new chemicals for chemotherapy, and it was a young chemist by the name of Dr Margaret-Ann Armour who looked at the situation and asked a different question. She asked, "What's going to happen to the medication that is not completely used up in the small hospitals and nursing stations in the far north? These are highly toxic substances. They can't just be dumped into the river." There were no suitable disposal protocols or procedures, and so she set herself to the task of developing such protocols.

She wanted not only to dispose of the toxic chemicals but also to do so by utilizing routines that were familiar, daily practice in small hospitals and nursing stations: routines using materials such as bleach, lye, and other ordinary chemicals to break down the chemotherapeutical compounds rather than introducing more complex chemicals to neutralize the toxins. In terms of chemistry, safely breaking down complex compounds is a tough job. It is not an easy task to dispose of toxic substances through processes that are no additional burden on the environment or on nurses, who are likely already pretty well burdened.

It took Margaret-Ann a number of years to develop new, environmentally suitable disposal protocols. Fortunately her work was financed by the Alberta Cancer Foundation – I say fortunately because neither the federal granting agencies nor the University of Alberta considered her research to be "cutting-edge chemistry" worthy of their support. Indeed, Margaret-Ann had a pretty difficulty time. Her department did not allot graduate students to her, because it was thought they would not learn "the right sort of chemistry." Furthermore, the protocols, once developed, were not the stuff that goes into peer-reviewed journals, nor were they intended to; they were to be published in manuals for nurses who serve on cancer wards. So there were no published and peer-reviewed papers, there were no graduate students, there were no grants, but there were these incredibly important results, derived from utterly pure chemistry, and applied to the specific deconstruction of complex compounds, rather than to their creation.

Eventually her work attracted several postdocs from abroad. In terms of the university's criteria for promotion and tenure, the lack of academically recognized support for her much-needed research presented a very difficult situation for Margaret-Ann. It took a fairly concentrated effort, until eventually the national recognition of her work and the pressure of a number of women scientists prevailed.

The University of Alberta granted tenure, and much international recognition followed. More postdocs and graduate students drifted in, and for her contributions Margaret-Ann Armour was given a major award by the governor general. It took not only an excellent chemist, but also a pretty sturdy soul and good friends to achieve that. Yet the award came, and the teaching Margaret-Ann is now asked to do internationally is in "chemical waste management," a field in which we cannot have enough competent and devoted prac-titioners. Again, different eyes seeing different things, combined with the courage to act on what is seen, brings enormous benefit to learning, to scholarship, to knowledge, and to the betterment of the human condition.

I could give you many more examples; however, I want to say there are some common characteristics among those who look at things with different eyes. They know, for example, that research is a social enterprise impacted by society's priorities. They realize, there-fore, that when scientists speak of "side effects" it is not a scientific statement; it is a social, political, or economic statement. Labelling an observation a "side effect," the researcher states that some facets of the discovery matter a lot more (often implying "to me and my friends") than others. Experiments yield information, facts, observ-able phenomena; it is society and the professions that rank phenom-ena into categories of "side effects" and "main effects," important and unimportant aspects. A different question, coming from a differ-ent standpoint, can open up windows that otherwise would remain closed. For instance, characterizing the product of a reaction as a "waste product" is an economic or social, rather than a scientific judgment. Since research is a social enterprise, it is vitally important to be mindful of the option of asking different questions.

You may ask, how can we look at things with different eyes given the reality of our lives, in which committees and work and grant applications so absorb even one view? I would answer to that, as I do to my young friends, "Never mind. That is not an excuse. Borrow somebody's eyes. Cultivate other eyes. You don't have to do it all alone." This is where collaboration comes; this is where conversation comes. This is where one uses all the things one has both as teachers and as learners – case histories, practicum, all those niches that are essentially ecological niches where one can ask, and must ask, different questions.

Now, as promised, I owe you some thoughts on what would I do if I were starting out as a graduate student or faculty member today. What questions would I like to pursue, knowing how research can absorb much of one's life?

If I may begin with the most narrow focus, I would stay in my own specialty. There are still a lot of interesting questions in the physics of the solid state, specially related to organic solids. I would be particularly interested in the characterization of materials. As scientists and engineers, we have usually attempted to gather all available information around a problem or a substance in the spirit of, "Let's try and learn everything about it," but this may not always be the best way of accumulating and assessing relevant knowledge. There is a real need for discernment here because one has to assess what it is that *can* be measured and how it relates to what needs to be known or predicted. Functional correlation is often crucial but not necessarily well established. Standard parameters, such as composition, conductivity, or colour are routinely tabulated and quoted – whether pertinent to the question under discussion or not.

I would also reflect on the utility of more and more detailed chemical analyses. Just because good and fast techniques to determine overall chemical compositions down to trace elements in parts per million or less are available, it does not mean that this information has bearing on all problems. A more discerning interpretation of *composition* would also involve a fresh critique of *distribution*; maybe we should revisit the concept of unit cells, clusters, and variable base units, such as domains, that were so helpful in explaining magnetic properties.

If I could expand from the issue of the meaning of composition and distribution, I would be very interested in the question of size and scale. In that drive to discover the smallest building block, I think we may have been pretty cavalier in the choice of what is considered a meaningful unit or building block. At any point there may be meaningful units defined in context, but rigorously defined. If one thinks of size and scale one can begin to expand from the narrow path of physics and crystallography into biology, into what an organism does, into the social organism. We all have lived through amalgamation, and we know it's pointless, but if we were asked, "Where's the evidence? What is the best size for the school board, for a hospital catch basin, for a transportation system, for a parks system?" we would not be able to cite such evidence. I would look with colleagues at size, scale, and the definition of appropriateness, and I think it would be worth doing.

Furthermore, I would revisit the notion of stability. In many ways we live in an extraordinarily pronounced off-equilibrium situation – whether one thinks of the production of materials under quite extreme and exotic conditions while using them in what one would call a normal environment, or one considers the growth and decay of living organisms, including social systems. I think our notions of stability, of equilibrium, of change, require a lot of scholarly revisiting, and I would happily be part of this.

If I had pots and pots of money and lots of people to work with, there are two areas that I think would deserve attention more than any other. One is quite obvious, and that is peace research. The intellectual mobilization for war, for destruction, and for violence is far, far greater, more complete, and better financed than the mobilization for trying to find ways in which people can indeed live together. Peace research is one of the great underexplored questions.

Finally, I want to suggest another area of research. I may be absolutely the only person interested in it, but I've been interested in it for many years and often spoken about it at science conferences. I have called this area of missing research "machine demography." We have a flourishing discipline on population demography that has been well developed over more than a century of scholarship. Initially the field was developed by people who took a dim view of high birth rates in Europe in the eighteenth and early nineteenth centuries, who assumed the resources of the world would run down rapidly with all these mouths to feed. Drawing on information from statistics to public health, people can tell you today how large the population of

China will be two years hence. We know the life expectancy of citizens in almost every country, we know their numbers, and we know
how much they will multiply.

To the best of my knowledge, however, we do not have a corresponding body of scholarship on machine demography; but machines
do work, they use energy, they produce waste products, and they
are around as incredibly important social forces as well as a part in
the total energy balance. While we have a great deal of information
on human demographics, we haven't a clue about devices. We don't
know the expected lifespan of the microphone that sits here, or anything else.

The questions to be asked regarding machine demography are
essentially the same as the questions to be asked of population demography. First the census: what is there? Then the taxonomy: how
do you classify what is there? People have normally been classified
first by locale and then often by age and gender. Once you have the
inventory, machines might be classified by function, by energy use,
by lifespan, or by the type of place they have in society. A clock is
different from a tractor, but so is a child from a mother, so is a professional from a farmer.

We now have a taxonomy of population that is very finely
detailed. I think if one began collecting information on machine
demography with inventory and coarse classification, one could
then use the information to answer a range of questions just as we
do with human projections. Are there enough? What do we need?
Can we feed them? Can we bury them? One sees China go for a one-
child family. In contrast to a one-child family, do we need a one-car
family? Do we need a one truck per block policy? We don't even ask
whether the world would be better off with a one-car family than
with a one-child policy, and these questions need asking.

Gathering information on the demography of machines – even just
learning what devices there are, how many of them, and how long
they might work – may seem like an impossible task; yet the demography of populations must have looked as confusing and intractable
to those who began to look at church records and old legal documents to get an idea of population growth and decline. Their initial
evidence wasn't any clearer than what we have before us now, yet we
still have no machine demography.

In closing I say again, in the end research is a social enterprise in
which society and practitioners ask questions, and it might be nice if
a few different questions were asked. Thank you.

25

The However Paragraph

(Guest lecture, The Toronto Congress of the Canadian Association of Physicists, Toronto, 2010[1])

Let me thank you not only for your very generous introduction but most of all for your presence. The fact that you have chosen to give me an hour of your time is a gift I respect and cherish profoundly. Time is, after all, the most precious of all nonrenewable resources. No one can give back to you the hour you are now giving to me. I will try to use this gift responsibly and respectfully, as one has to use all nonrenewable resources.

I will take an approach to the subject of Women in Physics that may be somewhat different from speakers of the past who were mainly concerned to explore how women could make a contribution to physics as physicists. In contrast I want to explore, from the perspective of someone who is nearly ninety years old, whether and how physics might have benefited from the presence of women practitioners.

I began teaching at the University of Toronto in 1967. It was a year after the call for a Royal Commission on the Status of Women had been made, and three years before the Commission's groundbreaking report was issued. The report made it very clear that at that time Canadian women were second-class citizens, and nowhere more so than in the academic fields I will call "the professions." In the wake of the report, many discussions focused around two questions: "What is wrong with women? Why can't they hack it?" and secondly, "Is there something wrong with science and the professions, not just in their practice, but in their structures?"

Now, fifty years after the commission, many of the professions and their self-images have profoundly changed. Today, you could not be a lawyer, a doctor, or an architect using the same textbooks that were used thirty years ago by just adding new factual material. Different templates are now the basis of the pedagogy in law, medicine, and architecture.

But what about physics? Is there really a profound change in the self-image of physics based on the insights and scholarship of feminists such as those who shaped the Report of the Royal Commission? In other words, is there a difference in how physicists are taught today because of what the reflections of feminist scholars revealed about the structure of knowledge and the structure of social power? At this point you may want to say: "Hold it – medicine, law, and architecture deal with people. Physics is science. Physicists deal with facts. In their world, facts must be reproducible and independent of the observer. Physics, as all science, is thus less affected by social consideration."

I would like to say that this is not in fact so. I want to set aside the issue that research needs funding and all the problems that the search for funds and means involves. My consideration here is the realm of physics and "the scientific method." When initially preparing this talk, I had intended to do a curriculum analysis of physics and other professional courses over the last decades and look at changes of subject and content. However, I find in the program for this congress, right here and now, an excellent illustration of what I would like to bring to your attention. Look at the large array of subdisciplines and then ask yourself, "Is the sum of these separate, hyphenated, and specialized skills and perspectives *physics*? Is this all that there is to physics?" Assume you brought a student with you to this congress who would be able to take in each and every session. At the end of the week, would she know what physics is in Canada in 2010? Could you say to her, "Now you know what physics is all about"?

Were I with you and the student, it would be at this point of the discussion that I would want to insert my "however paragraph." I have always had an intense interest in however paragraphs because they continue the discourse. They accept the existing work and knowledge but *supplement* it by saying, "Hey, maybe you should look a little further, cast your view a bit broader, or listen differently to the reality that presents itself." In other words, can there be, should there be, more to physics than the collection of hyphenated specialties in your Congress program?

Let us reflect for a moment on "the scientific method" that is the foundation of many of the presentations at this conference. Basic to

the scientific method is its reductionist focus. The ability to deal with
a problem in the laboratory, by regarding the problem's context as
either constant or of no consequence, is in some ways the root of
both the greatest triumphs and the greatest liabilities of the practice
of science. As scientists started to bring part of reality as a separate
question into the laboratory, it was assumed their insights would
return to the reality from where the problem came and as a result a
better understanding of that reality would follow. This assumed series of events actually happened very rarely. The isolated facts began
to create their own problematic and questions arising from them
occupied the discourse. The return to the contextual reality became
more and more tortured and more and more rare.

The question of the context of scientific findings became crucial again when feminists looked at the professions. Their critique
showed that one cannot practise medicine with "men" as the standard: women are citizens just as their male counterparts, and women
and children occupy public and private space as well as men. The
disciplines began to change their templates of teaching and practice
under the weight of these arguments. It became clear that the scientific method, in fact, investigated a deprived reality not corresponding to the reality of life.

Already in the 1940s, philosophers had pointed out to what extent
reductionist methods produced impoverished realities, yet it is only
now that one finds, for instance, that the medical profession redis-
covers context. Our medical colleagues begin to teach patient-centred
medicine, realizing that the patient is a human being with family,
work, and community, and these parameters cannot be ignored
when bringing scientific knowledge to a contextually defined problem. Students are no longer satisfied with the old-fashioned situation
in which, let's say, the great surgeon does a complicated operation
after which the patient is wheeled out into the care of nurses and
nurse practitioners with little or no feedback.

Yet physicists, to this day, may have very similar practices. They
may come out with fundamental insights that they then dump on
the engineers – the nurse practitioners of science – if I may call
them that. The reason I give this example is that I want to suggest physics could explore an approach parallel to that of medicine. Physicists, in fact, should consider "nature-centred physics"
because the problems of physics come from nature and need to be
brought back there. Evelyn Fox Keller gave us a wonderful insight

when she said: "Nature cannot be named out existence; nature is real." Let's stop and think for a moment. *Nature cannot be named out of existence.* Nature is not a sum of ecosystems. It is not a set of streams interacting on this or that. Nature is real, just as a patient is real.

On this table I put three books I brought to describe the territory of my inquiry into nature-centred physics. I want to put them together, each book making one side of a triangle. Within that triangle is the realm of what I think should preoccupy physicists in the near future. One side of the triangle is Margaret Benston's paper, "Feminism and the Critique of Scientific Method."[2] The second side is the transcript of David Cayley's CBC series "How to Think about Science." The bottom of the triangle is delineated by the program of this Congress. Within this territory, I would locate the neglected contextual issues that physics could address.

My point is that physics has extraordinarily good tools for many of the tasks that face us as citizens. First and foremost, there is thermodynamics, that great universal glue. Just imagine you could make politicians understand thermodynamics. Just imagine what that would mean to nature and to peace. But even if you don't think in terms of thermodynamics for politicians, within our own work questions of thermodynamics are often neglected. Physicists could bring to the civic discourse insights on systems' boundaries, concepts of size and scale, and a concept I am particularly fond of, the concept of "domains." Anyone who ever worked in ferromagnetism and similar fields knows the immense utility of the notion. The reality that boundaries exist and that they change under the influence of force is a useful, universal, and transferable concept.

Physicists have been increasingly preoccupied by the small building blocks of the universe, but there is also the large-scale ordering of structure. Superstructures are as prevalent and as fundamental as substructures to complete our impoverished view of reality. Today, as a woman and a Canadian, I would happily enter the field of physics. I would again want to have the joy of looking through a microscope, thinking of structures, and understanding how things work. But I would ask questions of size and scale of thermodynamics in the broadest sense, and I would attempt to look at nature as the source of questions as well as of solutions. Most of all, I would hope my courses and instructors would never let me forget that there is a difference between a mechanism and an organism.

Nature is an organism, while much of our impoverished reality tries to reduce it to a mechanism. Kant made it clear that a mechanism is a functional unit in which the parts exist for one another in the performance of a task. For example, all the parts of a clock can be made separately in suitable dimensions and then assembled to fulfill their collective function. However complex, the mechanism is fundamentally different from an organism because an organism is both a structure and a functional unit in which parts exist for and by means of each other as an expression of a particular task. Thus the parts arise on the basis of the interaction and of the functioning. It is the function of a seed that produces the leaf; the parts exist and come into being and function together. In an organism the parts cannot be assembled from pre-existing stock. They need each other to come into full function.

Physics as a discipline is equipped to deal with both mechanisms and organisms; however, the scientific method, with its reductionist emphasis, has led physicists to make problems of mechanisms a preferred choice. It is precisely the lack of attention to the workings of organisms that helped bring about the impoverished reality I am trying to address. The influence of feminist scholarship brought context and enrichment to the outlook and service of other academic professions. It is my sincere hope that a more nature-centred physics would result in a similar enrichment of both the practice and the practitioners of physics.

NOTES

1 Later published in *Physics in Canada* 66, no. 3 (July–September 2010), 171–3.
2 Margaret Benston's paper can be found in *Feminism in Canada*, A. Miles, and G. Finn, eds (Montreal: Black Rose 1982).

26

Reflections on Public Health and Peace: Ask How Are You? NOT Who Are You?

(The Dr Zofia Pakula 2012 Inaugural Lecture, Dalla Lana School of Public Health, Global Health Division, University of Toronto, 26 November 2012)

I am really quite overwhelmed not only by the size but by the quality of the audience. There are so many people who could sit here in my place and have a great many valuable contributions to make on those questions we all would like to address – What about peace? What about public health? I hope you will talk to each other as much as you can, because it is not only a very urgent but also a totally collective struggle as we try and think: how on Earth do we proceed from here?

I feel honoured to give the first of these lectures and have come equipped with what one needs at my age: a timer, cough drops, and a reasonably sensible manuscript. What I would like to do and why I chose that title, "Ask How Are You NOT Who Are You?" is to say that we have to care for each other's wellbeing even if it is for the most selfish of reasons: that we cannot be well when others are sick. We know it in the family. We know it in the community. We know it from the very notion of public health with its history. Think of the nineteenth-century conferences on sanitation, when people knew that even the rich and powerful cannot be well forever when others are sick. There's a collective notion of wellbeing that is not just fuzzy niceness but *real practice*. We cannot neglect the wellbeing of others, and that is physical, mental, and political.

The indivisibility of wellbeing is an issue I would very much like to address. It's the central issue of these lectures, and I would like to try to examine it in the spirit of Dr Zofia and her commitment to the advancement of health and the securing of peace. I'd like to reflect on these goals in terms of her life, looking at the point when the war ended and the horror of what had happened began to be clear to the world in two revelations: the horror of inhumanity and war signified by the horror of the Holocaust – what supposedly civilized people are able and willing to inflict on others – and the knowledge of nuclear war – the knowledge that there is no way to opt out, no way to be neutral. I would like to reflect on those revelations.

I will start at the time when Dr Zofia returned to what was supposed to be peace and show how these realizations shaped that generation, because honouring her will mean honouring that generation of survivors. I would then like to look at what happened to that interlinked, twinned concept of health and peace and at what it means to us in the here and now. I'm talking about collective attributes; as I said, you cannot be healthy when not attending to the health of others.

I did not know Dr Zofia. It's rather funny that we never met, being of the same age, the same conviction, being in that smallish circle of the university, and still we didn't meet. Yet I feel I know her, and I feel I know her well, because my life as hers – and as the lives of many others – was shaped by forces outside our control. Our traditional lives were torn apart, and as they were rewoven they were rewoven in that same atmosphere of the knowledge of the past, and the knowledge of having survived it.

In many ways Zofia is emblematic of the generation of survivors of the Second World War in its broadest implications: survivors that were for the rest of their lives under that burden of knowledge, and under that question, "What does it mean that I survived and others did not? What does that mean for the conduct of the rest of my life? What lessons have I to transmit?" That experience has been to many people, particularly to many women, a mortgage – a moral mortgage – on their lives: the mortgage of the survivor who cannot free herself from the demands on her life of the obligation that this very fact – of having survived when others hadn't – would place on her.

I want to honour that generation of survivors whose lives changed drastically and profoundly, and changed in heart, mind, and hand, what they felt, what they thought about, what they did, and how they conducted their lives across the board. The survivors had that common solidarity that brought so many together, who thought, "Never again." It was different from the "never again" in the First

World War, when one thought it was possible by reason, by structure alone. Here we were on a much, much deeper level. It was a level that changed lives to a new solidarity. It meant that women across the country, across the world, said "If our children are going to grow up healthy and sane, *all* children have to grow up healthy and sane. It is not good enough any more to look after oneself, after one's country." In A.J. Muste's words, "There is no way to peace; peace is the way," and we have to figure out what that way is. The peace movement, the women's peace movement that I know so well came out of that common mortgage, the mortgage of profound obligation.

Let me give you one example, and only one out of the many I could give: the example of the baby tooth survey that was conducted by women in the early 1960s, when the fear of nuclear testing, new preparation for yet another war, and the danger of fallout were such that women were alarmed at what that would do to their children. What would be incorporated in these young growing bodies, wherever they are, whatever the politics, skin colour, passport of their parents would be? In order to produce a baseline, we collected the milk teeth of young children who had grown up before atmospheric testing. It was an incredible experience – in both solidarity and pedagogy – to show that peace and health are so intricately linked that whether we talk about one or the other, we talk about both.

This understanding reemphasized that peace and public health are collective; they involve all of us. Whether friend or foe, we are dependent on each other. Out of that knowledge of interdependence came the string of activities that many of you in this room know well: be it Science for Peace, be it Veterans against Nuclear Arms, be it physicians organizing. It is that discharge of the moral mortgage of obligation of those who, by luck more than merit, survived to shape their lives so that nobody again has to face what Dr Zofia and others faced. For her it meant a change in her career, the attention to the victims, but also as a professional to see that where justice could be restored, where compensations could be made, where obligations could be discharged and responsibilities could be assumed, it would be so: it would be done. It meant a different structure but it also meant a different sense of collectivity.

I remember long and very frequent meetings in church basements, talking about fallout, talking about pollution, talking about laws, and then almost point-counterpoint the collective writing of briefs, the going to the government to say, "Look you guys, that is not right." I don't know how many briefs I wrote, but I do know my role in a brief on the Defence Production Sharing Agreement that blew away Canada's fig leaf of neutrality in the beginning of the Vietnam War. I want to just leave in your mind the recollection of that point-counterpoint: the solidarity on a daily level with others on that basic knowledge that *survival is collective*. Those who by the grace of God and no merit survived one of the most colossal disruptions of society carried for the rest of their lives the obligation to act so that nobody would be a survivor again.

I should make one other point about that period. It was very clear that one tried to deal with the root causes. It wasn't a question of fixing it up for tomorrow morning; it was a question of root causes both now and in the future. We had a great interest in school books, in proper nondiscriminatory description of other people, revision of history books, but also in war toys. I don't know whether Zofia let Andrew play with guns. We certainly didn't have any in our house. Children's books and war toys were important to us because we tried to nourish that part in everyone's mind that looks at other people as those who will help us achieve peace rather than those we would like to push off the flat Earth of our convenience.

During that period in addition to the preoccupation with root causes of war, the question of the economic consequences of disarmament was also clear; we don't want arms not only in the playrooms of our children but also in the arsenal of our politicians. There were, of course, the "tut-tutters" who said, "Well, what about jobs?" and those who, in a good scholarly fashion, pointed out that there are better things to do. We suggested that there were many additional things to do arising from the collective wish to focus society's best knowledge on addressing the root causes rather than the manifestations of war and intolerance.

We also knew that governments left much to be desired. There were those who run for parliament, but there was also the conviction that the alternative to bad government is good government not no government. There is no substitute for good government. Dealing with the root causes both of lack of public health and community health and lack of peace and justice is related causally to the presence or absence of good government, and it is *government* not just *governance*. It's not just, "Somebody ought to take care of this and do that efficiently." It is that peace, order, and good government that Canadians have been promised. The survivors were willing to shape their lives, their work, their activity, their profession so as to produce a soil that made good government possible, but government *per se* is not negotiable. We were convinced that we had the right to be governed rather than administered. Out of that comes the solidarity, the conviction, the hope, as well as the preoccupation and the obligation.

Let me take you on a fast-forward to the midpoint between the time the war ended and the here and now: a period of two if not three generations. Take the midpoint, somewhere in the mid-late 1970s, and stop for a moment and say, "Where were we in terms of discharging that moral mortgage? Had we gotten somewhere? Had we discharged some of this? Is the mortgage smaller?" If you put yourself into the mid-1970s, you may say in Canadian parlance, "Not bad." It wasn't that good, but it was not bad because in the early 1970s Canada had abolished the death penalty. In 1972 the Soviets and the US had signed an Anti-Ballistic Missile Treaty, which later in that decade was followed by the SALT 1 and SALT 2 Treaties. It wasn't bad. The Vietnam War had ended in 1975, hopefully giving one more lesson that war doesn't get anybody anywhere. True, we have made no progress in banning nuclear weapons. True, the US in 1976 or 1975 had just vetoed the UN a resolution for an independent state of Palestine, but then the US had brokered a peace agreement between Egypt and Israel, so we said, "Not bad. We haven't gone as far as we could, but at least the mortgage was somewhat paid back."

Then I take you on a fast-forward to the here and now, to the months when we are horribly worried about what's going on in Gaza, what's going in the Republic of Congo, in Syria, in various places. I would take you to the library, and as good academics should, I would say, "Let's look to the best knowledge we have both on peace and peace research." Remember that peace research was progressing fairly well in the mid-1970s. George Ignatieff was just ready to move into Trinity College. Peace Studies became part of the University.

Now we'll look at what the best minds today have to say about that interlocking central piece of our thoughts: public health and peace. Do they understand that they hang together? I would show you the wealth of literature. I would show you, for instance, in a respectable journal on social science and medicine, a long paper, nine typed pages with lots of references, called "A Public Health

Framework to Translate Risk Factors Related to Political Violence and War into Multi-level Preventative Interventions." I would take you to Johan Galtung's most recent paper, entitled "Cultivating Peace, Preventing Violence."

What do we have? We have in our memory of that generation of the moral mortgage, the knowledge that the personal is political and therefore the political is personal. We have to care, and here we are, three generations later, and I read learned papers in which war and violence are calculated as "a risk," one of those risks of being around, not a disaster we need to prevent, not a threat to us and our children, but a calculated risk, and I say "What's going on?" and so would Dr Zofia. "What is going on? What is going on with that junction of heart and mind and hand, where indeed the personal is political and the political is personal?"

What we see is a horrible disconnect. Suddenly it seems as if the misery of others becomes the road to tenure and promotion for the rest. It seems that from that solidarity of the survivors the communality of our fate has gone, that there's a distance. There's a paralysis of analysis. You could not wish for a better analysis of what to do to prevent what is labelled as "the high risk of violence and political conflict," but sanitized, abstracted from the literature: an incredible disconnect from our neighbours phoning their friends in the Middle East and hearing, "My cousin died this morning." And here we are.

Now, I don't say we have to go back – or should or could go back to the 1970s – but I say, and I'm sure you are here because you ask the same questions, "Where is the expression of our humanity? Where is that very thing that made women care for the health of other people's children? Where did it get lost?" I think back to the church basements and the briefs to government. If I asked students in this building now, "Have you ever thought of writing a brief to a parliamentary committee?" they would probably say, "What parliamentary committee?" We haven't had a decent interparliamentary committee for a very long time.

For me the answer is that we have lost the institution of government, as have others. What has happened is privatization and globalization. What has happened is that the communality is a communality of the stock market and of gain. What happened is that *we have not lost our humanity but we have lost our collectivity.* And I think we cannot afford it. If we look at the process that has at this point deprived us – apparently without much process – of the instruments with which we could collectively express our concern, when it is possible without much rumbling to prorogue Parliament, to say, "Go home, we don't want you; you just get in the way," I also think it is blatantly obvious that any critical argument makes no difference in the conduct of Canadian affairs.

I'm glad my good friend Senator Nancy Ruth is here, because we agree that it is utterly unacceptable not to care for the health of others, whether we like them or not, while spending inordinate amounts of money on weaponry, as well as on unneeded drugs. But her choice to work from within and my choice to work from without have shown me that even very good people from within seem not to be able to give us what we really need. The church basements are fine, I would think people are alright, but we have no way as I see it to promote peace and the just use of natural resources, the care of the environment.

The generations of survivors symbolized by Dr Zofia, speaking still through my voice, are effectively gone. We will not be there very soon. Our message, however, is not gone. It is not gone that there are and were people who said, "The personal is political, and therefore the political is personal, and I refuse to have things done in my name that I find both immoral and dysfunctional."

So what then is ahead of us? I think what is ahead of us is not to deal with manifestations but to come back to root causes. Be it those in this building who study global health, be it those who concern themselves about peace or weapons, we cannot afford to deal with manifestations. We have to deal with root causes. Why is it that the need for intervention arises? Many of these root causes are not at the place where the manifestations of ill health or political violence occurs. They are caused somewhere else, and that brings us home, and that brings us here. I would, maybe because of my background, suggest that *we cannot let the lack of being allowed to be political stand* because this, to me, is the beginning of fascism.

I see, probably more acutely than others, that what we are facing is a very serious case of technofascism: the fact that some people matter less, that some people for others are dispensable, is terribly serious. So I can only say when we leave the library, when we leave the excellent plans, good logic, perfect thought, and no reality, for heavens sake don't get into more analysis, more structures of health governance, more designations of more things to administer, to do, to research, to observe. Let us close the door to the library for the day and look: look at ourselves, look at the mortgage we tried to discharge, and say, "It all started with fascism. Don't overlook the seeds of new fascism, because the greatest danger to both health and peace is the assumption that some people matter more than others."

That is what I would like to say to you in memory of Dr Zofia, and in memory of the generation that really tried. Thank you.

27

An Interview with Anna Maria Tremonti[*]

(*The Current*, CBC Radio, 6 May 2010, recorded at the
Toronto studio[1])

AMT: After decades of pushing for social justice, Ursula Franklin is
just getting started. Ursula Franklin is a Canadian giant – a world-
renowned physicist, feminist, Quaker, author, pacifist, professor,
Holocaust survivor, public intellectual, mother, and mentor. Ursula
Franklin is with me in Toronto. Good morning.

UF: Good morning, and thanks for having me.

AMT: You have been working for peace and social justice for decades. You have lived through a World War, through the rise of
nuclear weapons, the end of the Cold War, the spread of pollutants.
What is your primary concern as you look around you in 2010?

UF: It's really the future of my grandchildren – of everyone's grandchildren. The world has changed, and I'm not convinced it has
changed in the direction that would make it more liveable, more
peaceful, more joyful for all of its inhabitants. That continues to
concern me profoundly because wellbeing is not a private affair.
Peace is not divisible or a commodity that one buys and some have
more and because of that others have less. Peace is indivisible. In
fact the very nature of modern war as well as modern commerce
makes it necessary to care for all and to understand that nobody
can survive at the expense of anybody else. That has been a very
difficult lesson both to teach and to learn.

AMT: Well, we can't talk about that without talking about democracy. What concerns do you have about the state of democracy?

UF: I am profoundly concerned not just about the state of
democracy but about the absence of democracy: the erosion of

* We gratefully acknowledge the CBC for permitting us to include this interview.

democracy. For somebody like me, who grew up under Hitler, with parents keenly aware of what was coming on, intellectuals who argued with their friends abroad to say, "Don't you see what's coming – how easily fascism can take hold?" I am super-sensitive to the erosion of democracy. I came to Canada by choice because it is a democratic country, and I see our parliamentary institutions are more and more eroded.

In fact I came here today because I thought I would introduce you, Anna Maria, to a new word, and that word is "scrupling." Just as we make in our daily parlance a verb out of "google" and say we are "googling," there is of course a word scruple and way back during the debate and struggle on slavery, the old Quakers used the word "scrupling." In that time it was of real currency, and they went scrupling with their neighbours: sitting down and saying, "We have a horrible problem. Many of us think it is not right to own people. We better scruple about that."

AMT: Scrupling. So in other words, if you have scruples you "scruple."

UF: Yes. You do something. If you have the need for clarity beyond your own private concerns you'd better scruple: that is talk with people and make it clear it's not my problem, it's not your problem, it's a problem that is bigger than all of us.

AMT: Let me pick up on something there. You talk about your experience in Nazi Germany and the Holocaust, then you talk about slavery, and in the same conversation you talk about our democracy and parliament in Canada. Can you connect those things? Some people would be offended that you connect those things.

UF: I would say indeed not only that you can but that you must connect those things. You cannot look at the tree and not look at its roots. Things don't come in a plain brown envelope. Things grow and you need to look both at the soil and at what is planted in the soil. What things grow and what things shrivel? I see democracy shrivelling and it is shrivelling at the institutional level. It's not whether you or I vote, or for whom we vote. It's not firing the coach or getting a better player: it's looking at the game. What has happened to the game?

AMT: And what has happened to the game?

UF: The game has become a ritual. It is not doing what it is supposed to do, and the players know it. That's why, in a scrupling session a month or so ago, we invited three sitting members, one of each party – people who wanted to represent us and got the job – to scruple with them. We said we feel unrepresented, and we knew from our contact with some of them that they felt severely constrained in representing us. What stands in the way? Let's not have a debate, not have something to blame, but be concerned about the structure we need to enable representation in the institution that we have, which is the House of Commons.

AMT: So you point a finger at the institutions. What responsibilities does an individual citizen bear in either the growth of democracy or the erosion of democracy?

UF: I think the first obligation is clarity. I find one of the real contempts of parliamentary democracy right now is the discussion on the coming immigration bill in which the minister went to press conferences about a proposal discussing the pros and cons of something that to this point has not been voted upon. Now the citizen cannot stop this. Many people who feel strongly about it want to talk, but they have to precede their talk by saying to the minister, "Listen, this is not the place. We have to have hearings. There is a process. When you have ideas of change, introduce them in the House, let the members go back to their constituencies, have first reading, have hearings in committee." There's a lot of difference between consultations, having tea with your friends, and hearings, which I would call "listenings" if I could. The ordinary citizen cannot produce hearings, but the ordinary citizen can remind the minister that he has an obligation to due process.

AMT: Take us back to your life, your early life in Germany, so that we can understand how your views were shaped. What happened to you and your family during the Second World War?

UF: My mother was Jewish, and my father came from a long German family. I was the only child, and I had wonderful parents in the wonderful atmosphere of pre-Hitler Berlin. My parents, particularly my mother, were intensely aware of what was coming in terms of the assaults on human rights and social justice. We got stuck, and it was very, very difficult. My mother, father, and I were all sent to different concentration camps but survived partly by luck, partly by the kindness of people. I went back, and it was postwar Germany that taught me how mindful one has to be of the roots of democracy. Having survived war in Berlin, and having known totally – intellectually and viscerally – that violence is pointless, leading only to more violence and more hatred, I wanted involvement in the citizenship of another country that had firmer groundings, so I accepted a postdoctoral fellowship to the University of Toronto.

AMT: So after all you learned from the traumas you faced, when you came to this country it was not solely about your personal space and what you might want to learn; you came to this country to speak out.

UF: And mostly to act out. Not to *tell*, but to *do* what I think good citizens are supposed to do, and can do, to nourish democracy.

AMT: You became the first female professor at the University of Toronto's Department of Metallurgy and Materials Science. How difficult was it to be a trailblazer in those days, which were the late 1960s?

UF: It's hard to say. Personally I met a great deal of helpfulness and courtesy. Since I knew what I was doing and I was prepared to work hard, I found my lot far easier than that of other women who met far greater discrimination. It was more difficult collectively than individually.

AMT: You took on the issue of pay equity. What happened? Why did you do it?

UF: There were women who retired before the law forced equal pay on the University, so they retired with a final salary substantially lower than that of their male colleagues. It was necessary to address that as a group. There were so few, there were only five of us who could be the representative claimants in a lawsuit, and so as in all these things you do it because there is, unfortunately, nobody else.

AMT: That goes back to the issue of the responsibility of the citizen.

UF: It does, except I do not think that everything is everybody's business. We have developed a structure of sharing work and sharing responsibility. It is the strengthening and not the shortcutting of the institutions we have that profoundly concerns me at the moment. Our basic parliamentary representative democracy is so curtailed by a variety of shortcuts and factors. I see that with great fear because the not working – at times things seem intentionally choreographed not to work – is an invitation to fascism, is a dream of the strong guy who cuts through all this nonsense and gets things done. That's where it links to my past experience of my parents' horror about the social unrest, inequality, inflation, lack of loans in Germany, that produced a situation that cried out for the strong decisive male and totally wrong and totally authoritarian action. I see this as being far closer to the Canadian reality than many of my friends.

AMT: Don't you think we have enough checks and balances in our democratic system here?

UF: We have them; we don't use them. One of the big ones is the opposition – both parliamentary and extra-parliamentary. I was horrified to hear the prime minister say that members of the opposition couldn't be trusted. If people elect a representative and they happen to be from a party that is not the prime minister's, that does not mean they are not trustworthy. We don't want a country in which people who may oppose this or that are considered untrustworthy. They make a contribution that we may not like, but they make it out of good intention.

AMT: A lot of this debate, as it were, is happening against a backdrop of increasing political apathy. There are a lot of people who will say that the public doesn't care about these issues, that these issues don't affect the public. Do you agree with that? Do you see apathy out there?

UF: Yes, I see apathy out there, but I also see a reason for apathy, and that is the non-response of governments. The cure for apathy is a bit of response. Any teacher knows if you want any engagement of your students you have to involve them, and you involve them not by saying "Put a lot of work in, but I'm not going to read your paper." You read it, you make marginal notes, and you show in your conduct, in what you teach, that you have heard what was said.

Kids are intelligent. Kids learn. They just often learn the wrong thing. These kids have learned they can intelligently work with other people provided it's a voluntary, often temporary, association, but the idea that as citizens our instrument is a policy of our government has been so discredited by the inaction of the government that the young say, "We aren't stupid. Why should we work with you guys? You haven't a care in the world for us."

AMT: What does that tell you about how you see the future? I mean you're basically saying they've learned that government isn't something to be involved in or to get interested in.

UF: Yes, then we have to change and that's where the scrupling comes in. That's why I say look at the process. It's not impossible to change. You can give power to parliamentary committees; that really makes a difference.

AMT: How do you define peace?

UF: I define peace not as the absence of war but as the presence of justice and the absence of fear. There's peace when people don't have to be afraid, and people don't have to be afraid when there is genuine justice: period. It seems to be so, so difficult, although it is so, so obvious.

AMT: Do you think many people who actually agree to go to war understand what you just said?

UF: Those who go to war do so because they have no more attractive or more available choices for what they want to do with their lives.

AMT: I should clarify, when I say those who go to war, I'm not necessarily talking about soldiers, I'm also talking about the people who send soldiers to war, who make a decision to go to war.

UF: I think these are totally different things. The people who make decisions to go to war have what I consider evil intent. They have no feeling either of alternatives or of responsibility for what happens not only to those whom they send but also to everybody else.

AMT: But they would argue with you they are going, for example to Afghanistan, in order to uphold the very democracy that you say is threatened.

UF: Well, good luck. You know, this is not without historical examples. There are a good number of eloquent people who will say if they want to do nothing but uphold democracy, there are a good deal easier and better ways of doing it.

AMT: Given all of this, what kind of society do you dream about for future generations?

UF: I used to say, and I wrote it in the foreword of one of my books, that to me the dream of a peaceful society is still the dream of the potluck supper: a society in which all can contribute and all can find friendship. Those who bring things bring things they do well, and bring a variety of things. Those who can't cook can still organize, help clean up, and all belong. However idiotic it might sound, that is still the society that I dream of: not that everybody runs everybody's business, but that we create conditions under which a potluck is possible.

AMT: Ursula Franklin, thank you for sharing your thoughts.

UF: Thank you for having me and listening.

AMT: Ursula Franklin is a celebrated physicist, author, and activist. She spoke to us from our Toronto studio.

NOTE

1 The audio recording of this interview is available at www.cbc.ca/thecurrent/2010/05/may-06-2010.html.

Afterthoughts

While preparing this book, it has been my great privilege to spend many hours with Ursula. As we worked to restore and select these speeches for publication, the insights she shared were often so extraordinary that I asked her if I could record some of our conversations in order to inform the introduction and conclusion of the book. Since the leitmotif of the collection is thoughts and afterthoughts, we felt it appropriate to share with readers some of the recent afterthoughts that Ursula expressed in our conversations. While the excerpts in the introduction are broad, those here touch on specific aspects of certain speeches in this collection. We present these "afterthoughts" by way of conclusion.

THE CONCEPT OF STRUCTURE

JANE: Ursula, in your speech, "Monocultures of the Soil, Monocultures of the Mind," you note the "red thread" through many of the things you do is *the concept of structure*, and you often refer to the link between structure and properties in both physical and social structures. How did you first come to recognize the relationship between structure and properties?

URSULA: This relationship is the substance of much previous inquiry because *structure has a profound influence on properties*. From the time people made stone tools, it has been known there were suitable rocks and unsuitable rocks. Those of us interested in the relationship among materials manipulation, human knowledge, and imagination cannot overlook what is given, and what is given are materials with specific structures. What people choose,

with increasing knowledge and understanding, are materials that
allow certain useful properties to be focused on, highlighted, and
exploited. For example, you can hammer a piece of metal into a
thin sheet. You bash it if you want, heat it, and it becomes a very
thin sheet. Early copper metallurgy was done like that. On the
other hand, if you try that with a piece of salt or rock, you get
smaller and smaller powder. That consequence is entirely related to
structure, from the atomic to the crystalline.

JANE: Could you give an example of the connection between structure and properties in the social realm?

URSULA: Look at the family: the role of parents vis-à-vis children.
Look at teaching: the changing role of the teacher and the student.
Look at the view of divinity: the saints vis-à-vis the parishioners;
God vis-à-vis priests; the priests vis-à-vis the congregation. These
are structural relationships, and those change. Sociologists, anthro-
pologists, politicians, priests have all built their teaching on those
power structures. There was a time when students could not question a teacher. The faithful could not question the priest. Any reformation, any change in pedagogy, is a change in the power relationships that, when transposed to the image of a physical object, is a
change in binding and structure.

The best use of the concept of structure is the knowledge that
the whole and the parts have structural relationships; the whole
cannot be assessed only as the sum of the parts. The way the parts
are arranged – whether they are atoms or community members –
allows the collectivity to do more than just the random sum of the
parts. In the family, the community, the classroom, if you have an
understanding not only of who is there but also of what can be
done by rearranging their relationships, you suddenly gain clarity
on what is possible and what is not – not because of the attributes
of the parts but because they are inadequately arranged. They cannot interact in the way they might.

You learn from the materials world, for instance, that small
amounts of impurities or deliberate additions make a major
difference in the properties of steel. Another example is semi-
conductors, in which parts per million additions determine the
properties of silicon and germanium. Now human beings are not
atoms, but they are also not independent, so it's easy to see how
changes in structure make some things possible and other things
difficult.

JANE: The collectivity can do more than the sum of the parts, and yet in your lecture "Reflections on Public Health and Peace" you say that in recent years we seem to have lost our sense of collectivity. How do you think that happened?

URSULA: I set out in the hope I would contribute to systemic changes. I hoped to advocate systemic approaches that would give us a better system. Over the decades, the really drastic change has been that questions that had previously been framed and addressed as systemic have become privatized. The past decades of technological development have allowed – and propagated – a shift from systemic approaches to problems of society, to totally privatized approaches in which each and every person has to change to eliminate discrimination and to eliminate war.

I find myself seeing the students of my students being deeply concerned about the world but seeing their response totally as their private decision. They seem to have lost the sense of collectivity and seem to feel the sum of a large number of private actions is equivalent to a collective action resulting in systemic change, and in fact it is not. I think only in retrospect will we understand how profoundly this turning away from collectivity will affect our future.

DESKILLING

JANE: One of the social impacts of technology you draw to our attention in your SciMaTech lecture is deskilling: the fact that the availability of a new technology allows certain skills to be developed while preventing others from being developed. Could you talk a bit about social deskilling?

URSULA: We might want to begin again with my definition of technology as practice. Now when, because of advances in science and engineering, certain tasks can be done differently – when you have machines to dig holes – then the skills of practitioners change. Certain skills aren't needed anymore, and other skills are developed. That's inevitable and part of normal life. The moment printing started, all things changed for those whose livelihood was related to reading and writing, and the number of people who could read and write suddenly exploded.

Now, not all lost skills are either obvious or are skills one can afford to lose. Some of those are particularly social skills. I used to speak about learning and "by-the-way learning." When people work together, they not only accomplish the goal of a particular

project but also *learn something about working together*. When
the practice changes, and in consequence the working together also
drastically changes, the by-the-way learning goes. In the classroom,
for example, work can now easily be broken up into individual
tasks on computers so students can continue at their own pace, but
as a consequence students don't learn how to work with people
who have a different pace.

Classrooms, workplaces – anywhere people need to work
together who otherwise would not meet each other – are places of
enormous social learning, particularly in an immigrant society like
Canada. As the structures of classrooms and workplaces change,
where does anyone have the chance to meet and develop ease with
people who may have different food, different habits, different language, and different social manners?

This loss of "by-the-way learning" is even more evident when
one considers social media, where there is the impression of inti-
macy, the idea of knowing somebody, without in fact knowing
them at all or knowing them fully.

JANE: How do we respond constructively to the deskilling in the
social realm that occurs because technologies are allowing people
to socialize differently?

URSULA: I would think one has to create the opportunities that the
common tasks previously produced by-the-way. One has to set time
aside, whether for potluck or for deliberately creating a common
task such as cleaning up a neighbourhood park, in order to recreate
the context that the workplace previously produced. It can be a festive occasion or a helpful occasion, but I think it has to be a attempt
to provide opportunities the previous structure contained *per se*.
Certain capacities, such as compassion and tolerance, cannot grow
without the soil of communal activities. If absolutely everything is
privatized, where does the knowledge and scope of a collectivity
develop? If one changes a structure, one cannot expect conduct that
was normally patterned by another structure. Certain structures
cannot facilitate certain conduct; you can hardly get entrepreneurial
zeal in a monastery or collective responsibility on the stock market.

DEFINITIONS

JANE: We talked earlier about your interest in definitions. How did
you become interested in things that define themselves by what they
are not?

URSULA: I have, because of my interest in nonviolence, a great deal of interest in entities that identify themselves by what they are not. You have organizations that are NGOs doing a vastly different collection of activities, defined only by the fact that they are not government. What does that mean? What can they do and what can they not do?

Now, my interest in pacifism is practical. I'm not a philosopher; I'm a citizen. I'm interested in what do you do after you've taken a dim view, and so nonviolence, which is so central, becomes a question of definition. What do we mean? What's left if you say you will not be violent? What then? I define violence as resourcelessness, and therefore nonviolence is resourcefulness. In the fullness of available resources, which are most appropriate to the situation at hand?

In terms of thoughts and afterthoughts, the main thread to make clear is that, while the principles of pacifism remain unchanged, the practice of pacifism depends on the social situation. Between my beginning to talk about that topic, Quakers talking about it, and now is a vast change in the way people relate to each other because of new technologies. Just imagine what any early uprising would have been if there had been radio, telephone, or internet; imagine the impact of social media on any current or future protest movements.

JANE: Your idea of the "however paragraph" seems to be another way of expressing dissent without being aggressive about it. How would you define a however paragraph?

URSULA: I love the notion of a however paragraph because for me it means one is in a different mode of discussion than to say "no, no, no." It's not an argumentative statement. It means accepting the argument that was presented and supplementing it, saying, "Yes, I accept your argument; however, there are additional angles one has to consider." The "however paragraph" comes out of my fondness for the notion of standpoint. We all look at reality from a certain standpoint. We can't help it. We are the people we are. We are where we are. We have learned what we have learned. The honourable thing is to be as clear as possible of one's standpoint, and at the same time to accept the reality that what one is discussing can be seen in a very different light from a different standpoint. The "however paragraph" is a way to bring in that different view, legitimately and respectfully.

JANE: Your interest in coexistence also resonates here, doesn't it?

URSULA: Yes, indeed. The notion of coexistence is based on the realization that "we" and "our community" are not the only inhabitants of this world. There are others who have a legitimate desire to live in their own communities and by their own values. In the Polanyi Lecture I traced the notion of coexistence in its geopolitical application as well as pointing out the need for coexistence between the bitsphere and the biosphere.

JANE: In that lecture you say of coexistence that both parties have to be committed to the existence of the other. Could you give me an example in the geopolitical realm?

URSULA: Think if there were a commitment – a genuine commitment – to coexistence between Palestine and the State of Israel. The absence of a genuine commitment to coexistence is what stands in the way, never mind the fact that the people are there. Then you can say, to what extent is there convergence because there are similar projects, there is similar technology? Or, is there a technology that is tied to the entity of the state? For instance, there's a long discussion on Islamic banking. How do faithful Muslims fit into a capitalist system that charges interest? These are real questions, and you can't dance around them.

A SCIENTIST'S PERSPECTIVE

JANE: Through our conversations I've become increasingly aware of many very specific ways in which your training as a scientist has profoundly shaped the way you see phenomena in the social realm. In "The However Paragraph" you say that anyone who has worked in ferromagnetism knows the immense utility of the notion of domain. How you have found the notion of domain helpful when applied to the social realm?

URSULA: The scientific concept of domain is very much borrowed from the literary and political fields, in which you say it's the domain of the church or the state. It signifies a region, and in the study of the magnetic properties of materials it's a physical region, that changes its size in response to external forces acting on the material.

A domain is a group property. It's a collectivity that's characterized by a response to an external stimulus. As the direction and strength of that stimulus changes, the size of the domain and the

number of participants change. When physicists discovered they
were able to see under the microscope the boundaries of domains
– that some grew and some shrunk without any physical movements of the atoms – they looked in their language repertoire for a
word that signified a collectivity characterized by one and only one
parameter, and they found the word "domain." The domain of the
church or the sovereign did not necessarily mean different people
but people who responded to a call in a similar way. If you think of
a domain of people called to prayer, who then all at a given hour,
turn in a given direction and bow their heads, you conceive why
the physicists chose the word domain when they suddenly saw
there were atoms that, on a given force, all bow their electrons in
the same direction.

You can also see how useful the notion is when one clears it from
any prejudice and trapping and says, "Here are people who on a
specific stimulus do the same thing and therefore provide a body
of strength and force." To have the awareness of the existence of
domains, of how forces act on materials, I think wouldn't do any
harm to people who deal with prejudice, with bias, with hate. With
a bit of literacy in scientific matters, one can say "Look, that's how
domains form, and that's how they can be undone." Because one
can demagnetize. I think just thinking and talking about domains
would help the discourse. Think of Twitter and the new social
media. The dynamics of domains might help us understand Twitter.

JANE: In "The However Paragraph" you go on to say, "Just
imagine you could make politicians understand thermodynamics.
Just imagine what that would mean to nature and to peace." What
principles of thermodynamics do you think would be particularly
useful for politicians and others to understand?

URSULA: There are two points I would want to make. One is that
the paper was meant for physicists, and there are assumptions one
cannot quickly paraphrase in lay language; however, what can be
done is to let people have a glimpse of how the world looks from
the standpoint of knowing about thermodynamics. The essence for
the lay person is to acknowledge the dominance of the principles of
nature on all we do. It doesn't matter whether one knows in detail
the first or second laws of thermodynamics; what matters is that
one knows in one's bones that a *perpetuum mobile* is impossible:
one cannot create energy, one can only convert energy.

One has to know in every fibre of one's being that humans are part of nature, and whether we like it or not we work under the laws of nature. Otherwise you get the hubris we see that people in power think they have power over everything, including nature, and do not understand they are part of a system in which they are subject to rigorously enforced laws. No change in government changes the laws of gravity or the laws of thermodynamics. Now if that were clear – that there are laws under which we work, whether we acknowledge them or not – then many political decisions could be viewed from that standpoint. We can't opt out of the laws of nature; there is no opting-out clause.

JANE: What laws of nature do you think are most frequently overlooked?

URSULA: I think the essential laws of nature that are overlooked are those regarding the conservation of energy: the fact that one cannot create energy but only convert energy, and the fact that there is entropy – wasted energy that cannot be used to produce work. All the laws of thermodynamics deal with the fact that *energy is the currency with which we trade with nature*. They provide one of the most useful ways through which we can assess, utilize, and monitor our interaction with nature. Energy is the universal currency, the universal language, but one has to understand the banking system of those with whom we interact. We go into nature's storehouses of energy, and there's nothing evil about it, but it needs knowledge of consequences. Science has accumulated knowledge about the nature and magnitude of those storehouses, and it's as much civic knowledge as knowledge of history and geography. Nature has a banking system, and energy is the currency.

JANE: How might a better understanding of entropy be useful in the social sphere?

URSULA: Entropy is a difficult concept. Think of it as waste, as energy one cannot use any further for the purpose intended. Imagine you have friction and you create heat. If you don't have any use for that heat, then it becomes waste heat: it's energy not available for anything else.

Now imagine a workplace that is unhelpful and disrespectful. The amount of energy needed to get a certain level of work done will be much higher. Those who work in such an environment will likely be much more tired at the end of the day and their immune system will be much less resilient than those of people who do the same amount of work in a respectful workplace in which workers are contented and don't have to fight stupidity. In terms of the conservation of energy, a disrespectful workplace creates heat when heat isn't needed.

ENGINEERING AND SCIENCE

JANE: What's the relationship between engineering and science?
URSULA: I'm happy to talk about the relationship between engineering and science, which is in many ways the relationship between the hand and the brain. I have always held, and feel so most strongly today, that it is the knowledge of the hand that drives the knowledge of the brain, so that engineering, *doing things*, is the first step. In fact, it's the seedbed from which the questions arise. Why does this happen? How can I repeat it? How can I use it? The mind, the intellect, has to have something to think about, and it is the incredible ability of a human being to observe, to create, to communicate, to feel materials, to smell, to observe keenly. The doing and observing is the seedbed.

Although scientists frequently think of engineering as an afterthought, the observation of what people do, and usually do collectively, is in fact the beginning of the inquiry. You do something, it works; I do it, and it doesn't work. Is it just that I am dumb, or are we actually not doing the same thing? The knowledge of the hand is the seedbed for the transferrable knowledge of the mind.

WHAT DO WE DO AFTER TAKING A DIM VIEW?

JANE: I have often heard you ask a question I like very much: you've asked, "What do we do after we take a dim view of something?" There is so much discouragement, so much complaint about political structures, economic structures, academic structures. In some speeches it seems you're answering that question in particular contexts. Do you think that is the case?
URSULA: Again, in terms of thought and afterthought, I would say that in the earlier part of my career I was particularly interested in what one would do after taking a dim view. One saw the horrors of war, one saw the dangers of fascism, one saw the increasing threat to the Earth by industrialization. The essential question often arose,

"What do we do?" I helped to write many briefs to parliament or its committees. Well informed organizations proposed and pressed for constructive changes through existing channels of government. In terms of afterthought thirty or forty years later, I say people have really tried and many good consequences, for instance in education and in nondiscrimination, have come about because of people having taken a dim view and acted upon it.

What is needed now is a different and fresh attempt at collective discernment, which is required to understand the changed structures of power, responsibility, and accountability. For instance, when I began to be interested in public policy, I thought our government was well intentioned and ill informed, and so I joined others to rectify "the information gap." After a while I realized that most authorities I was dealing with were well informed but ill intentioned. Correcting "the structural gap" that prevents clarity of a new power situation requires a level of collective discernment not yet reached among citizens. I desperately wish to contribute to this discernment through sharing these speeches. My old thoughts and afterthoughts, preserved in this book, are awaiting the young practitioners of a new age.

CONCLUSION

In conclusion, we would like to quote an excerpt from the most recent speech in the book, the speech in honour of Dr Zofia Pakula, "Reflections on Public Health and Peace":

> In many ways Zofia is emblematic of the generation of survivors of the Second World War in its broadest implications: survivors that were for the rest of their lives under that burden of knowledge, and under that question, "What does it mean that I survived and others did not? What does that mean for the conduct of the rest of my life? What lessons have I to transmit?" That experience has been to many people, particularly to many women, a mortgage – a moral mortgage – on their lives: the mortgage of the survivor who cannot free herself from the demands on her life of the obligation that this very fact – of having survived when others hadn't – would place on her.
>
> I want to honour that generation of survivors whose lives changed drastically and profoundly, and changed in heart, mind,

and hand, what they felt, what they thought about, what they did, and how they conducted their lives across the board. The survivors had that common solidarity that brought so many together, who thought, "Never again." It was different from the "never again" in the First World War, when one thought it was possible by reason, by structure alone. Here we were on a much, much deeper level. It was a level that changed lives to a new solidarity. It meant that women across the country, across the world, said "If our children are going to grow up healthy and sane, *all* children have to grow up healthy and sane. It is not good enough any more to look after oneself, after one's country." In A.J. Muste's words, "There is no way to peace; peace is the way," and we have to figure out what that way is.

The generation of those who feel themselves under that moral mortgage is almost gone from this Earth, but the work needing to be done is not. It is our hope that this book will help preserve the values, and the process of discernment, that motivated that mortgaged generation beyond its lifespan.

Appendix

Speeches Clustered by Theme (interviews are listed separately)

COMMUNITY

EDUCATION

FAITH

RESEARCH AS A SOCIAL ENTERPRISE

THE STRUCTURAL IMPACT OF RESEARCH FUNDING

SCIENCE, DISCERNMENT, AND RESPONSIBILITY

THE SOCIAL IMPACT OF TECHNOLOGY

WOMEN, JUSTICE, AND PEACE

INTERVIEWS

Index